WINE, WOMEN AND SONG

A SPITFIRE PILOT'S STORY

WINE, WOMEN AND SONG

A SPITFIRE PILOT'S STORY

COMPILED FROM DOUG BROWN'S LETTERS AND REMINISCENCES

HAMISH BROWN

FONTHILL

Dedicated to my Comrades in Arms 485 (NZ) Squadron and 130 (Punjab) Squadron

I make particular mention to the families who made considerable sacrifice to provide us with home comforts and rekindle our spirits while we were at war in the air. My personal thanks go to the Rickerby, Cavaghan and Dias families of Cumberland, Leuchs of Tadworth, Fergusons of Oxted and the MacCullough family of Canada.

In memory of:
Pvt Harold Cavaghan, Border Regiment, died France 1/8/1944 aged 19
Sgt John Ferguson, RAF Volunteer Reserve, died 10/10/1942 aged 20
Sgt Donald McCullough, RCAF, died 12/12/1941 aged 24
and Joe Rickerby, a good friend who died in a car accident in 1973

Frontispiece: Doug Brown, NZ405225

Fonthill Media Limited
Fonthill Media LLC
www.fonthillmedia.com
office@fonthillmedia.com

First published in New Zealand, 2011, by Stayer Ltd
This edition published in the United Kingdom and the United States of America 2012

British Library Cataloguing in Publication Data:
A catalogue record for this book is available from the British Library

ISBN 978-1-78155-035-9 (print)
ISBN 978-1-78155-131-8 (e-book)

Printed and bound in England.

Connect with us
facebook.com/fonthillmedia twitter.com/fonthillmedia

CONTENTS

FOREWORD

It has been a real pleasure and privilege getting to know Doug Brown and his fellow 485 Squadron pilots through my involvement with Spitfire restoration and the establishment of the Fighter Pilots' Museum in Wanaka. These are men who deserve our gratitude and admiration, and while the 485 reunions are perhaps a bit more sedate nowadays than the original gatherings, new stories are still being told and they are well worth listening to. The Spitfire will continue to fascinate generations to come. Knowing Doug as I do to be a great adventurer, I'm sure his story will make a wonderful read.

I congratulate Hamish Brown for getting Doug's story into print. With the establishment of the 485 Wing at Whenuapai, the history of 485 Squadron is becoming well documented and Hamish has done an excellent job of contributing to that with the publication of this book.

Sir Tim Wallis
Patron, 485 Squadron
Aviation enthusiast, pioneer of live hill-country
deer capture, founder of Warbirds over Wanaka

PREFACE

This work is based on letters Doug Brown wrote to his family while serving with the RNZAF and Allied Air Force during World War II. Doug was a prolific writer. It was of great concern to him that, should individual missives not reach their destination, his family might think he had 'bought it'. The text faithfully draws from the original transcripts, with some minor concessions: omissions made by the war censor have been reinstated; where letters went missing, Doug has endeavoured to fill the gaps; and any repetitious or redundant material has been deleted. Where supplementary text expands on the original letters there may be some overlap – especially where Doug had a near miss and played down any dangers or risks encountered.

Over the years Doug has been interviewed by historians and filmmakers interested in recording first-hand reports of the period. Use of these transcripts, speeches he has been called upon to give, and other reminiscences have been included to complete the picture of this important part of our history. Doug's log book has been used to verify dates and actions. We are also fortunate that at 91 Doug still has full mental faculties and is able to recall most dates, places and faces from his war time 70 years ago.

This is not intended to be a technical manuscript on Spitfires, or the theory of war in the air. Neither is it intended to be a complete record of 130 and 485 Squadrons, nor their personnel.[1] Those who did not serve with Doug, or were only briefly in the squadron or on another flight, may not have been mentioned. When a new pilot joined a squadron they were often posted on before becoming operational, or it may have been some weeks before their first operational flight, which for many inexperienced pilots was often their last. No offence is intended by excluding pilots who may have come to know Doug after the war.

There is no doubt many airmen were lucky to survive, as indeed many who were in the wrong place at the wrong time were killed. Despite their near misses, Doug and his comrades firmly believed that in order to get through you had to make your own luck and have a positive attitude. When an element of doubt or fear of going on operations set in, this was often a forewarning to pilots that their number was up. You had to have confidence to survive.

---

1   A detailed history of 485 Squadron can be found in *No 485 (NZ) Squadron 1941–1945* by Sortehaug and Listemann and *An Illustrated History of the NZ Spitfire Squadron* by Kevin Wells.

The Battle of Britain recognised the need to replenish personnel from the Commonwealth. Within two years of the outbreak of war, over 3000 New Zealanders were serving in the RAF. Some had trained in the RAF prior to the outbreak of war and others came through from the Empire Training Scheme. As well as the provision of men and women for the cause, £126,000 sterling was raised to provide aircraft for 485, the first NZ Squadron. These 'subscription' Spitfires carried the name of the province that funded the purchase, which in those days cost over £5000 each.

Doug joined 485 Squadron at the end of 1941 at Kenley under Fighter Command's 11 Group. Not that he knew it at the time, but he would spend four Christmases away from home. It is a large chunk of one's life – about the same length of time we spend at secondary school.

This book provides insight into the effects of war on the human being. The average casualty rate in squadrons Doug served in was well over one killed each month. In excess of 30% of those serving in Fighter Squadrons did not return home – this figure excludes those lost in training. The statistics for those in bombers and the Fleet Air Arm were even worse.

Somewhat akin to the fatalistic 'Eat, drink and be merry for tomorrow you die', Doug's Spitfire was named 'Wine, Women and Song'. In order to cope with the rigours of combat in the air, life on the ground was lived to the full.

ACKNOWLEDGEMENTS

Many of the images are from Doug's photograph collection. A fire at Milfield in March 1944 destroyed much of the collection. Some of these were replaced at the time by copies from Sport and General, London. Others have been supplemented over the years from the collections of colleagues and have been acknowledged where the original source was known.

Auckland War memorial Museum staff

Authors Brendon Deere *Spitfire – Return to Flight*, Mark Hillier et al *Westhampnett at War* and Peter Macky *Coolangatta A Homage* and *Wartime Correspondence*, for their guidance and encouragement

Bycroft Biscuit Tin images from June and Don Bycroft

Dave Russell-Smith for his account of Pam Barton from 184 Squadron archive

Fletcher McKenzie, Executive Producer, FlightPathTV, www.leadingedgemedia.tv for the transcripts of his interviews with Doug

The Francis Frith Collection www.francisfrith.com

François Dethier for image of Diest-Schaffen and images of Michel Donnet

Getty Images

Harvey Sweetman for the use of his early photographs of 485 Squadron

Imperial War Museum London (www.iwm.org.uk)

John Rickerby for his image of Scaur House, Carlisle

King's School Auckland, Jo Baynes, Carolyn Prebble, Tony Sissons, Isabel Sutherland

W/O Marty Fitchett of RNZAF Whenuapai

Matthew O'Sullivan of RNZAF Museum, Wigram

Marion Heasman for the use of Ferguson family photographs

Mary Denton, The RAF Heraldry Trust (www.griffon.clara.net/rafh/)

Max Collett for putting names to faces on later 485 Squadron images

Michael McLeavey for use of his rendition of the *Awatea*

National Archives of the UK for the use of Combat Reports

Noel and Margaret Taylor

Nola Tucker for the use of Hugh Tucker's photographs

Pam O'Connor for use of Ken Law's collection including photographs of EFTS Whenuapai, on the *Awatea*, and others en route to Bournemouth

Peter van Bommel

Rolls-Royce Heritage Trust

Sarah Shand for the use of MM Shand's photographs and combat account

Sealand Aerial Photography

Shaun Churchill for use of images of Aston Down and Kenley airfield ww2airfields@aol.com

Family, friends and 485 Squadron colleagues and their families for their comments and contributions

Between the Wars

*

AN INTRODUCTION

Doug had two uncles on his father's side, both of whom were killed in the Great War. Stanley Gordon Brown was an Able Seaman in the Royal Naval Volunteer Reserve, Hawke Battalion. He was killed at Gallipoli on 19 June 1915, aged 23. Gilfred Elliot Brown was a 2nd Lieutenant with the Border Regiment. He was killed in France on 18 November 1916, aged 23, and is buried in Ten Tree Alley Cemetary at Puisieux.

Doug's father Edward (Ted) Broadley Brown was born in Aspatria, Cumberland on 21 September 1892. He emigrated to New Zealand around 1910 and resided at 'Indore', Mt Eden – a significant move for an 18-year-old.

From August 1914 Ted served for eight months in the 3rd Auckland Regiment of the Samoan Expeditionary Force prior to serving with the 2nd Batallion of the NZEF in the Middle East and France. In January 1916 he was admitted to hospital in Cairo with enteritis and that same year received the Military Medal. In October 1917 active service was waived by the Military Service Board and Ted was discharged 'in view of the Appellant's record, and that he was the sole surviving son of his parents.'

Edward Broadley Brown married Louisa Francis Pendock Tucker in 1917 and resided at The Cliff, 7 Bourne St, Mt Eden until his death in 1964.

ABOVE LEFT Gilf, Gordon and Edward Brown, circa 1900
ABOVE RIGHT Ted Brown and his mother Gertrude, circa 1910

ABOVE LEFT Doug's parents, Lou and Ted Brown at Brandraw House, Cumberland, 1921
ABOVE RIGHT George Todd Brown (right) and Viscount Gillan share a joke

There is some evidence the Browns (*Brun*) and Tuckers (*Tooker*) came to England with the Normans in 1066. The Duke of Normandy granted land in Cumberland to the Browns for their help at the Battle of Hastings.

The Tuckers from Milton, Kent colonised Bermuda and Virginia from the mid-1600s as the Civil War took hold in England. The Tuckers of Bermuda had large families and, despite holding positions of power in the colony such as the presidency, the original lines dispersed within 200 years to neighbouring United States, the Navy, the Army and Civil Service in India. Henry St George Pendock Tucker was a director of the East India Company.

Doug was born on the kitchen table at 7 Bourne St on 6 February 1919. This event was followed by the arrival of his sisters Peg and Shirl.

Doug's primary school education was at King's School in Remuera from 1925 to 1932. His parents had sent him as a boarder, rather a surprising decision given the family home was only 2km away. In his year group at King's were Bill

Boxing on the lawn, King's School, Auckland 1930s, with 'The Towers' behind. Doug boarded in the dormer-style roof space. The showers were in the basement three levels below

Caughey, with whom Doug served on the King's School board, and Ken Lee, who later served with Doug in 485 NZ Spitfire Fighter Squadron.

Doug's first 'near death' experience occurred when he contracted scarlet fever and diphtheria early in his school years. The up-side of this enabled him to miss school and convalesce at Bourne St. There were other close calls when playing with Ewie Johnston in a disused water storage tank on Mt Eden and when he was buried in a sand tunnel which collapsed at Manly beach.

Ted Brown and Laurie Taylor developed Manly beach, Whangaparaoa, as a holiday subdivision. Unlike developers today, the two made no money out of the scheme. It was their intent to retain a section in the development and build their own holiday homes. In the early days the family used to go by barge from Auckland to Little Manly where they were collected by a Mr Smith who took

Manly Beach 1929

The three at top left are still friends today. Bill Caughey was on the King's School board with Doug. Ken Lee flew with Doug in 485 Squadron

In front of Ted Brown's house at Manly. Bob Gyllies, John Meuli, Doug, Paul Hayward, Peter Jacobson

ABOVE LEFT In front of Ted Brown's house at Manly, circa 1939.

ABOVE RIGHT Peg, Shirl, Lou and Ted Brown with Airedale.

them by horse and cart over the hill to Big Manly. He also supplied a large block of ice to keep food cool for a couple of weeks. When the barge was destroyed by fire the wharf was dismantled and they made the arduous journey by car on metal roads. The Browns and the Taylors still have a bach at Manly today.

Following primary school it was off to Wanganui Collegiate, where Doug lasted four years. Depite the fact that he did not enjoy secondary school, Doug made many lifelong friends there, many of whom were also pilots in 485 Squadron.

Auckland University beckoned after school and, following in his father's footsteps, Doug studied law, although he never completed his studies. He also had a keen interest in rugby and other sporting activities.

Hamish Brown

Outbreak of War

*

TRAINING IN NEW ZEALAND

Friday, 1 September 1939 – War is Declared

I was at the Château on the Saturday when war was declared. There were about eight of us boys there and we had a great weekend. Included were Bob Gyllies, Digger Robertson and Peter Ellis.[1] On the way down, at Taihape, we called on a relative of Peter Ellis. She did not seem at all pleased to receive us at that time of night. We eventually reached the Château for a late breakfast. The party went on well through that evening and after the dance was over the three-piece band retired to one of our rooms to continue activities. There were of course many complaints from adjacent rooms regarding the noise and the language. The affair terminated when the manager told Bob Gyllies that he did not want to see his face in the Château ever again.

We came up to Auckland on the Monday and we all decided to volunteer.

---

1 Peter contracted polio during the war and was rehabilitated back to Queen Elizabeth Hospital, Rotorua in 1943. He lost the use of his right arm and learnt how to be a leftie and play golf one-handed.

While we were keen and excited to get away it was not as simple as that. Les Robertson, who was in the RNZAF, managed to have us transferred into the Fleet Air Arm and we were scheduled to leave for England in April 1940. Fortunately for me it did not work out that way as the Fleet Air Arm proved later to have a particularly high attrition rate. I did not pass the medical as I had broken my nose at rugby. One side of my sinuses was completely blocked and I had to get an operation privately before going any further.

I spent a few months filling in time farming and shearing in a gang at a place called Aria, between Te Kuiti and Awakino.

Prior to the serious business of training we had a three-month session in Auckland doing Morse code and other such things. Then it was on to camp at Levin into what was previously a borstal.

22 December 1940 – Initial Training School, Levin

My introduction to the Air Force was 7 a.m. on Sunday, 22 December 1940 at the Levin Railway Station, where our course members arrived by train from Auckland. It seemed rather harsh to be starting camp just before Xmas, but that was the way it was – there was a war on!

We were met by a number of corporals and sergeants and I well remember a red-haired Sergeant Robertson who from the outset considered me a rebel and hounded me during my days at the Initial Training School in Levin.

The six-week course was devoted to teaching us discipline. This was achieved by the Army method of drill, drill and more drill. We also participated in educational courses covering engineering, gunnery, Morse code and aircraft recognition.

Following our 'Levin Experience', pilots, observers, gunners and radio operators were then posted to various RNZAF stations within New Zealand.

John Grierson and I, among others, were posted to Number 4 Elementary Training School, Whenuapai, Auckland. I knew John from Auckland University. We had played rugby together and of all things had won the doubles ping-pong championship together too.

Sunday, 9 February 1941 – No 4 Elementary Training School, Whenuapai

I will always remember my first flight in a DH82 Tiger Moth on the afternoon of 10 February. My instructor was F/O Hansen and the training came under the heading of 'Air Experience'.

ABOVE LEFT Doug, Jack Brockett, Peter Dunn, John Grierson at Levin

ABOVE RIGHT Doug's father EB Brown and Doug at 7 Bourne St

Following take off F/O Hansen gave me 45 minutes of this experience in which he turned the aircraft every which way. It took some time to recover my equilibrium after coming back to Mother Earth. There was a limitation on the number of flying hours available under instruction before flying solo so I was concerned the emphasis was on aerobatics rather than basic flight instruction.

Squadron Leader Jack Seabrook, a WWI RAF pilot, was Commanding Officer at Whenuapai and coincidentally a friend of my father. How fortunate I was that the day after my first dual flight he met me and asked how I was progressing. I explained my experience with F/O Hansen and that I was supposed to be going solo within a set number of flying hours and all I had done was 45 minutes of aerobatics. I miraculously found myself with a new instructor, F/O Barnett. He was excellent in manner, attitude and ability and I remained in his care for the total flying period at Whenuapai.

At that time Whenuapai had no sealed runways and all our flying was completed on a grass landing field. Runways soon followed and the drome became fully utilised by the RNZAF and US Air Force.

My first solo was 20 February 1941. F/O Barnett said, 'It's all yours', so with the formalities over I took off in the Tiger Moth. All I had to do was one circuit and land. The Tiger Moth had no wheel at the back, just a skid. I came in and it made a hell of a noise so I thought, 'Christ, I had better go around again!'

The same thing happened on the second landing and the noise made me think I had misjudged it. On my third approach I had become a bit panicky and

TOP Aerial view of Whenuapai around 1941. RNZAF MUSEUM

ABOVE LEFT Ken Law flying dual in Tiger Moth

ABOVE RIGHT Tiger Moths in front of main hangar Whenuapai

No 4 Elementary Training School, Whenuapai (Doug is on the left in the second row)

decided I had to drop down to land, whether I broke something or not. After landing the instructor asked why I had gone around a second and third time. I said I was concerned about the noise from the rough landing and he explained it was the skid and was normal!

Our time at EFTS was completed on 28 March, at which stage I had completed the required flying hours.

We then had the choice of further training in NZ or Canada. John Grierson and I decided on Canada as they had Harvards – more modern than what was available in NZ.

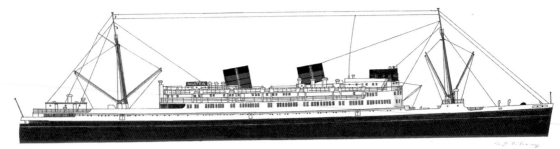

TSS. AWATEA.

The *RMS Awatea* was commissioned in 1937 by the Union Line to compete on the Trans Tasman Auckland–Sydney–Wellington route with Matson Line's *Mariposa* and *Monterey*. Built by Vickers-Armstrong at Barrow at 13500 tons it was reputedly the fastest and most comfortable ship in the Southern Hemisphere. Captain Davey told me he would try to do the run in record time and used to pull up alongside the wharf without the use of a tug, just like parking a car.

The *Awatea* was requisitioned as a transporter. Only minor refits were carried out, including a 4" gun aft. The first of five service trips started in November 1940 on the Auckland to Vancouver run transporting airmen for further training in Canada. I was on the third run from 29 April, arriving 14 May 1941.

In September it was then requisitioned by the British. Some repairs were carried out in Vancouver after a collision with a tanker along with provision of additional armaments and accommodation. In October 1941 the *Awatea* and *Prince Robert* transported 2000 Canadian troops to Hong Kong. The Japanese attacked on 8 December. Hundreds were killed during the attack or in the years following while POWs. (Ironically the *Prince Robert* also assisted with the evacuation of Canadian POWs in 1945.)

She then went on to the Philippines and Singapore (evacuating civilians), Ceylon, South Africa and Trinidad. The ship was completely gutted and refitted in Liverpool. A busy few months followed carrying troops from Britain and India (where Captain Morgan took over) to South Africa, and transporting troops from Halifax to Britain.

Later in 1942 an extensive refit was carried out in Glasgow to prepare *Awatea* as a troop landing ship. Lifeboats were replaced by landing barges, accommodation capabilities increased further and armaments strengthened. Training took place in Lock Fyne and the *Awatea* then took its place in the Convoy AT20 destined for Allied Landings in North Africa. It was while we were on patrol and the convoy was passing through the Irish Sea that I spotted *Awatea* painted in camouflage grey.

Operation Torch successfully took place on 8 November with 3000 troops disembarking into Vichy-French North Africa, but the *Awatea* was bombed and sunk on the 11 November 1942 off Bougie Bay, Algiers. This was to be the end to a ship that had escaped U-Boat attack, survived a number of collisions with friendly ships and been stricken with a smallpox outbreak.

ABOVE *TSS Awatea*, rendition by Michael McLeavey.

At Sea on the Awatea

*

AUCKLAND TO VANCOUVER

Wednesday, 30 April 1941

Dear Mum, Dad and Girls,

Well here goes the first epistle from the 'Younker' while he is setting off on holiday.

I was glad to see you at the wharf, Dad and Shirl, and was glad you were not there Mum, as you can understand. You were great, Mum, when I left, and I'm afraid I was the boob, however, let's forget it. Glad you got the penny, Dad. Keep it, it may be a good luck charm – worth little in money but maybe invaluable in luck.

After we left the wharf we got under way fairly rapidly and were soon followed by our escort. I watched all the nooks and crannies up the coast, especially Whangaparaoa – my wonderland. Since we went inside Tiri, we had a fine view of the end of the peninsula. Unluckily rain came at this stage and it blotted out the land so we did not see much of the coast from there onwards. The bar opened at five. At that time we all popped down to the bar. As the ship was a luxury liner in a previous life, Dave Waters decided to celebrate with French bubbly. The rest of us sat back sipping iced beer before tea which we sat down to at 6.30. I was pretty tired and headed for bed early, and after a nice hot shower I was soon asleep. This morning I did not arise till about eight and after shaving I gaily strolled into the dining room for breakfast – very good too. After breakfast we had a lifeboat drill, followed by a parade which was a waste of time but passed the time until lunch. We were to have another parade after lunch, but that came to nothing and we were free all afternoon, most of which I spent up on deck with a few Aussies and our men.[2] We had a few beers at five and then dinner. After dinner three of us went down aft and watched the water swishing by – a pleasant occupation indeed.

It has been rolling a bit today and the *Awatea* is nosing under a bit. I must be like Dad as seasickness hasn't affected me. However, the majority of the boys are not themselves and many of the meals eaten a waste of time – not money, as the Government is paying! John has managed to hold out – as a matter of fact we have had no sickness at our table yet: the first of us who does not appear for a meal due to seasickness shouts the table. I'm not going to be the mug anyway.

We start on a routine tomorrow. P.T. at 6.30 a.m. and lectures until 4.30 p.m. It sounds quite a bit, but it won't be bad.

Our escort, the armed merchant cruiser HMS *Monowai*, is like a picture. Every time I look out our porthole she is in the same possie about a mile away.

The climate is getting warmer as we near Suva.

I will close for the present and get a bit of sleep but will probably add a note tomorrow evening.

Tons of love,

Doug

2   There were 146 men on board and 70 died in service. [ref *For Your Tomorrow* by Errol Martyn]

Thursday, 1 May

We've been hard at it this morning and as I have a few minutes to spare I thought I would put in a few more lines before posting. This letter has to be in the purser's office to catch the Suva mail. I will send this from the boat and if time permits send a card from Suva.

The flying fish have been sighted and all during Morse I watched the little lads flitting over the water – great to watch, aren't they?

Well I must away, so will close now. All is well on board.

Cheerio, and tons of love,
Thumbs up, Dad

Doug

P.S. Please give me Mr Beaufort's address.[3]

Awatea, Back at Sea

Friday, 2 May 1941

Dear Mum, Dad and Girls,

Here we are as they say 'like a painted ship in the ocean', but no albatrosses so far.

We reached Suva at about 9 a.m. and had leave from 10 till 4.30 p.m. The first port of call was the Bank of NZ where we hoped to get some cash. We were only meant to change a quid, but with a bit of wangling, I managed to exchange three. First of all we walked to a rather nice hotel and settled down to a very long beer. After posting the card we went shopping. I thought I would get a coral necklace as they look rather nice. We then split up a bit but Alan Robinson, John and myself stayed together. We wandered through the slums and went on to the Garrick Hotel where we met some great friends of Alan's, Mr and Mrs Wiseman, who entertained and introduced us to a

3   Beaufort had been an assistant Chaplain at King's College and later Headmaster at King's School, Auckland, NZ, 1931–1934.

Ken Law on the *Awatea* at Suva

mob of Suva-ites, including a couple of Army sisters through whom I got in touch with Tad Morpeth. We yarned and drank beer with them for a while and they asked us to have lunch with them. We wanted a Chinese dish so we went to the 'chop suey' restaurant and I sampled crab omelette. After a feed, we tootled off and met Tad Morpeth at the Wisemans' and spent the afternoon thus till about four o'clock. We wandered back to the ship, bartering with the natives on the way. The wharfies who incidentally only get two shillings and sixpence a day did well as the guys threw the silver they had left. We left Suva at about 7 p.m. and were sorry to see the last of it. Even though it stinks and is pretty rough, it is good to get your feet on a bit of terra firma. Must close for now as the tea gong has sounded.

Monday, 5 May 1941

Just finished morning parade and have got about 15 minutes before I go and guard the 'gun' and look for subs.

Where did I get to? We had left Suva so will continue this episode from there. Friday was a big day as we had it twice – darn funny Friday night, still Friday and more Friday, and both were darn hot. This day was my first watch: it is a good job as I have it from 10 a.m. to 12 noon and do not have to attend lectures. There are a couple of gun crews: the boat crew and a crew picked from the Aussies. I have not seen the Aussies in action but I watched the boat crew hard at it the other day and they were pretty good. The swimming pool was opened up and though small it is appreciated as the atmosphere is becoming hotter, especially at dinner when all the ship is blacked out. The sweat runs off the boys in streams and that is no exaggeration. The only interest on this day was a large school of porpoises, which played about for about 30 minutes and kept us amused for a while.

Saturday was even hotter, it would not have been so bad if it had been a dry heat but it is pretty muggy and that is not the best way to stay in one piece – I am nearly a grease spot now. John and I had a bridge session with Dave Waters and Toby Webster, and played from 1.30 till 10.30 in the evening, taking time off naturally for a bit of dinner. After all that time John and I won one shilling and threepence, being only 500 up.

There was a bonus yesterday as I was on guard I missed Church Parade. I went to the flicks again, 'Housekeeper's Daughter', which we had seen before in Auckland. It was said we passed the equator in the afternoon but I don't think we got over till early this morning. I'm sure I heard the props scrape over the line as we went!

Thursday, 8 May 1941

On Monday morning our escort, the *Monowai* left us. We were sorry to see her go but we picked up a message that we would be met by the *Prince Robert*.[4] Sure enough at 10 a.m. the Canadian ship joined us and there was quite a bit of cheering on both sides. We had another gunnery practice shooting at old boxes and other rubbish we threw over the stern. Another crew is training to handle a Maxim gun, which is perched up top and used to knock down aircraft.

I will try to give you an idea of our day on board ship. We are wakened at about six and have P.T. at 6.30 which is not very satisfactory, after which I go to the gym for half an hour or more. We are then free till breakfast – for me 8.30. The morning parade is at 9.30, and then we buzz off to lectures – except me for as I am a naval man now I have my gun to guard every morning from 10 a.m. to 12! The lectures finish at noon and we are then free till 2 p.m. when we have another parade and have lectures from then till 4.30, which are an absolute farce. We have some free time from 4.40 until tea at 6.30. In the way of entertainment we have an excellent pianist who plays two hours at

---

4   Canadian National Liner converted to Armed Merchant Cruiser.

lunch and two at tea. He can play everything from real classics to hot swing. We also have the flicks every night with a change of picture every second night. This Saturday and Sunday some of the lads are putting on a concert in aid of the Spitfire Fund.[5]

The lads aboard are all great chaps, including our Whenuapai mob of course.[6] Of the Aussies I see quite a bit off Cliffe, Bluey, Ward and Kennedy. Incidentally Cliffe and Ward were great rugby players and had trips to NZ.

By the way, I hope none of you people received Lord Haw Haw's message saying in effect that the *Awatea* had been sunk?[7] It may have caused you unnecessary worry – we'll hope not!

Sunday, 11 May 1941

We've run into rough weather. It's a real storm and quite a number of the boys are down with seasickness and what's more it is jolly hard trying to write. I was on guard this morning as usual but it was too treacherous to go up to the gun mounting. The boat has had to cut her speed down considerably and we are now going no more than about 9 knots. The nose is digging in. We expect to hit Vancouver on Wednesday. We spend no time in Vancouver but go straight from the port to the train, which is not so hot. I saw my first albatross yesterday. It appeared during my watch and was still following us this morning together with a mate. We saw a ship a couple of days ago and all reckoned it may be a raider. The *Prince Robert* hopped over to give it the once over so all was OK.

Can you send me the *Weekly News* to keep me up to date with what's happening in Auckland and NZ.

Well I must close now and catch the mail. Cheerio for now.

Tons of love to all,

Doug

5   Many Spitfires were partially funded by NZ provinces and Pacific nations. NZers contributed £126,000 sterling to provide funds to buy Spitfires for members of 485 Squadron to fly.

6   From my section at Whenuapai were: Feisst, Freshney, Grierson, Hunt, Latta, Madden, Mosen, Robinson and JD Webster. Ken Law and others were in the other Whenuapai section. Of those on the Awatea 'Hori' Copland, John Davies, Ross Falls, Marty Hume, 'Rosie' Mackie, 'Mick' McNeil, 'Mick' Maskill, Deane Palliser, Austin Smith, and Gray Stenborg all served at 485 Squadron.

7   Lord Haw Haw was the name given to the Nazi propagandist who broadcast from Germany during the war.

Canada

*

Medicine Hat
Monday, 19 May 1941

Dear Mum, Dad and Girls,

As you can see, we are at a place called Medicine Hat in the State of Alberta, 65 miles north of the US frontier.

Let me travel back a day or two. We hit Victoria, Vancouver Island at 10 a.m. Wednesday and were taken off the boat, assembled, marched up the town and back again to the ship, which left at about 12.30. We put on a fair pace to Vancouver and most of the time was occupied in checking kit bags. In the time remaining John, Dave Waters and self went up and saw the skipper who shouted us beer and showed us over the bridge, which was very interesting, especially a type of gyro which records the depth of the sea on a chart, the bottom being sounded 90 times a minute. We reached Vancouver at about six and were marched straight onto a CPR train (all the NZ pilots and Aussie single-engine trainees). The qualified guys, observers, gunners and multi-engine trainees went on CNR. The Aussies went to MacLeod and the NZ twin-engine chaps went to Brandon, Manitoba. The trip during the past night was uninteresting but the food was fresh and appreciated. We had

Awatea arriving in Vancouver

carriages, which were classed as second class but quite comfortable. Buster Kennedy, Toby Webster and I spent an hour and a half with the engine drivers. The engines certainly are large and you go along as though you are riding a horse and get bucked all over the place. We had one stop that evening at about 11 o'clock and of course there was a rush to look for the nearest bar 'parlour' which was never found. In this part of Canada there are no bars as we have. They sell beer in beer parlours, which are similar to our NZ lounges. No one is allowed to drink standing up or carry a glass of beer from one table to another! If you want to buy beer or spirits to consume at home you need a license, which is similar to a benzene permit and costs 50 cents.

Next day, Thursday, was wonderful and we saw most of the Rockies. We were lucky to see bear, deer and moose. The railroad through there is certainly a great bit of work and I was very much taken by it, especially the large tunnels and the spiral. We had only one real stop on the way over and that was at a place called Field. There was a rush to try out Canadian beer but we got a shock when we tasted it! It is terrible stuff but not so bad if you put a bit of salt with it. We buzzed on from Field and our next stop was Calgary where we had nearly two hours from 6 p.m. We had a look round the town and had a few beers and then went and had a go at skittles, which was a bit of fun and filled in time.

Calgary seemed quite a prosperous town and it was full of Air Force chaps, some from NZ. In Calgary there are four Air Force stations. On the train from Calgary to Medicine Hat we had Canadian Air Force and Army. We reached Medicine Hat at 12.30 a.m. and we were bundled into trucks like cattle and brought out to the station. As we arrived we got the shock of our lives to see an aircraft in flames. It was one of the Harvards we had heard so much about and it put us off a little.

It was now nearly morning and we were exhausted. We were shown our barracks, a dormitory filled with double beds, one bed up above the other, similar to bunks aboard ships. We decided to lock ourselves in the barracks. We were exhausted from the journey and did not want to get up at 7 a.m. for breakfast.

The next morning the Corporal had other ideas but had some trouble getting

Rockies

us out of bed. At 10 a.m. we opened the door and went to the mess but they wouldn't give us any breakfast. We were assembled and were ticked off by a sergeant – evidently we are on an RAF station – and we just laughed at him so he left us in disgust. We were paraded before the Station Adjutant, a Scottish Flight Lieutenant and a jolly nice chap, and after a few preliminaries he told us we were only to stay here for a week and the boys started to clap and cheer. He looked over at the drome and said, 'I wish they would invent a Harvard that didn't make that much noise.' Unfortunately they are very noisy machines! We had a free afternoon so I buzzed off to the hangar and went into the officers' room and asked one of them whether there was any show of a trip in a Harvard. He said OK so up I went and he gave me the full works for about an hour.

Why we are here for a week I don't know. Our next stop is Moose Jaw, where there are two stations – an RAF and RCAF – we naturally hope to strike RCAF.

Medicine Hat is a great place. The population is about 11,000 and you would never hope to meet better people. They are so good to us they embarrass us at times. Friday we got leave at about 5.30 and met a great mob who asked us out and we landed up at a dance at 11.30 – they do the real jitterbug here! We finished at 1 a.m. and after a yarn with a few chaps we met one who took us for a tiki tour. He had a great place and a whopping St. Bernard dog. He took us to see the neighbouring towns, mostly to show us the beer parlours, I think. Anyway, we got him home at about 6.30 in the morning, very much under the weather, while we were perfectly sober.

On Saturday morning we formed a funeral party for the chap who was killed here the night we arrived. I've never seen such a disgraceful exhibition as the RAF chaps put on. They took half an hour to arrange us properly according to height and we could have done it ourselves in half a jiff. On Saturday night we went to the cabaret and finished up at a party at a flat, which we had arranged previously. It was a good night and the girls are numerous, pretty, and very sociable.

Yesterday, Sunday, we went and watched baseball in the afternoon. It is a terrible game and almost ten times slower than cricket! In the evening I had supper as they call it here with a lass I have met and who has given me a great time, called Frances Sinclair. Polite and well behaved as well. How do you like that, Dad! The town is about three miles from the station and I've never had to take a taxi here yet. We get into the street and after a little while we are piled into a car and brought home by one of the locals.

I will try and give you some idea of this town. As for the name, it originated back in the old days when some Indians were crossing the river and the Witch Doctor lost his hat. The place mainly runs on the CPR and also a big flour mill – one of the biggest, I believe, in Canada. There is a river running through and it is rather a pretty sight. The shops are similar to NZ and are well kept and goods reasonable in price. There are also plenty of snack shops, which do us well. Last night I had steak, sausages, fried potatoes, peas, apple pie and ice cream and coffee for 85 cents – a real whopper steak about a yard long. Porterhouse too! The sausages were the ones you were talking about – small sausages, but very nice indeed to eat.

This place is noted for rattlesnakes. I haven't seen any in the wilds. A chap down town had a couple in the shop window but they did not look too inviting. We have been asked to go snake shooting by a son-in-law of the chap who took us out last Saturday afternoon. He said the Sunday before they got 35 snakes.

It was rather amusing on the first day. While I was up in the Harvard the boys went over the prairie to have a look at the plane that crashed. As they were wandering along they came across a snake which was about six feet long and not knowing what it was Alan Robinson grabbed it by the tail and started acting the goat. It was called a Black Rat snake, which is non-venomous but eats rattlesnakes.

Sunday is a funny day here, they have church. I think they are more sincere than us, in fact I had tea at Frances' that night and they tried to get me to go along. In the afternoon they have baseball.

They do it in style and have what they call a high school band, which has girls and boys in it up to the age of 19 and they are good. There are about 50 or 60 in the band and they wear white shirts and long white pants with cloaks purple outside and yellow in. The drum major is a girl – who is amazing to watch and can do anything with the stick.

I heard today it would be another week before we go to Moose Jaw – I hope so as we are having a grand time here – a holiday. We have a syllabus of sorts, you'll laugh when you hear it. We are divided into two squads and on alternate days we have an hour's drill, 10–11 a.m. The rest of the time we can rush about the footy field and we are trying to get a team of rugby players to play the officers. We have leave every day from 4.30 p.m. till midnight which doesn't mean a thing to the NZers. If they feel like it they get back at three in the morning and nothing is said. This afternoon I am going to play golf on the local course after I have been to the bank. We were told we had no show of getting any money – I hope the information is wrong as the boys are in need of finance!

I sent you stockings, Peg, for your birthday and also one pair for Mum. I got silk and not nylon, or whatever you call it as the local girls say nylon are no good as they do not stretch. Anyway, you've got no choice!

Yesterday we got leave in the evening and the first thing we did was to have a good feed as we can't tackle the tucker at camp yet. Later we went jitterbugging and had a great time.

Well, I'll close now and try and catch a boat home!
Will write again from Moose Jaw if not before.

Tons of love,

Doug

Medicine Hat Golf Course: Toby Webster, Doug, Dave Waters, Dutch Stenborg, Colin McPherson, John Grierson

Medicine Hat
Monday 26 May, 1941

Dear Mum, Dad and Girls,

Well, we are still here having a small holiday and everything is grand except lack of cash. I have heard we leave late tonight but in this outfit seeing is believing. The boys like it here as the people are so kind but there's a war on and we all want to get into it and have a go. After all, we are here to fly.

Last week passed very uneventfully. One night while we were on leave we were stopped by a pommie officer and his gang of service police. We were asked for our passes for after midnight, which we did not have. Toby Webster had a piece of the officer and we all chipped in. At one stage Toby was under close arrest. There is more in it than I can tell and the story is all round the station and town as the officer is much disliked by all.

I went to a dance out at the station on Tuesday night, which wasn't so good even though they had a good hall and an orchestra of about fourteen. Saturday

WINE, WOMEN AND SONG

night here was a bit of a celebration as it was the anniversary of Victoria's birthday. It is celebrated like Guy Fawkes Day over here and the rockets go for quite a while. All the farmers come into town and have a day at the pub and there are a few dances.

There was another accident here on Friday night. Two were killed, pilot and instructor – I think they must have been acting the goat. The parade is today so I expect we will be raked in again.

On Saturday morning Toby Webster, Alan Robinson, John Grierson, Colin McPherson and self went about six miles over the prairie and near the South Saskatoon River looking for rattlesnakes and anything else we could see. We met a couple of young Canadian lads who had .22 rifles. We had a go at a few geese and in the end managed to shoot a snake. It was a six-footer and was weaving its head from side to side as if about to strike. Alan raised the rifle and shot it through the head.

At present the weather is about on a par with mid NZ summer – quite hot, but it can be very cold in the morning when we get up.

This is how our future trainers, the Harvard greeted us on arrival at Medicine Hat

32 Service Flight Training School
Moose Jaw, Saskatchewan
Thursday, 29 May 1941

Dear Folks!

Plenty has happened since I last put pen to the paper. We were told on Monday we were leaving for Moose Jaw the following morning and were given leave till midnight, which didn't mean a thing as most of us stayed on till about 2 a.m.

Tuesday was very wet and the mud around the station is terrible – there is no tar seal and there seems to be no seepage. There is no mud that can beat Canadian mud! In one way we were glad to get away from Medicine Hat on account of the mud, but the mud here in Moose Jaw is even worse. There was quite a mob at the station to see us off – the boys seemed to live up to the usual NZ tradition and there were some very fond farewells. The journey progressed without event. Toby Webster, Dave Waters, John and self played bridge most of the way. We left the Hat at 12.30 and covered 280 miles to Moose Jaw by 7.15, which was not bad. We were met by buses at the station and then put in billets, had a feed and went to bed.

The Commonwealth Training Scheme was established in Canada early 1941. I think we were the second course from New Zealand. This was a wonderful training area as the flat prairies were ideal for airfields and the country was easy to navigate. Most roads ran north–south or east–west. Moose Jaw was a very small town, a railway stop for CPR from Calgary. Our station was under RAF rather than RCAF control, with the Commanding Officer, instructors and administration all from the UK and primarily ex Battle of Britain pilots.

As we were at an RAF station we got RAF allowances and this was 50% less than a food allowance on a Canadian station. The food therefore was lousy. There were quite a few Chinese restaurants around town and one in particular set himself up at the station gate and did quite well out of us.

[Letter continues]
Yesterday was spent in interviews: the CGI, CFI, accounts, medical and so on. We were not free till about six and then we went to town. The station is an RAF show and a bit of an improvement. By the way, the CO at the Hat told a yarn to us and, after cracking the NZers up properly, said that as we

were of such a type we were all to train in fighters! So it looks as though we'll all be fighter pilots. We are training on Harvards and today were interviewed by our flight commanders and ours seems OK. There are two NZ pilots here as instructors. The way they run flying here is that we are split up into two shifts. Half are on duty for 24 hours flying from 12 midday. The next 24 hours is taken up in lectures about six hours a day. As for leave we get every second weekend from midday Saturday till Sunday midnight. The other weekend we will be flying.

Moose Jaw is considered the toughest possie out west and we have been told to look out for ourselves. There are of course some fine families, but apparently a few of the boys like to shoot one another now and again – seems strange but true. As for the women I'll leave that to your imagination. We keep at least fifty yards' distance anyway. The town is quite different to Medicine Hat.

I start flying tomorrow – I hope – we also expect to get weekend leave.

Well, that seems to be all the news for now so I'll buzz off. A few of the boys got reply cablegrams today, which is the first news received since leaving.

Tons of love to all

Doug

Moose Jaw
Monday, 2 June 1941

Dear Folks!

Well we have been here nearly a week now and are more or less settled down. The boys are still going crook because we have been promised fighters instead of bombers.

Regarding our instructor, John Grierson, Gray Stenborg (another King's lad!) and I have got a great fellow, F/O Bell, who has seen service this war in Blenheims and is suffering slightly from nerves. He is fairly quiet and very thorough but he yarns and treats us as one of his own 'tribe'. Flying has been negligible and I only have 30 minutes to my credit.

Our course was initially upset because we had all volunteered for flying twin-engine aircraft with the intent of a posting to bomber command in the UK. The way things were going there were only single-engine planes. The 65 of us decided to sign a petition to the CO a W/C Morrison who had reddish hair, ginger moustache and distinctive sideboards. Our petition was received and we all were summoned to the Assembly Hall and were read the 'Riot Act' according to Air Ministry Orders. Our action constituted 'mutiny and was punishable by death!' The entire course burst into laughter whereupon 'Ginger' Morrison left the room.

We were later advised we would be changing places with another course flying 'twins' but this did not eventuate either as the exchange course contracted mumps.

From this point we were instructed on Harvards and at the end of the course most, including John Grierson, were posted to Twin Engine Operational Training Units. Of the 65 on the course, about 80% went on 'twins' when they got to England and only about 15 of those will have survived the war. With hindsight I was lucky.

[Letter continues]

The rest of the trainees say the Harvards are great machines to fly and as long as one is careful there is very little trouble. If we get transferred we will probably get into night bombers, which will be pretty good. We have to put in at least 72 hours flying here in 10 weeks, after which we will get some leave.

The first mail arrived from home a couple of days ago and the hut was quiet for once as many of us were a trifle homesick. It was wonderful to hear from you and glad to see that you received the silk and though you did not mention the cards I sent I expect you received them.

Last weekend we were off and we had a jolly good sleep in a pub in town. We went and had a few pots of beer, went to the swimming baths which are mineral water and fairly warm. After a couple of hours swimming we went to a local hop and got to bed about two and slept till 2.30 Sunday afternoon. On Sunday, what was left of it, we spent mostly in the baths – a good occupation as it helps maintain some fitness.

I have now had 2½ hours in the Harvard. They are quite different to the Tiger Moths. You cruise at 150 mph indicated on the instruments. This is equivalent to about 170 miles per hour [land speed]. In the air they are great to handle but taking off and landing is another story. We have to land on runways, which consist of tar sealing about a mile long and about 20 yards wide. With a cross wind it is hard to keep the plane straight. The gen is to fly the plane about two feet from the ground and then flatten out and wait for the bump.

These aircraft have retractable undercarriage, dual petrol tanks, dual timing gear, boost and artificial horizon and gyroscopic compass. We have to play around with the settings on a circuit in order to gain some experience. There isn't much time to think so we need to be very careful to let the right things off at the right time.

Although this school is very large (there are about four courses going through) we haven't killed any of our mob off yet!

Must buzz off now. Am fit and well.

Love Doug

Moose Jaw
Tuesday, 10 June 1941

Dear All,

We are meant to be flying but it has been a bit of a waiting game. It has been poor for flying as it is always clouding over and then we get recalled. Some of the boys have got good time in but a majority of us have had very few hours. I've only got 3½ hours so far and am by no means the lowest. My instructor is not too fit and I have been taken over by a new chap for the time being – an American – who joined up with the Canadian Air Force. He is only a young fellow and from all accounts a very good pilot. The sooner I go solo the better as once solo you can put your hours up rapidly. I had a very good flight the other day. The instructors (six of them), did some formation and I was lucky enough to go as passenger with F/O Bell. Great show! They fly with wing tips nearly touching the tail plane of the nearest Harvard.

By the way, I wonder if you could get me some NZ wings. We get RAF or Canadian wings here but NZ would be better. If you can, please send over two or three pairs. You may not be able to get any in Auckland but you will be able to get them in Palmerston North for sure.

John and I have kept up the swimming to keep fit. I can now at least run about ten yards! We are trying to pick a team to play the Aussies at rugby.

If we get it going we will play in Moose Jaw and give the local Canadians a treat.

I changed £7 in Medicine Hat. Unluckily the Moose Jaw Branch wanted it back so I went in and saw the Manager of the Bank of Canada and gave him the dollars. As a result I am a bit short again. He said it would be better for me to write to Mr Askew[8] and get him to cable the money out from England. I will drop him a line in any case and tell him I will be over there in a month or two.

The bank manager took John and me up to his house – a very nice home and asked us to have a drink. John and I thought we were on for a beer session. We got a bit of a knockback when he came in with a bottle of whiskey and poured out two whoppers. It was rather funny to see John and myself drinking it as though we drank nothing else. Oh for a bottle of Lion now!

We went into the CPR railway station and got some pamphlets advertising NZ. There was one photo of Auckland. How is the place – I didn't appreciate the climate till I came here. Just wait till I get my body in the sun at Manly again, whoopee!

From your letter, Dad, you seem to be having quite a profitable time winning golf balls. I wish I could get more golf over here on decent links like Middlemore. I've had one game here and that was at the Hat. The greens were wonderful – sand and oil. Some liquid to keep the sand moist and to bind it a bit. When you reach the green if your ball manages to dodge the castings you pull out a gadget like a carpet sweeper and obliterate all the footmarks of the previous players. Great fun! The mosquitoes there were like German dive bombers. Whoppers. They fly in formation and when they nip you they take out a chunk. Once one of them manages to bore into you they are all in boots and all, digging away in the same spot.

A few of the boys, including yours truly, have got colds. The lads at Brandon, the other half of us, have got mumps and are under orders and confined to camp.

Bad luck about Bob.[9] It beats me why they couldn't find out he had TB before. Pretty tough travelling around the world to have a party with Gyllies and he has to leave before I reach there! He may come home via Canada and if he is fit enough to do a bit of visiting I may meet him. Here's hoping! Mr and

---

8 Manager of District Bank in Carlisle, Cumberland.
9 Bob Gyllies was diagnosed with TB at his medical in England and deemed not fit to enter the forces. After the war he was best man at my wedding and Hamish's godfather.

Mrs Gyllies will be glad in a way to have him home though Bob will be sorry to miss out.

We have got a wireless between a few of us in the barracks – $15 and well worth it. We haven't paid for it so the sale isn't through but it is as good as ours. We get Hollywood every night and we get great music. I have not invested in a camera yet.

Well I'll get a bit of shut eye so will close. Love to all.

Doug

Moose Jaw
Tuesday, 17 June 1941

Dear All,

Another week and today I got mail from you all!

The hot weather has started. We have had nearly a week of perfect weather and the sun has certainly got a bit of heat in it. Today it is about 85°F in the shade but there is a nice cool breeze. On Sunday, which was a perfect day, we found a great spot to relax. They have an aquatic club down on the river where there are canoes and games of all sorts, diving boards and good people – including very nice girls. What amazed me was the water. Being river water I thought it would be fairly cold, but it is surprisingly warm and clear. They go in for these river canoe clubs over here and I think in the town of Moose Jaw there are about five clubs, which are very well organised. We enjoyed it so much on Sunday that after duties yesterday we happened down again, getting there after dinner. We had a swim and a paddle round in the canoes and a good sunbathe.

We had weekend leave but we did nothing out of the ordinary. We went to town and had a few beers then went to a dance and slept at the hotel. Oh yes! At about 12 a few of us were wandering along the road when I saw an airman in greatcoat with pyjamas, and on second looks I saw two good old NZ wings on the shoulders. His group had arrived about a week ago on the *Aorangi*. We chatted for a while and their CO S/L Wilton, John and I knew at Levin. He is over here for a few months to see how the Canadian scheme differs from NZ.

I wrote to Jack Seabrook, my S/L at Whenuapai and gave him a very vivid description indeed about the stations over here.

We have a new complaint now. We have not been getting paid! Since we have been in Canada we have only received $25 advanced to us by the RNZAF. There were some real stories going around last Friday, I can tell you, and all the blame fell on the NZ Government. Believe me they were well praised! A few of the boys were in Regina and saw the Accounting Officer in the hope of settling the affair. He was up poste haste on Monday and we are apparently going to get our back-pay soon. Will the boys go mad when they get paid! I wrote to Mr Askew and asked him to send $50 to $100, whatever he thought fit. A draft of English and Norwegians has just finished and they are showing off their wings. The Norwegians have great wings and they look very fine in their officers' uniforms. They have ten days at Banff at the expense of the Norwegian Government and the boys are looking forward to it.

You mention the war effort of Canada in your letter Dad. As a matter of fact it is very difficult as there are many Cannucks of German and Italian descent and they naturally won't sign up. Financially I think they help the cause but otherwise not so hot. An instance during our stay in Medicine Hat they had a recruiting hut in the town and after running it for a week they got three recruits at the expense of $1500!

This climate is very changeable. Today we had a perfect day and at 2 p.m. the sky looked rather black and soon we got lightning – fork and other kinds, quite a show. Down came the rain, hail and everything else. It only lasted about half an hour but it was quite a storm. The kites, heavy though they are, even with brakes applied went for a dance. It was all hands on deck to get them in: we were sopping before we had gone a couple of yards. A couple of the chaps in our flight were solo in the storm and they had a lot of fun.

Some of the boys have as much as 30 hours flying up while some of us haven't gone solo. I have been told I go solo tomorrow morning. F/O Bell expressed his regret at not getting me away sooner and said that as soon as he gets me solo, he'll bump my time up quickly. John, who has the most time up in our flight, had some fun tonight. He went up to practice slow rolls, which are the most difficult in the aerobatic line. He rolled OK but when he finished he was shooting towards earth and pulled her out a bit fast and had a beautiful 'blackout'. He lost over 3000ft in that lot. He is not so keen on aerobatics now.

We got a new draft of Englishmen. They don't look too healthy. The trip over knocked the stuffing out of them.

You would like the cafés over here, Dad. The food is very cheap and good. They have great salads, shrimp, chicken and wonderful fresh asparagus. I had a 50 cent meal the other day comprising: fruit cocktail, soup, celery, olives, radish and asparagus, shrimp salad, roast turkey and veges, ice cream, buttered toast, coffee and all that goes with it – not bad.

I haven't sent you any mail by air, and I would think you can understand that at 70 cents each my pay wouldn't last long on its present basis. However, when I'm holding I'll pop you one or two.

Tons of love to you all,

Doug

Moose Jaw
Sunday, 22 June 1941

Dear Mum, Dad and Girls,

Today is the hottest day we have so far experienced – 90°F in the shade – but the wind is blowing at 50 mph, which means no solo. The wind is warm and brings clouds of dust with it. Last week was rather rough though fine and I did not get in any solo till later in the week. I was getting a bit worried but the Flight Commander told me not to and I've got away now and all is OK. As a matter of fact I went rather well! One of the Norwegians had bad luck. The night he got his wings he went night flying and when going around again he pulled his flaps up instead of his undercarriage – an easy thing to do but disastrous – he made a beautiful mess of the plane but was lucky enough to come out with a small cut on his head; a great way to finish a course. This station has had very few crashes and has a great record by exceeding the monthly flying hours of all other stations in Canada and now we do no flying on Sundays.

On Sunday we spent most of the day on the river – from midday till late. It was great down there and a Canadian and I paddled in the canoe a fair way upstream where there was some nice scenery. I have got quite a tan up now. The water is very warm and I think that most of the leave we get will be spent by the river. We still have not received any pay apart from another $10 advance but it is rumoured that we get it this week. Three of us have been asked down to Regina for the weekend by three lucky lasses who have a nice big Pontiac car.

You want to see the tropical kit they have issued us: 'Rompers' – all we want is a bucket and spade and we would look the part! We will get a photo taken of us in them and post them over. We certainly look tricks.

One of our boys had a weekend about 100 miles south of here. He went on a cross country to Swift Current and back and he lost his map on the return journey. It got down among the fuselage and he had no show of getting it. For some time he looked for Moose Jaw but finally had to make a precautionary landing at Mossbank, a bomber and gunnery school. He apparently had a great time there and was billeted in the sergeants' mess where there is a team of Aussies.

A few of our lads have now got the mumps – about ten of them – which is pretty bad luck as they will miss our course. The boys at Brandon got them pretty badly and the whole camp was put under quarantine, which we have so far steered clear of. In my opinion the whole thing started on the boat where one of the boys got them.

We got our first mail by boat today and I received a *Weekly*, *Free Lance* and *Observer*, which were much appreciated. I also got a letter from Ruth[10] with a couple of photos taken at the wedding. Some of the lads got as many as 20 letters – not bad.

Good-bye for now.

Love Doug

---

10 Ruth Taylor married Bruce Craig.

32 SFTS
Moose Jaw
Monday, 30 June 1941

Dear Mum, Dad and Girls,

We had the misfortune to be raked into a parade – a victory parade, they called it – through Moose Jaw. The fair is on so we have to show willing. The hierarchy said we only had to go about a mile and then would have the evening free to look around the show, free of admission. We went about ten miles more like it! Mr McKenzie King[11] took the salute. The funny part was there was an Army band leading – a good band – and the Home Guard had to be in and they had a boys' bugle band. All was OK while the Army band played but when the boys played the result was not so hot as they had a time of their own which was half as fast again as the leading band. The boys were doing the polka and it reminded me of a Laurel and Hardy picture which I saw long ago when they were in the Army in India – do you remember it?

Last weekend was our weekend off and we went down to Regina and had a wonderful time. We got in touch with the girls we had met a couple of weeks ago. Starting at a Flying Officer Wettel's place we had a few beers and proceeded to give the town a good look over. The girls had their Pontiac again so no taxis or walking needed. Believe me, we can pick them! On Sunday they took us to a place called Regina Beach, about 40 miles away. It is quite a nice spot on Regina Lake and we had a great time.

We had a great day and what surprised me was the cheapness of cherries, which are equivalent to about a bob[12] a pound and tasty. The Wettels are taking a bach for two months and have asked us down for our next weekend which will depend primarily on 'swot' and secondly on money. We stayed down there till 8 p.m. and caught a train home, arriving at 11 p.m. Some had very little sleep last night but will make up for it tonight.

Toby Webster and a Canadian and I went to a bit of a regatta at the aquatic club last week. They had canoe races, a swimming race and then had a sing-song around a fire with toasted marshmallows. All this was followed by a dance which was a good show. It was a pity we had to be in by midnight. Poor

---

11 Prime Minister of Canada during WWII.
12 Slang for shilling.

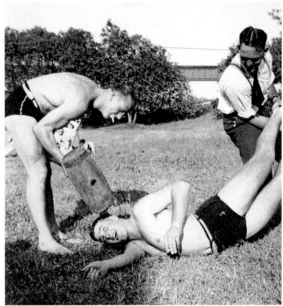

ABOVE LEFT John Grierson and Doug with lucky Tiki

ABOVE RIGHT Outside the Aquatic Club: Toby Webster, Doug, Alan Robinson

old John was not too fit that night as he had an abscess on a tooth and had it taken out.

I have now got 25 hours up. I had a good cross country which was really enjoyable – 200 miles of prairie – but it is quite easy to get lost if you don't use your wits. I will be going on a 400 mile within the next day or so. These planes are certainly the goods and the more I fly them the more I like them, however they are much noisier than the Tiger Moths. It will seem strange when I get on to night and formation flying. John has started night flying and he thinks it is pretty easy. We have to do 40 landings here which are meant to take 10 hours.

We got a bit of back-pay last week – $53 – so the boys are pretty happy.

I am enclosing a few more photos and I sent a parcel which you ought to get with this mail.

Love to all.

Doug

Doug

32 SFTS
Moose Jaw
Monday, 7 July 1941

Dear Mum, Dad and Girls,

It is getting more like the tropics every day.

Last week was just the usual – doing very little apart from lectures and flying. One night I went to town and had a jolly good feed. Group Captain Isitt[13] came over one day last week. It was good to see an NZer. He had a yarn to us and said that he'd learned from news he received that his racehorse Kindergarten was still going well. A fine chap and he asked us all our troubles, though he could do little for us.

13   Great War veteran of the Somme who transferred to the RFC. In 1940 he was in Canada as the NZ representative on the board of the Empire Air Training Scheme and in 1942 was posted to Britain as Air Commodore.

Back: Doug, Gray Stenborg, John Grierson, John Davies / Front: Charlie Croall, Alan Robinson

The 'Wings' exams are due on the 21st of this month, so I will have to do a bit of 'swot' to help get the NZ average up.

I started formation flying last week and John and I went for our first solo formation together and had quite a bit of fun. We were tootling along, me leading when I spied a plane on our tail, which proceeded to shoot us up. It played about for quite a while and then joined the formation and who should it be but my instructor. When he got tired of our faces off he hopped in a dive and proceeded to do a spot of low flying. I have also started going on solo aerobatics – screaming dives have nothing on me! When I was doing them dual I had the peculiar sensation of 'blacking out' in a loop.

I have done some night flying and it is a thrill. F/O Bell sent me off solo after three landings and away I went. I managed to get down every time and the instructor seemed to think the landings were good. The bumpiness of a landing is exaggerated to a great extent and you think the end is near. It is strange when you get the stick back and you are starting to sink and you begin to wonder whether you are going to drop two feet or fifty.

This weekend was mucked up for me as I was night flying till three in the morning and had to sleep till midday. John and I went to the aquatic club in the afternoon and had a bit of sun. On Sunday there was a dust storm which completely obliterated the town. However we dodged most of it as the dust kept away from the river.

I received a good luck charm from Nanna. Please thank her as I wrote to her the night before I received it. By the way, I lost the tiki you gave me, Dad, when flying the other day and I can't find it anywhere. Would it spoil my luck if you gave me another?

Well, I'll say cheerio for now. Love to all.

Doug

32 SFTS
Moose Jaw
Canada

Monday, 21 July 1941

Dear Mum, Dad and Girls,

Our exams start tomorrow. I am beginning to think I know very little, but hopefully enough to get through and get a decent average. Tomorrow we have armament oral, which I know quite well; the next day we have signals; and the next two days are taken up with navigation, armament written, airmanship, engines and maintenance. We had an exam in 'identification of aircraft' and though it counts very little towards 'wings' I managed to clock 94% as did John and Toby Webster who took second place – I wish I could do the same with the other subjects. As for flying I expect to get about a dozen more hours in before the course finishes. I had 'Wings' Cross Country this afternoon and passed and I had my CFI final test the other day and from all accounts did well getting 'high average' for the flying and 'exceptional' for the blind flying. We have a choice on leaving here as to which aircraft we wish to fly, and I am going to put in for (1) coastal command, (2) medium bombers, (3) heavy bombers, and hope I get on to a Sunderland. It is jolly hard to pick and choose as now I am very keen on single-engine aircraft as well.

We spent the weekend in camp except for late on Saturday afternoon when the temperature reached 110 degrees and we thought something ought to be done about it. As a matter of fact it is very hard to concentrate on any work in the heat we have had during the past few days. Next weekend exams will be over. John and I are going to Medicine Hat where we should have a pretty good time.

Tons of love. Goodbye for now.

Doug

Moose Jaw
Monday, 28 July 1941

Dear Mum, Dad and Girls,

Exams are over but I don't think I did that well, in fact 'B All' but that can't be helped. I've passed navigation and the only mark we have received besides is oral armament in which I got 73%, which was very low. Old John must have written a snappy paper heading the list with 93% the highest mark yet attained in navigation since this station started, the previous highest mark being 92%. The NZ boys are showing them how as another one of the boys got 92%. In the oral armament both John and I got 93%.

I spent this last weekend in Medicine Hat. John and I went with four other lads, leaving at 9 a.m. on Saturday morning and getting there in the afternoon at 5 p.m. We stayed at the Cecil Hotel, which is run by a fellow who was in the RFC in the last war and who made a bit of a fuss of us when we were there for ten days in May. I took Frances Sinclair out on Saturday night and spent Sunday at their place and I got to bed just after midnight. Sunday was spent eating, mostly – guess what we had for tea? Corn on the cob with plenty of butter, pepper and salt. Taken straight from the garden and put into the pot. Sweet corn over here is hard to beat!

Back: John Grierson, Gray Stenborg, Toby Webster, Alan Robinson, Doug / Front: Colin McPherson, Dave Waters, John Davies

We had a quiet night at the Sinclairs' and spent most of the time talking. I caught the train back to Moose Jaw at 1 a.m. this morning and was in camp by eight o'clock.

We were pretty tired and my instructor thought it was a great joke and immediately sent me up for an hour's formation – pretty rough it was! When I got down I was stonkered and slept from midday till nearly six this evening. We went along the road to a 'Chink' who gave us a jolly good feed for 40 cents. Tonight I had veal cutlets, peas, chips, soup and banana pie.

When in England I think it will be better to address letters to Cumberland, to the District Bank. I could give Mr Askew the address of my station and I would get mail a lot faster than mail going to NZ House.

Well that is all for now so I'll close. Love to all.

Doug

ABOVE Doug in Harvard.   BELOW John Grierson and Doug

32 SFTS
Moose Jaw

Dear Mum, Dad and Girls,

As we are setting sail for the East Coast the day after tomorrow, I thought I would send this letter airmail.

We receive our wings and stripes tomorrow, so I'll be a fully-fledged pilot. As far as commissions are concerned we will not know whether we have received one or not till we get to Halifax. We get three days' leave included in our trip across Canada and John and I will spend some time together.

I finished my flying test Friday and was sorry to see the last of the Harvard. The past 40 or 50 hours in them I have had complete confidence and the more flying I got the better I liked it. We were told that these planes are absolute death traps but most of our course agrees that they are the 'goods'. We were interviewed by the CO the other afternoon and from what he has said we now seem to be certainties for fighter planes and to tell you the truth I will not be sorry now I have had time to think about the other option – bombers!

Since flying finished we have had two nights entertaining our instructors. The first was last Saturday night and little parties sprang up through the town with about eight of the boys and two or three instructors apiece. Last Monday night we hired the Elk Club, and took all the instructors down there and gave them a bit of a do. From all accounts the instructors enjoyed themselves. As the licensed places have to close at 11 we all went down to a café in town and had a feed and a jolly good yarn and got back to camp at about one after a very hectic evening.

Yesterday we returned the equipment issued to us during our stay and we had to make up our log books.

After running us round the camp they told us we could have a local leave pass which ends tomorrow morning. All yesterday and last evening was spent at the aquatic club lying in the sun, canoeing and playing a game of volleyball. Last night we spent playing ping-pong and swimming. I am writing this letter at the aquatic club prior to a piece of the good old sun. Tonight they are having a dance here, which I will no doubt attend, and from all accounts it should be a jolly good show. I don't really know what we would have done without the aquatic club as we have had no exercise in the camp at all and have to depend primarily on the exercise we get down there in the weekend to keep us fit. Toby Webster and I had a run or two around the aerodrome but we had to give that in.

From all accounts when we get to England among other things we will find a shortage of cigarettes as they are now rationed. If it is no trouble to you, would you send odd parcels of Grey's cigarette tobacco, together with papers? We are led to believe the kind of cigarettes you can get in England are tripe and may not be the best for health's sake.

In your last letter, Dad, you mentioned Moose Jaw and the lightning displays. We get some wonderful shows and many of the boys attempted to get photos but there were not many successes. They seem to come on perfectly clear nights and are not even followed up by rain. The Aurora Borealis is also seen here but so far all I have noticed is the continued light from the sun up north – quite a good sight and very useful for night flying. Talking about photos, there is one thing I should have brought over with me and that is a camera. I intend to buy one but so far finance has not been absolutely A1 in indulging in this sort of purchase. As a matter of fact I have spent most of my last pay on clothes – slacks, shirts, pullovers and shoes, all of which I believe are very hard to procure in England. If I find I have got a few spare dollars before leaving for England I will buy a camera, even if it is just a cheap one.

Talking about clothes, I sent two pair of nylon stockings to you, Mum, which you should receive in time for your birthday and yesterday I saw some rather nice ties similar to those you brought out with you on your last trip. They are quite expensive so I hope you like them OK. I sent some slippers and a wallet previously, which ought to reach you before you get this letter.

John and Toby have just arrived and John tells me we are going to stay at Fort William with people by the name of McCullough whom his family met in NZ through Rotary. If they give us as good a time as we've had from most of the Canadians we should do well.

We had a visit from an NZ officer Squadron Leader Gilkinson who has only been away from NZ about a month and he said we will meet the boys from whom we were separated in NZ. Great! The *Awatea* and *Aorangi* are now off the run and the boys will be landing on the east coast and not the west so in all probability we will go over to England in the same ship.

We now have the final results through for the exams. I did not do so well but John held the fort, taking second position with an average of 88%. My average was OK at just under 82% – but my position was twentieth. I lost marks in the one I reckoned I would get near 90% – quite a shock was received when the colours went up and I only got 71%. I managed to head the list

Dr Crawford McCullough, Grace and Donald McCullough (killed 1942)

in one subject – airmanship, which includes engines and maintenance – in which I got 180 out of 200. As for the other subjects, in signals I got 83% in the written and 100% in the practical. In navigation I did badly and only got 145 out of 200. Oral armament gave me 83%.

I received Colin McGruther's letter which you forwarded to me and from his note he seems to have been through Crete as well as Greece and I'm glad to hear Jock McGruther is not very badly injured. I have started a letter to Mrs McGruther and it should be finished next month sometime.

Well I seem to have reached the end of my ration as far as paper goes so I'll close.

Cheerio for now and tons of love.

Doug

Training at Moose Jaw was intensive and professional and we all qualified for our 'wings'. Flying was mainly solo and we completed cross-country navigational flying, night flying, formation, aerobatics, steep turns, spinning and forced landings.

The Harvard was well advanced on the Tiger Moth but nevertheless we were flying solo after six hours dual. From the first flight at Moose Jaw on 30 May to course end on 1 August I had completed 97 hours flying and achieved a proficiency assessment of average!

The weather in Canada was generally good for flying and the grid layout of the roads made navigation easy. We had a few problems when the storms came up. Firstly the wind could go around 180 degrees very quickly and overshooting the runway became a problem. Secondly we operated with flares rather than electric lighting. Consequently when it was windy the flares would go out making landing at night difficult.

Halifax
Monday, 18 August 1941

Dear Mum, Dad and Girls,

Well here we are in Halifax waiting to be shifted on.

We were given eight days to get to our destination. The few days prior to leaving Moose Jaw, parties were frequent with officers, ground staff and friends, so we were kept busy. The farewell was good and there was a good muster of girls. Instructors and ground crew were very sorry to see us go as they got on well with us and we were the first course to be farewelled by the ground crew. A great honour, indeed!

We left Moose Jaw at 5.30 and when we arrived at Regina we had another farewell to contend with. We reached Winnipeg at 6.15 the next morning after a good night's sleep. Most of the boys stayed on all day there – all except John and I who pushed on a couple of hours later. We reached Fort William at about 11 p.m. to be greeted by Dr McCullough. He took us up to his beach house, which is about 25 miles from Fort William. It was a great place called Birch Beach on Lake Superior where they have a diving board and speedboat. It very much reminded me of Auckland with islands dotted here and there and all that was missing was the salt in the water. We were at Fort William from Saturday night till Wednesday. Most of that time at the beach and it was far from quiet! Dr and Mrs McCullough were always trying to get us into trouble and their married daughter Isobel was a real menace. Isobel took charge of us on Tuesday and took us on a sightseeing tour in the morning around Fort William and Port Arthur, which are only a few miles apart. As a matter of fact I think these are two of the prettiest towns I have ever seen. On Tuesday night we went on a 'spree' and started with a cocktail party at a millionaire's whose wife has modelled in New York for Elizabeth Arden. She is pretty snappy too, very much so! The party did not finish till after one. We then all went out to one of the bootleggers' by the name of 'Uncle Frank' who had a place with a wireless pickup and sold grog at terrific prices. At the end of the evening – or should say early morning – we proceeded to a café and had a good feed of steak and onions.

CNR ticket Montreal to Halifax

The Doctor had a big job waking us but he managed to get us down to the train at 6.45 a.m. They are certainly wonderful people and kept John and I on the go. We had a letter from Mrs McCullough and Isobel today and they are dropping you a note and some photos. So much for Fort William.

We headed out in great style on Wednesday and reached Toronto next morning at 6.30. We did not look up any addresses there but had a good look around including the Bank of Commerce building. It is a big town and, from what we saw of it, very nice. We left for our next port of call, Kingston, at 4 p.m. that afternoon. You may say, why Kingston? Well it's a long story. The night before I left Moose Jaw I had a letter from Bob Gyllies and he told me that Digger Robertson and Nook Fenwick were at 31 SFTS Kingston training for the Fleet Air Arm.[14] So we took pot luck. We arrived there at about seven and after booking in at the hotel I got on the phone and rang through to the station but they told me I could not see them. John and I popped into a taxi and got the guard house working and we saw Digger and Nook. They are looking very fit and both have earned their wings though they haven't got them up yet. They have to do two more months there and then they will be off. Billy McManemin is finishing his course in England. As Dig and Nook were night flying they could not get into town but we stayed yarning to them

14 The Fleet Air Arm boys had a tough time of it. While my peers and I already had our 'wings', the Fleet Air Arm were only just starting their flying training. When they reached England they were given Able Seaman's uniforms and spent nine months doing menial tasks before getting to camp.

till about 11 o'clock and then we caught the bus back. We met two other NZ boys in town and had a few beers with them. Next day we hoped Dig and Nook would be able to get into town but they could not make it, so their place was taken by two other lads.

We left Kingston for Montreal at one that afternoon and reached our destination at about 5.30. The train for Halifax, *The Ocean Limited* left at 7.30 so we had a couple of hours and visited the rougher part of the town around Chinatown. The trip on the train was not very enjoyable as we were six hours late due to failure to fill the engine with water. One of the engineers forgot to look at the gauge. We reached Halifax at 2 a.m. yesterday. Camp is the worst I've ever seen though it is a pretty fair depot and handles many thousands of men.

All the boys we trained with at Whenuapai are here. The entire 10 and 11 courses have had a good reunion. All fit and many commissioned. We have now worked out that none of the boys in 10 course were killed while training, which is a great record. We may go over with the boys from the *Dominion* if we get any Monarch ham.[15] Comprenez vous?

During my leave I bought a second-hand camera, a real cheap job but I reckon it was a bargain and I hope the photos come out OK.

Well, I'll buzz off now. Tons of love to all and thanks for everything.

Cheerio, Doug

P.S. You may get some photos in an envelope from Moose Jaw. We got Dave Waters who contracted the mumps to take some snaps of us with our newly acquired wings and stripes.

15 Coded message to pass censor. It was thought the transport would be the *Dominion Monarch*.

At Sea Once Again

*

CANADA TO ICELAND AND
TRANSIT TO BOURNEMOUTH

At Sea
Sunday, 23 August 1941

Dear Mum, Dad and Girls,

We have now been at sea three days and at the speed we are travelling we will be going for a fair while yet.

To get back to where I last left off. We were drafted on Tuesday morning last and given our orders on Wednesday as well as some pay, which is always handy. We were then told to pack bags and to be on parade at 5.45 that afternoon which did not give us much notice. John and the boys commissioned were not drafted with our lot and when we left on Wednesday afternoon they had still received no news. John and I had the afternoon together and brought a few things to send home. When we got back to the parade ground we found that we had to march to the wharf, a distance of about five miles, which naturally enough no one approved of.

Atlantic crossing, view
from *HMS Worcestershire*

We got down to the wharves and as we passed the ships we wondered
which one we would get. All our guesses were wrong as we ended up on an
auxiliary armed merchant cruiser, the name of which I cannot mention,[16]
but its size I should say is about 11,000 tons. We were then shown our
billets. We expected cabins but no show! The 140 of us, all sergeants
needless to say, are piled into a couple of staterooms about the size of our
big living room with a mattress and two blankets each. It was a bit of a
come down after the trip over the Pacific but I find I sleep very well indeed
in spite of the type of accommodation. The food is good – it is the same

16 HMS *Worcestershire*, an armed merchant cruiser similar to HMS *Monowai*, the escort from
Auckland. Built by Fairfield Shipbuilding, Glasgow, in 1931, this 10,500 ton ship spent much of
the war transporting troops. It was hit by a U-Boat in April 1941 during an Atlantic run and on
6 June 1944 sailed for Juno Beach with troops for the Normandy landings. After the war she was
returned to Bibby's and converted back from a 2000-man troop carrier to a 100-passenger First
Class Liner.

Convoy out from Halifax

as the sailors get and they certainly get fed well. We have to run the mess ourselves. We get our own food and wash up afterwards. The Royal Navy certainly can't complain about food. I had my first feed of fresh herring the other day and very good it was too.

We were entertained all Thursday morning by a medical parade and also by watching a convoy leave the harbour – a steady stream of boats of all shapes follow one another out to sea for a period of about four hours. As it happened, we led the convoy and the escort together with a couple of destroyers and a couple of corvettes. Our pace is terrific! A steady 6 knots. It is a wonderful sight to see this convoy. There is half a century and a score boats all lined up in about six lines and they keep their dressing in every direction. Every time you look at them it appears you are still at the same spot in the middle of the ocean – reminds me of the 'Ancient Mariner'. Up till now we have been watched over by coastal command planes, which scout out every inch of the ocean. They are a great asset and I expect we will be watched over by Sunderlands for many miles prior to our reaching England.

Our routine on board is quite easy going. We have breakfast at 8.30 and are then free till 10 a.m. when we have a parade and boat drill. From this time we can go and do as we please. Our meals are at 12.45, 4.30 and 7.30 – respectively lunch, tea and supper. We have a job or two, one is a watch at the anti-aircraft guns, the object being to identify any type of aircraft that approaches and also we may be detailed by orderly sergeants.

So far I have been lucky and only struck gun watch once although I am on again tomorrow afternoon and I hope it is nice and sunny. The weather so far has been good and the wind is quite fresh but I expect there will be a change soon. We have had the flicks once. Every quarter of an hour or so the film had to be changed causing some delay but it was quite good fun with a lot of Aussies and Cannucks. We have had a bit of Housie – a nickel in – but so far I have drawn a blank. My only complaint is the living quarters and lavatories, which are really filthy, and I don't think I'll ever see another bath or shower till I reach England. However, it is all experience.

Doug

Still at Sea
Monday, 31 August

We still plug on and so far have sighted no land. It is rumoured that we will leave the convoy on Tuesday or thereabouts and head north to an island shaped like an animal[17] and from there will take another ship 'home'. As a matter of fact I don't mind how long we are on the water, as I must say I like the sea. Seasickness aboard has been slight in spite of some rather dirty weather, which reached a climax yesterday. We had to spend this morning picking up some of the stragglers in the convoy.

We've seen no subs or other enemy craft, although there was a bit of a scare a couple of days ago. Two ships were sighted at about three o'clock and off we went with the destroyer well in the lead. As we got nearer we could distinguish them as schooners. We stopped them anyway and after putting a shot across

17 Iceland

their bows a boarding party was sent over armed to the teeth both with guns and provisions. They turned out to be Portuguese fishing boats, which had been at sea about three months and all that the Navy got out of them was a request for cigarettes, which they readily gave.

I can't say enough about the Navy as they do their work thoroughly with few complaints and they have treated us boys very well indeed, giving us more or less the run of the ship. It is not as good as the *Awatea* where we could do our 'watch' in shorts. Here we have to get well wrapped up. I will feel the cold a bit this winter as I have just had two summers on end, the second of which was very hot. My blood will be thinner than usual and not exactly welcome the cold.

As for finance, I think I've worked things pretty well in that by the time I get to England I'll be broke! Cigarettes are apparently in short supply at 'home', and I will look forward to a stray tin of Grey's. I have got a fairly good stock at present, which ought to last a few weeks, also some tea and sugar, which I will deposit in Cumberland for their use when I get the chance.

I've seen another movie 'Three Sailors' with Claude Hulbert and a couple of other comedians – it was a very amusing show. Some of the boys go as many as four times to pass away the hours. I have heard we are going to have a concert aboard but like everything else I will believe it when I see it.

I have just done a couple of hours watch and it was darn cold though the sun has come out and the sea has gone down a considerable amount. From what I could see the convoy seems pretty well intact. The few stragglers I expect will catch us up.

When we first got aboard many of the boys let their faces have a rest and did not bother to shave and at the end of the week there were some rather funny beards on display. For my part I have got quite a snappy 'mo' but I will get it removed one of these days. One of the boys who has red hair has shaved all except his 'mo' and has left extensive sideboards – he looks a real trick and has earned himself the name of 'Nancy'.

Monday, 1 September

We are into another month and I expect by next month, if we go on fighters, we will be thinking of going in boots and all, but don't let it worry you for, as you know, you can't keep a good Brown down.

We are expecting relief anytime now so that we can shoot off on our own which will mean a bit more pace towards land.

We sighted a plane today. I don't know whether it was hostile or not, but he kept well clear.

The weather has been much milder the last few days since the blow out and it is quite pleasant on deck and doing watch, which I again have to do tomorrow morning at 8.10.

Tons and tons of love to all and keep the old chins up. I'm damned if I know what I'll do when I do get back to NZ. I've been trying to bring my mind to bear on the subject but it will all work out and I'll probably end up on the farm. Goodbye for now.

Doug

Troops building huts in Iceland for US arrival. GETTYIMAGES.COM REF 3065110

WINE, WOMEN AND SONG

Iceland
Saturday, 6 September 1941

Dear Mum, Dad and Girls,

We are not in England yet, but are at an island not far off.

We had an uneventful journey except one night when a sub was picked up on the detectors but nothing came of it. We left the convoy last Tuesday morning when it was taken over by several destroyers and we headed off on our own accompanied by a corvette. We sighted land next day and were anchored out in the Gulf Stream by about 3 p.m.

We did not get into the town that day. The next morning only one boat got ashore with about 30 of the boys. When they were seen, the embarkation officer came out to the boat in a hell of a stink and no more shore leave was to be had. The town from all accounts was not so hot and the lads did not altogether enjoy their trip. That afternoon the anchor was pulled up and off we went and ended up around the coast in a sheltered anchorage.[18] You should have seen the fishing lines go over when we got here and a fair number were caught – mainly whiting and plaice.

Most of the boys had quite a yarn to the Army boys ashore and they can have their jobs. They have been here about four months. The first three days spent without sleep building a shack or two for their accommodation. I wish I could tell you a bit about this country but it will only be chopped out by the censor and so is not worth it. I can tell you there are naval boats here to the extent of the number of our place and Hughes.[19]

In the years prior to the outbreak of war there was some German presence in Iceland, even at a diplomatic level. At the outbreak of war, Iceland declared itself as neutral. Germany and Britain saw Iceland of strategic use due to its position in the north Atlantic.

Officially known as Operation Fork, British troops entered Reykjavik in May 1940 despite protestations by the Icelandic Government. It was at this time Germany invaded the Low Countries. A naval complex was established at Hvalfjordhur and occupied forces steadily grew.

18 Hvalfjordur (whale fjord), the site of a British and US naval base.
19 Code for 75. From 7 Bourne St and the Hughes number 5.

269 Squadron Hudson from Kaldadarnes, Iceland drops depth charges on U570 and gains its surrender (27/8/1941). IMPERIAL WAR MUSEUM – IMAGE C002068

In July 1941 US Marines occupied Iceland to support the British occupation and gradually replaced and surpassed these forces.

On his return journey from a meeting with Roosevelt, Churchill visited Reykjavik in August 1941, assuring the locals that the British and Americans were there to keep the war away from Iceland.

Many of the locals were less than welcoming to us in our role of so-called Allied forces. There had been a suggestion that Germany would underwrite capital development harnessing geothermal activity for heating and power generation and provide an economic boost.

[Letter continues]

Yesterday afternoon we had a game of rugby against a naval team and managed to beat them on the muddiest football field I have ever seen in my life. I got a game and was pretty fit considering. We, the Air Force, had no rugby gear and played in singlets and shorts and sandshoes, which made the game interesting. You could get no grip at all and your legs would be going about 30 revs and your ground speed would be nil. The added complication was the field was on quite a steep incline. However, to make a long story short, the Aussies and NZ boys won 9–0 after a darn funny game. On the way back to the boat all went well till a wave decided to shoot over where I was sitting and I got the lot, which caused some amusement. Today we are going to play the Aussies, which ought to be fun.

This morning we had quite a spectacle. Two converted trawlers came in, one leading and one trailing, towing between them a German submarine[20] and it was a jolly good sight to see her brought in. It did not look much damaged and will be used no doubt by the British when it is again made serviceable. I think the Hun has done his dash in the Atlantic.

Cheerio for now and love to all,

Doug

Bournemouth
Tuesday, 16 September 1941

Dear Mum, Dad and Girls,

Well here I am in England at last after an unexciting voyage across the Atlantic.

I will start my story where I left off. When I last wrote we were in a Fjord in the Land of Snow and Ice and were preparing to transship next day. Unfortunately for us that did not happen as next day we went round to the chief port [Reykjavik] and were taken off in lighters, luggage and all. Instead of going to a ship we went ashore and were sorry we did so as we were then taken 11 miles to an Air Force depot camp and it was not so hot. We only had two days there, but some chaps were there for a couple of weeks. We slept on floors with no

20 U-570. She had been damaged by British aircraft and towed to Thorlaks-hafn on the south coast and then around to Hvalfjordur for repair. The submarine was put into service by the British Navy as HMS *Graph*.

ABOVE LEFT Beer label

ABOVE RIGHT Iceland. Playing bridge in barracks at midnight. Don Beatty (Aus P/O), Mac McLeod (Aus Sgt), Mick Osborne, Doug, Clive Elliot on bed

mattresses and the food we got was little and consisted mainly of concentrated biscuits and stewed tinned meats. One thing that did fascinate me about this island was a stream that is made up of hot mineral water and was wonderful to swim in, especially after no bath for about two weeks. It was very funny – all the boys go there, undress and hop in, in the nude, and the girls swim in togs. The Americans are encamped there and we had a lot of fun with them and they could not do too much for us. We left the camp at about six o'clock one morning and got aboard our ship at about nine. What a ship – a real troop ship and we bunked in with the soldiers. We had over-cramped messes with poor food and we slept in comfortable hammocks. We nicknamed this ship the 'Altmarck'[21] and the name suited admirably. If the NZ Government is paying second-class passage for all airmen to the UK, they ought to claim a refund!

The way I looked at the whole thing, it was an experience. We were not escorted on this trip and went at a fair pace, though it took us four days to dock in a port somewhere in Scotland.[22] I was amazed at the number of ships we saw on our last day at sea. The Hun has got his work cut out if he wants to sink the British merchant fleet. We had some Hun prisoners aboard off

21 Actually the *Leopoldville*, a Belgian 11,500 ton vessel converted into a troop ship. It was sunk off Cherbourg at the end of 1944, carrying US reinforcements for the Battle of the Bulge. There were over 2200 troops aboard and about one third were killed.
22 Greenock, near Glasgow

Postcard of Bournemouth. Building with clock tower was sergeants' mess

the submarine. They are confident of victory and do not believe Hess is in England and could not understand why the British had so many ships. They did however look very fit men and they were getting good treatment.

We arrived in port last Saturday and went very crook when we found we had to spend another night on ship. We had an official welcome by an Air Commodore and he got a very bad hearing as the boys were pretty fed up.

We got put in the train at about midday Sunday and started our trip south to Bournemouth. We passed through Glasgow and though we were told it had been bombed quite a bit it looked OK. Quite a few bomb holes were visible in the open country. Our first stop was Carlisle and I was like a kid I was so excited as though I was coming home. I got off the train contrary to regulations and tried to scribble a note, which a girl was going to take to Mr Askew at the bank, but I got rounded up before I got far so I missed my chance. I wrote another note when I reached Bournemouth. The countryside was wonderful and I imagined I had seen some of the places before but I think it was all in my mind. I will hop up to Cumberland at the first opportunity which, with any luck at all, will be before I am posted to OTU.

We left Carlisle at about five and saw three more hours of country from there. It was interesting to see the number of brick walls – miles and miles of them. We only had one more stop on our way down here and that was Derby, which we reached at about 11 at night – I thought of Mac Wallace who is stationed there. We got little or no sleep that night, as the carriages were not made for that purpose. The next day – yesterday – we reached Bournemouth, at seven in the morning. What a beautiful summer resort it is and the weather is good. We are all put in hotels minus most of the 'trimmings', but it is a real treat to us. Our mess – there are a thousand sergeants here – is very good and meals wonderful.

So far Bournemouth has had few bombs. One wiped out Woolworths and the pier has suffered a little damage. The whole of the coast is a mass of barbed wire and anti-tank gadgets. Last night we had a night out on English beer. We all got very merry and had a lot of fun in the blackout trying to find our way home again. We got there more by good luck than good judgment. John Grierson has been here over two weeks. He is the only P/O of our lot. Good old John, just the same and he looks very well indeed in his uniform, but is

Barbed-wire protection on Bournemouth foreshore. GETTYIMAGES.COM REF 3470713

WINE, WOMEN AND SONG

very broke as are all the P/O boys. As for pay, the P/Os get a bob a day more than us but pay 2/6 a day mess bill compared to our sixpence.

Though I have not been posted yet I am sure I will be flying Spitfires or Hurricanes. I am not sorry, as they are good planes, whereas many of the Bombers are older in type and you may be unlucky and strike one that is rather out of date.

I have applied for fighters and I think all those trained on Harvards will get them. I don't know John's fate yet but his options are Heavy Bombers, General Reconnaissance or Torpedo Bombers. John is rather worried he may get on the latter, the average lifespan not much better than one torpedo.
Well I must away to a parade and hopefully some pay!

Goodbye for now and keep fit and well. Tons of love,

Doug

Bournemouth
Sunday, 21 September 1941

Dear Mum, Dad and Girls,

Well, I've been here nearly a week now and it is not a bad possie.

Every day last week we paraded for such things as identity cards, we had lectures, and in general there was a lot of mucking around. We even received £12 in pay the other day. We had an equipment parade yesterday and received another kit bag full of gear, mainly flying gear which is really good quality. We parade again tomorrow morning and hope to get some leave so that I can pop off up north.

Spare time has been plentiful. Last Monday night as I told you we all went out on the binge and had a really good night out, but a few sore heads in the morning. Tuesday night we had a quiet night. Phil Stewart and I went to a theatre where we saw a show starring Billie Burke and Mary Carlisle. It was not a high-class show but nevertheless jolly amusing.

On Wednesday night we went to a dance at a place called the Pavilion where there is a good orchestra and a beer is easily got. Brian Thomas and I – with girls – had the bad luck to get involved in a very expensive café,

Doug and Brian Thomas visit Christchurch

which charged us 3/6d a pop for fish and chips. Damn poor fish and chips at that. Thursday night was very amusing. Some of the boys from the course in Canada – Brian Thomas, Phil Stewart (I was at Wanganui Collegiate with him), Wig Webster, Peter Gawith,[23] John Oliver – and I decided we would go to the theatre preceded by a beer or two. We caught a bus out to Boscombe and booked seats for the 8.15 p.m. show.

One day last week Peter, John and I thought we would be very game and try the water – never again – it took me about two hours to thaw out, but I can say I have had a dip in England.

Yesterday morning was spent getting gear but in the afternoon six of us caught a bus for Christchurch about 12 miles out. A couple of the boys reckoned it was similar to its namesake in NZ. You even cross the River Avon. The main attraction is of course the Christchurch Priory. The church was

23 Peter Gawith was killed on 29 July 1942, and I coincidentally met his sister in Tutukaka at the Becks in 2006

Postcard of Cat & Fiddle, New Forest

erected in 1093 and so is quite an age. There is a document there that dates back to the 11th century. When I dropped you the postcard last night we had just eaten and were looking for a means of getting to a country inn. We took a taxi to a desolate place called New Forest, where we were shown the third-oldest inn in England, by the name of the Cat & Fiddle.

The front part is the original inn of 1033 and you have to stoop inside as the beams will hit you a beauty if you don't duck. The beer was very good and we played darts and shove-halfpenny with the locals and spent a happy hour and a half. There is a type of garden bar at the back with a buffet one end where we finished the evening with fish and chips. We headed back by train to Bournemouth, but it was late due to an air raid about 20 miles west of us. We saw quite a good show from a very safe distance. The planes were very high and the search lights could not pick them up. You could see and hear the ack-ack shells exploding. We had a very good firework display till the train arrived about 45 minutes behind schedule. And so we headed home after a very good night.

John Grierson has been posted and leaves us on Tuesday morning to train on heavy bombers and have a conversion course on the really big stuff, Lancasters. I had morning tea with him this morning and we all intend to have a really good binge at the Cat & Fiddle.

Well, I must away and have tea, so I'll leave you.

Tons and tons of love,

Doug

I was keen to renew my roots in Cumberland. The warrant officer in charge was very obliging and told me to: 'Go north, young man!' I gave him £5 to reimburse him for any costs to telegram me when required back. I spent five days in Carlisle before I was recalled and took the train all the way back again to Bournemouth. There I found I had been posted to 58 OTU Grangemouth, near Falkirk, not one hour from Carlisle!

Bournemouth
Saturday, 4 October 1941

Dear Mum, Dad and Girls,

I have just returned from Carlisle. We had a week's leave ending yesterday and naturally enough I headed north. I stayed with Mr Askew except for two nights and he took me all over Cumberland in the car. Late on Sunday afternoon we went for a drive north of Carlisle and had a good look around – beautiful country and I was very taken with the lanes with oaks growing on each side of the road to form a natural archway.

On Monday morning I visited the Cavaghans and arranged things for the next two days. In the afternoon I went with Mr Askew to Silloth on the coast. Instead of golf we spent a couple of hours in Aspatria at Dr Hodgson's – Brandraw House[24] – he showed me over the place and it looked pretty good

24 Brandraw House, Aspatria, Cumberland was at one time the Elliot family home. Gertrude Elliot married George Todd Brown – my grandparents. Tom Stalker was the groundsman.

to me. It cost him £75 to black the place out which is a pretty penny. He was talking about Tom Stalker and how he reckoned he was like Jesus Christ because he was born in a stable. He was apparently born in the stable on the right of his garage nearest the house. I took a few snaps of Brandraw and then visited the church and churchyard and I took a few snaps of our ancestors' gravestones.

After tea I took a taxi, gear and all to the Cavaghans. Mrs Rickerby and Joe came over and we all sat down to a night's Pontoon. Mrs George Cavaghan is staying there with her two children and has been there since Geo. Cavaghan was killed at Tobruk – it must be terrible for her. The whole family is very cut up. The other brother is fighting in that vicinity also. However, to get on, we had a very good night and Mrs Rickerby raked in the money. I think I won about threepence halfpenny after about five hours' play. The party broke up at about one and I slept soundly at the Cavaghans.

Tuesday was wet and we were unable to play golf at Silloth. In the morning I went through the bacon factory, as did Bob Gyllies when he was here. The same chap took me through who took Bob and he wished to be remembered to him, not realizing I had to go back to NZ to do that! In the afternoon the weather broke a bit and Mr Cavaghan and I went out to the local course and had a few holes getting back to the house at six. After a quick change Mr Cavaghan and I went down to the Silver Grill where we waited for the womenfolk to arrive not long before eight, during which time, Joe Rickerby, Mr Cavaghan and self had a beer or two. I met a Mr Redmayne that night, a tailor and he wished to be remembered to you, also the two Mr Diases. Dinner was a pretty bright do. After dinner we went to the local theatre and saw quite a good show after which we went to Rickerby's and had a few more beers and I stayed there the night, getting to bed none too early.

On Wednesday morning we went for a walk around the town and met Joe and after a couple of beers and lunch Mrs Rickerby and I had a game of golf. After tea at Askew's I came into town and had a few beers at the Crown & Mitre with Joe. I got lost in the blackout getting back to Askew's and it took me an hour. I slept in on Friday morning and had a lazy morning reading the papers. After lunch I said goodbye to the Cavaghans and Rickerbys and met Mr Askew at four o'clock. He drove me up to a dairy farm on the border – it didn't look too bad.

Thursday in the evening we went to the flicks and I caught the train south after midnight. I had a good trip down, sleeping most of the way. We reached Euston at about 7.30 and so I had an hour spare. I told the taxi driver to wander a bit while taking me to Waterloo so I could see a bit of London on the way. I caught the train for Bournemouth at 8.30 and got here not long before midday.

I have been posted to an OTU at Grangemouth not far from Edinburgh which will enable me to see something of Scotland. Seven of us applied to get to an OTU together, and five of us were lucky. We will be flying Spitfires. I am pleased I have struck Spits as they are the best fighters of the lot and are generally reckoned by the pilots as such. We set sail for our new station the day after tomorrow so I'll be able to tell you more about it in my next letter.

Our last few days in Bournemouth were pretty merry ones. A new course came in before we left and young Arthur Johns was among them. You can tell his folks he looked pretty fit on it. Kennedy was also among them. I had not seen him since we left the *Awatea*. Also Jack Brockett, who you will remember was my tent mate at Levin, and had to take another course there.[25]

Well, I seem to have come to the end of my ration of paper so I'll close. I'm enclosing a couple of photos if they don't make the weight go up too much. Tons and tons of love to all and I hope you are all as fit and well as I am – too fit in fact.

Cheerio for now.

Doug

P.S. Keep your fingers crossed and I may get home soon – hope so!

25 Jack Brockett ended up in bombers and was killed in October 1942.

OTU Grangemouth

*

RAF Station
Grangemouth
Scotland
Saturday, 11 October 1941

Dear Mum, Dad and Girls,

As you can see from the above address, I am in Bonnie Scotland and from what I have seen of it so far it is very dull and very cold. We arrived here last Tuesday morning at 11:30 after a rotten trip up. We left Bournemouth at five 'pip emma' and reached Waterloo at about nine where we had to unload all the kit bags. There are quite a number when everyone has three-a-piece. We unloaded from train to porter's trolley, from trolley to lorry, and then we all had to pile ourselves into a bus, which took us to King's Cross. When we got there the reverse of the loading process took place and we caught the Edinburgh express which left at 10.15 a.m.

In usual Air Force fashion we had reserved cars but they did not designate them so we spent about half an hour of travel time getting seats. The trip up to Edinburgh was not particularly comfortable. I slept because I was tired. We reached Edinburgh at about nine o'clock, a good two hours late, but we managed to get a cup of coffee and a couple of sandwiches which cleared the 'moss' away for a while. We had to go through the usual luggage procedure and, after another half hour's travelling, damned if we did not have to do it again! As usual there was no one at the train station to meet us and we had to wait a good hour before we were picked up by transport and eventually reached the base.

We were greeted by a few of our P/Os who left Canada after us but were posted immediately on reaching England, namely Russ Mathieson[26] and Rosie Mackie. Another one of the Moose Jaw boys, Snow Everiss, also a P/O, had the misfortune to crash and was killed here in early October. Very bad luck as he was a pretty good lad and it only goes to show it does not pay to marry before leaving NZ – he was married on final leave.

We were shown our barracks which are not A1, but comfortable, consisting of single beds – 18 of us to a hut. We have got a heater, which keeps the place cozy, so we don't fare badly. We have not got good conveniences: lavatories are handy but for a bath or shower we have to go back to camp, which is across the road from our huts. Our mess to which we were shown next is about half a mile from our barracks and is very good, consisting of a newly constructed hall. The dining room produces good meals well served and we are waited on. Take today's menu. Breakfast: cornflakes and bacon and eggs; for lunch: soup, cold roast beef with potato, red cabbage, mustard pickle and sauces followed by stewed apples and custard; for tea: sausages and mash. These meals include bread and butter and jam. We have a very large lounge with plenty of easy chairs, a wireless, and gramophone with plenty of new records. At one end there is a bar where the very best beer is sold and cigarettes aplenty. I don't think I'll need any tobacco from home, but will cable you if I do. On Tuesday afternoon we were issued with new helmets as well as oxygen gear, silk gloves and civilian gas masks.

On Wednesday we started hard at it with lectures on signals which lasted four hours. It was very boring and I think the majority of the boys were sound asleep. In the afternoon there was no flying. We had wireless practice from ground stations to air and it was very funny. Half of us are in the watchtower, taking turns at talking over the 'mike', and the rest of the boys parade up and down outside with full wireless equipment, wheeling what look like prams up and down. So much for the latest technology in R/T. Before we go into Spits we will have a few hours on Miles Masters. They are similar to a Spit, but fitted

26 Later in the war, I took over Russ Mathieson's flight in 130 Squadron.

out for dual. After a couple of hours dual spread over a couple of days I had an hour and three quarters solo today. They are great machines to fly and I expect in a day or so I'll be flying the Spit itself.

Our days here are very long. We have to be up early to have breakfast and be ready for a lecture, which starts at 8.30. From 8.30 till 12.30 we are hard at it without a break, doing lectures, wireless, and other training. We have an hour off for lunch and if we are flying it means a walk of about a mile from one side of the drome to the other and another half mile to mess, so you can see if we come from flying at 12.30 and have to be back for flying at 1.30 we have not very much time in which to eat! The same occurs in the afternoon. We get off at 4.30 and have to be back at 5.30, and if we are lucky we finish at about seven – not a bad day. Leave is a weekend off every second if we are up with our flying and we treat the other weekend as an ordinary day of the week.

So far I have not been into town but if we get leave in the coming weekend we will go to Edinburgh and see the sights.

I expect now you will be thinking of going to Manly and I only wish I was with you. This morning was very cold and the frost lasted till very near midday. It was bitter. The heater in the hut is fed by coal. Last night at about 10 p.m. after a couple of beers at the mess, we brought a loaf of bread and made toast as I had a pound of tinned butter. We then ended up frying some of our onions brought from Canada and we had the hut full of smoke and the stink of onions. They were good but the smell was still lingering at midday today.

My first flight since the beginning of August in Moose Jaw was 9 October in a Miles Master with instructor Sergeant Matthews.

The flights I had with Sgt Matthews were formatting on his aircraft, flying at low level up Loch Lomond. This was an exhilarating experience for a young pilot yet to face the reality of air combat.

I had only had three flights in the Master with Matthews and as many solos when he said, 'All right, off you go.'

I said, 'What do you mean, off you go?'

He said, 'There's a Spit, off you go.'

So, 14 October was my first solo in a Spitfire. I would never forget this first flight. The weather was marginal with poor visibility. The only instructions were where the speedo and throttle were located. Right from take off the experience was totally different from training craft to an aircraft with power and acceleration.

The cockpit equipment was very complex and instructors presumed from a quick review all could be absorbed – this was not the case.

In Spitfire Mark Is the undercarriage was raised manually with a hand pump and the pilot ideally needed three hands to control the aircraft during take off: one for the throttle, one for the joystick and one for the undercarriage pump. On this first flight, by the time I had the undercarriage up I was at 3000 feet and completely lost.

In these situations panic was often a factor in many mishaps. This is probably what happened to Snow Everiss when he spun into a large coke stockpile and was killed. Others disappeared, never to be seen again and presumably crashed into the sea. The conditions were not easy. It was a foreign landscape and with the regular occurrence of fog and mist landing was difficult.

On this, my first Spitfire flight, my mind went back to training by F/O Bell at Moose Jaw – when lost, always fly your reciprocal course. Fortunately I had noted my compass bearing on take off. Despite knowing this mentally it seemed to take ages to return to the drome. Instead of a 10-minute circuit and bump, the trip actually took 50 minutes. It was gratifying to get back.

At OTU we were left to our own devices with 'cross country' exercises, aerobatics, air firing, combat practice and formation flying a priority. F/O Bell's quality instruction at Moose Jaw had enabled me to cope with these activities.

The Harvard cruised at about 130 whereas the Spitfire Mk I did 250. Looping in the Spit was as easy as in the Harvard but rolling wasn't. When rolling in the Spit the nose tended to drop a bit so we made sure we did everything at height. I had done the necessary training and there was no sense of fear. The main perceivable differences were the speed differential from the extra power and the noise which is a beautiful sound.

Once the basics were mastered the Spitfire had few vices. It was a difficult plane to spin and when landing it never dropped a wing. Of course if you dropped down from too high you lost your undercarriage but that was no fault of the aircraft! The Hurricane on the other hand always dropped its left wing when you landed and just as you were stalling you had to put your right rudder on.

In combat the Spitfire had a superior turning circle and the engine, particularly the Rolls-Royce, rarely had any trouble. The golden rule was that if there was engine trouble or oxygen failure or R/T problems, then turn back. Many suffered or were killed as a result of not turning back when in difficulty.

Grangemouth
Wednesday, 15 October 1941

It seems hardly credible that about a year ago I would see a Spitfire's photo in the paper and to think that now I've flown one. All seven of us from Moose Jaw stationed here went off yesterday in the Spit. A great thrill! I got into the craft, had a good look round and after a while got her started. The plane felt a bit strange but I thought no more about it. The aerodrome control pilot gave me the signal and I taxied out onto the runway headed into the wind and opened the throttle. What acceleration! She was up in the air and at a thousand feet before I knew where I was so I did not attempt to continue in the circuit but had a fly round and got used to the controls. I was going at 270 mph at cruising boost and revs so I don't know what is going to happen when I open her out. The first time I came in to land I had to go around again as I headed onto the runway too soon which meant that I couldn't see a thing as the cockpit is well away from the nose and vision ahead is blocked. I came in next time round and made a pretty hairy landing but nevertheless the plane was still in one piece. You have to be very careful when landing as the undercarriage is very narrow and if you come down on one wheel you are liable to damage the undercart.

Our course here lasts six weeks in all which means we still have five to go and then we will be in the firing line. All I have to do then is push the button at the right time.

Tons and tons of love,

Doug

Grangemouth
Monday, 20 October 1941

Dear Mum, Dad and Girls,

We are back in camp again after a very good – too good – weekend in Edinburgh.
I finished the last letter to you last Wednesday night. Thursday, from what I remember, was just a usual day of flying the link trainer. I cannot explain the

Nº 13 COURSE.

BACK ROW: Sgts:- Potocki, Paszuki, Domiter, Szumski, Miles, Taylor, Burke, Morse, Glancy, Menzies, Rudkin, Webster, Walker, Sweney.
CENTRE ROW: Sgts:- Samiec, Zolcinski, Zbrozek, Pentz, Booth, Buckley, Marre. McFarlane, Smithson, McNeil, Stewart, Thomas, B.H., Brown, Thomas, H.G.
FRONT ROW: Sgts:- Slonski, P/O's:- Lagunski, Bednarski, Hume, Sgt:- Ryan, P/O's:- Grosvenor, Jones, Taylor, Doudy, Tucker, Snowball, Allen, Gordon, Dunbar, Wallace.

58 OTU Grangemouth No 13 Course. Samiec, Slonski and Tucker bit the dust before course ended

workings as it would be definitely 'chopped' by the censor. Friday was the same until I finished flying at five and headed poste haste for the barracks. After a very hurried tea and a quick dress I was ready by six when we were supposed to receive our passes. But, as usual, we had to wait 45 minutes, during which we had a pot or two. As soon as we laid our hands on the passes we headed for the bus stop and got a bus into Falkirk where we had another 45 minute wait as we misunderstood our meeting place with some of the boys who went in ahead of us. However, we eventually caught the 7.15 and reached Edinburgh at about 8.30. Our next move was rather doubtful for none of us knew Edinburgh, and being dropped there in the blackout did not help us much. We knew we were staying at the George Hotel, having booked rooms a few days previously, however we did not get there for some time because the boys wanted to go to the bar and it took a while to find. When we reached the pub – as the Scots call them – we were given very nice rooms and thought it rather a toney place. We were expecting to pay through the nose but we found the tariff very reasonable.

Once settled we went to the bar and enquired as to where we would be able to have a good night out and ended up at a place called the Havana which is considered a low dive by the generalissimo of Edinburgh. From our point of view we did very well for ourselves as they have got a great orchestra.

Phil Stewart and I were the only ones who made breakfast. We got quite a good feed of cornflakes, Finnan haddock, toast, jam and coffee, which there was plenty of. As for the Finnan haddock I reckon it is better than smoked cod.

After lunch, Phil, Long Thom, Mick McNeil and self went and had a look at the castle.

Saturday night went much the same as Friday night though we got home earlier due to the early closing of the dance halls. They close at 11.30 on Saturdays. I took a girl I had met earlier in the day, a rather nice lass called Kay

Mick McNeil at 58 OTU

McKenzie. The highlight of the night was the seven of us having a beer at our pub with a couple of cops and an Army chap who had a crown and two pips as well as RFC wings. Wig, card that he is, had one of the cops' hats on and was giving orders right and left. Sunday morning was rotten but we all made breakfast and I had another go of Finnan haddock. We did not go out in the morning due to the rain but sat back and read the local chat. After a feed it cleared up and while Phil, Long Thom and Mick went to Holyrood Palace I took two boys up to the castle. We took a Rolls-Royce taxi up and though most of the castle was closed up we had a beer or two.

Wednesday, 29 October 1941

I had two lots of airmail the last few days, including mail from Peg and Shirl. I was very sorry to hear about Nanna, but judging from the last mail she seems to be making a grand recovery. Give her my love and tell her I always wear the good luck charm she sent me in Canada under the left lapel of my tunic just above the wings and so far luck has been good. I wrote to

Great-Uncle Alex[27] a week back but did not mention Nanna was unwell. I got a reply today and judging from the letter, which was completed by Aunty Eva, he is not very fit. He will be 80 years of age this coming Sunday which is pretty good. I also wrote to Auntie Sarah and will write to Miss Graham before long. It was pure bad luck I did not see her when last in Carlisle.

Have not been over fit the past week or so, suffering from a real chesty cold and to crown it I am deaf in one ear – only temporary so don't worry – due to going too high with the cold and getting it knocked a bit and fixing it properly in the decompression chamber.[28]

We had a real do in the mess last Friday night. We had the lounge for dancing to an eight-piece orchestra and the dining room as the bar. It was certainly a good show. On Saturday night I went to a place called The Rink, which is a favourite hide-out of the boys. There is an ice rink and a dance floor, as well as a first-class restaurant and bar. The orchestra was really good and last Saturday night they had a real swing artist by the name of Scot Wood playing. You should have seen me doing La Conga! The price is amazing, 9d for the night on either the ice rink or the dance floor.

A new course came in yesterday consisting mainly of Belgians, Canadians, Poles and South Africans with a couple of NZ boys and an Aussie.

I don't know whether you knew Bill Middleton or not? Bob Gyllies knew him. He was with 485 NZ Fighter Squadron but was killed in action. I was talking to a P/O in the same flight and he said he saw Billie go down.

I had a big day yesterday and as a consequence of being Duty Pilot from 9 a.m. yesterday till 9 a.m. this morning I got no sleep last night and at present am rather tired. It is one of those jobs in which you can never leave your post – so to speak! I spent all last night giving weather reports to local airports and receiving the same. The funny part is I make the met report up and I hope all goes well. I was a bit worried last night for if we'd had an air raid alarm we would have been in the poop properly as I told a couple of the boys in Battle section to hop it and leave their telephone numbers. They hopped it OK but left no telephone number!

Tons and tons of love, and chins up,

Doug

27 My mother, Louisa's (Tucker) Uncle Alexander living in Overton, Wales
28 The pressure is reduced to simulate altitude flying until one is almost unconscious.

Grangemouth
Monday, 3 November 1941

Dear Mum, Dad and Girls,

What a pleasant surprise tonight – I received my
first parcel from you, sent through the District
Bank. Biscuits all the way from Bycrofts and
though a few on top were broken they are in fine
order. They have been open five minutes and the boys
are knocking them back.

Bycroft Biscuit Tin. Food
parcels were regularly sent to
troops from family, friends
and manufacturers. Products
included Bycrofts biscuits,
tinned Whitebait, Toheroa and
Oysters and of course cigarettes

This morning we were up at seven and it was pitch
dark but we had one of our fortnightly boloney parades. I
have previously managed to dodge them. Two of the NZ
Sarges were pulled up for not shaving and they explained
they couldn't do it because we did not have the conveniences. We have been
told we are going to have some posh barracks, but I'll believe it when I see it.

Flying has been going on in the same old way and I have recovered from
my deafness. The new course I mentioned has just started on their first efforts
in the Spit and managed to crash three today, all due to overshooting and
failing to go round again.

We are now doing battle formation. The poor old kites we happen to meet
in the air get 'shot up' metaphorically speaking. We have also done some work
shooting with the 6-inch camera gun, and the photos are good. I had a go with
live ammunition the other day. I was surprised at the comparative silence of
them considering that on the Spitfire Mk I there are eight Browning 0.303
machine guns going hammer and tongs. I don't know what difference a couple
of cannons will make but we are told they make a mess. If we get into Mark
VBs four of the guns are replaced with two 20mm cannons.

Sunday, 9 November 1941

The weather has been very poor of late and consequently little flying. Since
I started this letter I have only managed to get an hour's flying, which is very
annoying. I had a great chance the other day of flying a Spit Mk II to the
Orkney Islands. We did not get there due to bad weather. I think we could
have got through but the leader had different ideas. I was rather disappointed
as it would have meant travelling back in some bigger craft. The main

difference from the Mark I being a slightly larger Rolls-Royce Merlin engine using 100 octane and producing a little more take off power.

I have just come down from a flight and what a time. I was low flying and ran into a snow storm and got properly lost; reported it over the R/T so no others would get into it but being low down could get no communication from them. Nevertheless I'm still here so I got back OK, most of the way hedge hopping.

We shifted our barracks and it is a definite improvement though it means about a mile walk to the mess for breakfast, but I think all approve. We have central heating! It is generally darn cold when morning comes, but still a jolly sight warmer than the other place and my cold is nearly gone as a consequence. We have basins with plenty of hot water, but we still have to have our baths at the camp, which is OK as we have them after P.T. each day.

We had a bit of fun the other day. Half a dozen Aussies went to Edinburgh for the day – just took the day off – and they had the bad luck to be caught and got a severe reprimand. Worse still, two of them went to The Rink full of beer and started to act the high hat. An Army 'one pipper' like a fool poked his nose in and one of the Aussies, a pretty tough sort of lad, took exception and poked the 'one pipper' fair on the 'geezer'. He is now under close arrest awaiting court martial and I think he will be very lucky to get away with it. It was a great pity for the other chap with him. Though he got off with a pretty good 'tick off', he is generally a very quiet lad.

I received the cash you sent to me the other day – thanks very much indeed, Dad, it will be very useful. I intend to bank it when I get my leave in about a week. I expect to get a week's leave when I am posted to a squadron and I intend to spend it with the Rickerbys and Cavaghans in Carlisle. I'll see a fair bit of Mr Askew, I expect, more especially as there is a snappy young thing working in the bank there, Rouse by name, but I doubt if she can cook, Mum.

During the last week I have been picture mad, going three times. I saw 'Adam Had Four Sons' which was quite a well-acted show with plenty of action. A couple of nights ago Rex Rudkin and self went and saw one of the Dr Kildare pictures which was quite good. The following night I saw the Marx Brothers in 'Out West', which I thought was very amusing. I also saw your friends, Dad – Laurel and Hardy.

There is no flying this afternoon as it is snowing outside and I think there are a few faces which look as though they are suffering from the night-before feeling.

Flying boots are well displayed today to keep the old legs warm. The Canadians love to display their flying kit and do so even in the street, which is darn sissy. Perspiration forms in them and they are not much advantage to you when you get up in the air a few miles. However, it is their funeral you can't tell them anything.

This week I will be fairly busy finishing the course and I expect every available hour will be used up for flying. We have to do dusk landings in the Spit, which will not be unlike night flying but I don't think we will overdo it. We'll be having shots at the drogue this week and no doubt one of the boys will put the wind up the poor old cock piloting the old Battle [aircraft] – we'll see what happens anyway. I had a lot of fun with the Cine camera gun and did pretty well and knocked my opponent over a few times.

Love to all,

Doug

P.S. Received two lovely parcels yesterday. What a great selection. I got the tiki OK and will look after it, I can tell you. If you manage to get them please get me a film or two: Kodak 24 x 36mm FY 135 or an equivalent. Noel Taylor will know what's what from Bruce Craig. They have 18 or 38 exposures – the 18 is handier.

Grangemouth
Sunday, 16 November 1941

Dear Mum, Dad and Girls

We are very fed up as we have to put in another week here. Due to the weather being mostly fog and Scottish mist 'the trainees are not up to standard.' The main annoyance is the question of leave. We were to have a week's leave at the end of the course. In fact we believe that as a result of an Air Ministry Order we are now doubtful whether we'll get it. There will be a riot if we don't. Another thing is we will get no mail this week as we all wrote to NZ House and cancelled any further mail and I also I wrote to Mr Askew and did likewise. All we can hope is things turn out for the best but judging by today we won't get much flying in this week either.

Yesterday there were about 20 lost, all wanting 'homings' at once. Most of them got down on dromes scattered around Scotland. Dutch Stenborg, who I trained with in Canada, got lost and ran out of gas and made a good forced landing in pretty rough country. He certainly had a tale to tell this morning. I had a letter from John Grierson yesterday and from what I can gather he will not be going on the really heavy stuff but flying Wimpys (Wellingtons).

We have a lad here, Instructing Flight Sergeant Don Kingaby, whom you may have heard about – being the only person with a DFM with two bars. Not bad going for a little chap. He is a great scout and comes around with our mob a fair bit and gives some very useful hints. He is the son of a parson but you wouldn't think so. We also have here Flight Lieutenant Bush DFC (cousin of Ron Bush the All Black) a real Kiwi and a wonderful flier. He has done his dash as far as fighting is concerned and is putting in time here till he is sent back to NZ.

While I think of it, Dad, I was wondering if I could get a car over here with the aid of some of your cash. I have got £24 sent from you and with a few more pounds I ought to be able to pick up a fair flyer. As far as benzene is concerned we do not do badly: we get the usual allowance plus enough benzene to go from station to station in the event of a change and also four allowances a year. I do not intend to get anything classy, maybe just an MG, which could be picked up for about £60.

Bruce Wallace has arrived OK. I had a letter from Mac the other day and he had a weekend with Bruce and all seemed well. I dropped Bruce a line and hope to see him soon. I also had a letter from Mr Beaufort and he is apparently on an RAF Station just north of his old vicarage. Today I got a letter from Digger to say he reached England OK although they ran into a sub or two on the way over. They were lucky enough to dodge trouble but saw one get it. Apparently Billy McManemin got 'scrubbed' which was bad luck as I thought he was doing very well. I don't know what he'll do now.

Thursday, 27 November 1941

I started a week's leave last Monday night and am at present at Mrs Rickerby's. We did very little flying during our last week in Grangemouth due to bad weather, and at the end of the week we had all had enough. On Sunday night the Aussies and NZ chaps decided to have a bit of a do at the mess. I'm afraid a number of the boys had too much – or, should I say, could not hold what they had.

Grangemouth seemed to be under the impression that I am a good flyer. They gave me above average assessment and I am going to a Spit Squadron in Hawkinge, between Dover and Folkestone, which is the real hot spot. I am proud and glad that I have been picked for such. Of the course at Grangemouth about a dozen altogether were picked as AA pilots and going to similar stations. There are five of us going to the Squadron I am lucky enough to get into, 4 NZ boys and an Aussie. Don't worry about me, I will always have a good plane under my control and I think I can handle it well enough to dodge most of these Huns.

My final flight at Grangemouth was 22 November 1941. I qualified with an assessment of 'good average' having completed 34 hours of Spitfire flying. We were posted to 11 Group in the south of England. I had good training in Canada in formation flying and qualified above average which helped me getting straight into 11 Group. I found the most difficult manoeuvre with the Spitfire was landing but the Battle of Britain boys only had 8–10 hours so you can imagine how they suffered.

[Letter continues]

Those of us who did not have leave cancelled for various indiscretions left Grangemouth on Monday evening. As it was after eight before I got my baggage checked through, and I still hadn't bought a ticket from Edinburgh to Carlisle, I spent the night at Edinburgh and came down to Carlisle on Tuesday.

As soon as I had lunch I went down to the bank and collected the mail. There were two from the girls, and also a letter from Bruce Wallace who struck it badly and got bombed a bit during his first few days. He has contacted Mac and spent leave with him. I had contemplated going to Derby this coming Saturday and spending the weekend there but it is rather awkward. I enquired at the station and I would have to change trains at Sheffield, which means a long wait before going on to Derby.

On Tuesday night I went to the Crown & Mitre with Doug and Joe Rickerby and their fiancées Pat Semple and Effie Gordon. It cost 8d for a couple of raspberryades and a dance.

Yesterday I finally had my photo taken. It was jolly funny. I went to the studio and started a coughing fit and an old girl came out with a cup of coffee

Carlisle studio shot

and told me to hog it, which I did, and was nearly poisoned at the first mouthful. When I showed my disapproval she said it was some patent cough cure of hers! Then, scene II, the husband led me into his studio – the real McCoy with all the gear – and when I had adopted the correct posture he commenced to switch on the lights and, lo and behold, no action. I felt the real film star, I can tell you. However, he shoved me back into the sitting room and I watched him pulling out fuses right and left, and after dashing about for 15 minutes he came in and said, 'OK now. It is a funny thing – the lights would not go on because I forgot to flick the switch.'

Yesterday I spent lunch with the Cavaghans and in the afternoon I went with Mr Cavaghan to look over one or two of his farms near Wigton. We went to the Silver Grill afterwards and had a few pots with the two Mr Dias and Mr Redmayne and got home in time for a jolly good feed of eggs and bacon – a real delicacy in this country at present. Mr Cavaghan told me to tell you he is a real farmer now and has at the Grange his own cow and fowls and they make their own butter, so they do not fare as badly as most. Mrs Rickerby and Mrs Cavaghan are kept busy as they have quite a few days in the canteens and they also do camouflage work for the war effort.

From your letters, all seems to be well with you, including your golf, Dad – another 'pewter mug' to add to the collection – you'll have to take on beer drinking, I can see that. This letter should arrive about Xmas time and all I can say is all the best for Xmas and the coming year and I hope the weather keeps fine and sunny, and I only wish I was with you. Here's to the next New Year's Eve party we have down at Manly, even if we have to drink lemonade all night!

Always remember a Spitfire is a small target!

Cheerio for now,

Doug

Kenley, Surrey
Monday, 8 December 1941

Dear Mum, Dad and Girls,

Things have taken a turn recently now that the Japs have come in. I wouldn't mind knocking them about with the Spit. If things get too hot I'll try and get out even if we take them on with training planes. When the Yanks stop yapping and get organised, the Japs will get bombed to hell. It is a fairly well-known fact that a Jap pilot cannot fly to any great altitude due to the bubble formed in the blood probably due to overindulging in starchy foods like rice.[29]

I think I had better get back to when I last left you at Rickerbys'. In the afternoon I went and saw Miss Graham and, as you can imagine, she was jolly glad to see me. I had to speak very loudly as she was deaf – she was probably the same when you last saw her. She asked me to have a cup of tea and I consented, being polite (wish I hadn't as I had just had lunch), but she brought out a big platter of Cumberland ham and eggs, as well as fruit salad which was jolly nice, but I was too full to appreciate it.

On Saturday afternoon we went to St Bees to watch a rugby match against Sedbergh College where Harold Cavaghan is. School rugby is always good. If I ever get the chance, Dad, I will go and look over your old school, Cranleigh.

That night I had the big date with my lass from the bank. There was quite a party of us there, Joe Rickerby and Effie Gordon, Dick Dias and Pat Semple, and Louise and myself, who assembled at the Silver Grill for a meal at about seven. Lady and Mr Creighton were also there, and four others who knew you who forced me to have another beer. I supped one and then had to have another, and when I was about to have my third a gentleman came up and grabbed me by the arm and said, 'Are you Ted Brown's son?' Upon the reply, 'Yes', I was dragged off to another table full of people, all friends of yours, Dad – what rough cobbers you keep – who pumped more beer into me. The chap's name was Mr Harrison and he wished to be remembered to you. To crown the lot, the two Mr Diases were there, and it got to the stage where Louise had no show of getting Dick and me out – it

29 Probably propaganda. The Japanese were short on fuel which restricted the mobility of their forces. They had no access to high-octane fuel, affecting the performance of their planes.

sounds terrible, Dad, but you shouldn't have so many hospitable friends.

Sunday was rather a lazy day. In the morning we were ordered up to Cavaghans' where we had a few beers and also Lady Creighton appeared and gave me a pullover. In the afternoon Joe and I went for a fair walk, during which I said goodbye to Mr Askew and did my stuff generally. In the evening Mr Dias, Joe, Dick and I had a go at poker and as usual I was the loser but it passed the time away while I waited for the train for London. It reached Carlisle three hours late and consequently arrived late into London. I hit out for the NZ Overseas League and met Arnold 'Mick' McNeil and Jim Burke, who were at 58 OTU Grangemouth, also going to 91 Squadron at Hawkinge with me, and Norman Smith, son of the Manager of John Burns Ltd – he was full of go and had just had a weekend with Mac and Bruce Wallace. I also saw young Johns there and a number of lads I had met in the Air Force since joining. I headed for the Sussex Hotel, the home of the NZ boys on leave in London, and ran into the rest of the Grangemouth lads. We had a farewell beer and went our various ways.

The five of us heading for Hawkinge caught a train at Charing Cross and at about three we were in Folkestone and got to the drome at 3.30. We then went through all the baloney attached to entering a new station. The Squadron was well represented by NZ and Aussie boys and when we got there we had quite a yarn and a few beers before a jolly good bath and bed.

The next day we went before the CO Jamie Rankin and he told us there were three vacancies for an NZ Squadron and, of course, all ears pricked up and being four NZers made it rather awkward. However, on the toss, Phil Stewart missed so Jim Burke, Mick and self considered ourselves the men as the applications for the NZ Squadron must run into hundreds. That night we celebrated in a place called the Odeon, a combination café bar and dance show. We missed the bus back but a copper helped us get a taxi to Hawkinge. Next morning was all hurry and rush. I lost my kit bags and had to leave them to fate as we had to get an early train. Fate had a day off and my kit did not arrive until today: five days later. We were jolly glad to reach Kenley safe and sound.

485 (NZ) Squadron

*

EARLY HISTORY

FORMED ON 1 MARCH 1941 AT RAF DRIFFIELD IN YORKSHIRE, THE 485 (NZ) Squadron was manned by NZ pilots, but controlled and on the payroll of the RAF. Fighter Command at that time was structurally divided into three geographical groups. 485 Driffield was part of 13 Group, which provided back-up to 12 Group in their role of defending the central region of England. 11 Group defended the south and south-east. The Spitfire Mark I, marked as OU, was issued to the squadron while undergoing initial training as a unit.

Founder members who joined the Squadron at Driffield in March 1941 included Bill Crawford-Compton, Lyndon Griffiths, Jim 'Pranger' Porteous, Harvey Sweetman, Hal Thomas, and Bill 'Hawk' Wells. On 1 July the move south to Redhill took place under the auspices of Fighter Command's 11 Group. Reg Baker, Dave Clouston and Jack Rae joined the squadron.

There were a number killed during the short stay at Redhill. The move to Kenley on 21 October 1941 came with an upgrade to Spitfire Vs and a further intake of pilots including: Johnnie Checketts, Reg Grant, John Palmer, Tony 'Slim' Robson and Mick Shand.

Marcus Knight, permanent Air Force, was the first CO through to mid-November 1941. Although I did not serve with him, we were at Wanganui Collegiate together.

Ka Whawhai Tonu 'We will fight on'. RENDITION BY MARY DENTON/RAF HERALDRY TRUST

Bill Wells was a Flight Commander during the Battle of Britain and, being a fairly aggressive fellow, he had the CO position by November.

Mick Maskill, Evan 'Rosie' Mackie, Ross Falls and Marty Hume were with me at 32 SFTS course, Moose Jaw, Canada and all were posted to 485 Squadron in the latter stages of 1941.

ABOVE The boys in front of their new Spitfire VB August 1941. Back: Jack Strang, Tusker McNeil, Jack Frecklington, Gary Francis, Max Krebs / Middle: Wally McLeod, E Cochrane, Don Griffith, Bill Crawford-Compton, Marcus Knight, Andy Kronfeld, Dave Clouston / Front: Jack Rae, Dickie Barrett, Harvey Sweetman

OVERLEAF Original Squadron members at Driffield, March 1941. Back: French (Ground crew), Donald McGregor, Dickie Barrett, Bill Middleton, Gary Francis, Allan Shaw, John Martin, S/L Marcus Knight, Frank Brinsden, Patrick McBride, Athol McIntyre; Ground crew: Smith, Bongard, Erridge, Murray, MacGibbon / Front: George, Neville, Martin (Ground crew); Hal Thomas, Dick Bullen, Bill Crawford-Compton, Jack Maney, Jim Porteous, Austin Smith, Harvey Sweetman, Kevin Cox

ABOVE Ground crew reload Spitfire, August 1941. GETTYIMAGES.COM REF 3322119

OPPOSITE Armourers load ammunition into the wing of a Spitfire at RAF Driffield, March 1941 Aircraftmen Martin (on wing), Bongard and Neville. RNZAF MUSEUM

BELOW Squadron ground crew re-arming a Spitfire, believed to be at Royal Air Force Station, Redhill. On wing: Aircraftmen Erridge and Martin. Under wing: Aircraftmen McGibbon, Bongard & Neville. RNZAF MUSEUM

Hal Thomas signed up for the RNZAF Reserve pre-war. On 485's first operation over enemy territory on 23 June, Hal's friend Dick Bullen was killed and Hal was lucky to get back to England, his Spit peppered with holes. Hal was posted to Aden in October where he spent a few months ferrying planes and then posted on to Cairo.

Jim 'Pranger' Porteous was so-called 'Pranger' as he destroyed more RAF aircraft than German ones.

Harvey Sweetman was 18 when 485 Squadron was formed. He left 485 early in 1942 to serve as Flight Commander for 486 Squadron, the second NZ Squadron, which was then night-flying Hurricanes. In July Harvey claimed the first victim for 486, a Dornier 217, which went straight down near the drome at Wittering. At the end of Harvey's tour his 'rest' period was spent as a test pilot for Hawker. On his second tour he returned to operations flying Tempests and completed his tours as CO No 3 Tempest Squadron. He married Gwen after the war.

Lyndon P Griffith was a likeable 'rogue'. Lyn rejoined the squadron in October 1943 and was in my flight at Biggin Hill. He borrowed a Spitfire one afternoon to visit his wife Mary who had just given birth and returned five days later at a time we were short of aircraft. 'Griff' had a colourful post-war career and always seemed to be in and out of trouble.

With the move to Leconfield in April 1941, the Spitfire Is were upgraded to Mark IIs and Jack Frecklington, 'Tusker' McNeil, and Jack Strang were added to the ranks.

I was not in the Squadron with 'Freck' as he was posted to Aden and subsequently Cairo with Hal Thomas. Later, in 1942, Freck flew Spitfires in the Middle East for 601 Squadron, mainly as high cover. Returning from a party one night in Egypt with the Hurricane boys, he was thrown from a jeep and badly injured with a blood clot on the back of his head on which the surgeons could not operate. He took 'leave of absence' from Cairo hospital one night and was found in the gutter. He had been hit on the back of the head with a bottle, which had dissipated the blood clot. He married Beryl and farmed at Rata near Feilding. For further reading, see *LJ Frecklington's account of his war.* (private publication)

TOP Harvey Sweetman
ABOVE Lyndon Griffith

Kenley

*

Life was relaxed with G/C Bouchier in charge of the station. The Wing Commander was W/C Finlay Boyd and Bill Wells was CO of 485. Gary Francis was Flight Commander A Flight and Jack Strang was my Flight Commander B Flight.

Two other squadrons formed the wing: 602 (RAF) Squadron with Al Deere CO and 452 (Australian) Squadron under Bluey Truscott.[30]

485 was a typical squadron with two flights of 24 pilots and 18 aircraft. In addition there were ground crew and support staff. Ground crew tended to stay with a squadron as it moved around. I had Vic Strange with me most of the time with Nobby Clark, Lee Jordan and Joe Roddis. I still correspond with Vic and Joe.

The squadron's primary function was to fly over to France at 20,000 to 25,000 feet. The squadron often took bombers over to hit aerodromes like Caen and Beaumont, south of Le Havre and Rouen also as a ruse to flush out the Hun. More often than not we did not run into any. When the Germans did attack they were quickly in and out – they did not hang around.

---

30 452 Squadron moved to Australia when Singapore fell to Japan. Based in Darwin many of the squadron were killed in combat with the Japanese or as a result of flying accidents. Truscott was killed in an accident with 76 Squadron, flying a Kittyhawk in WA.

Kenley was a pre-war establishment with elaborate officers' and sergeants' messes. The runways had been lengthened for Spitfires but were still on the short side in a no-wind situation.

The sergeants' residential part of the mess was occupied by Grenadier Guards on Aerodrome Defence. The sergeants' billet for 485 Squadron was a private house opposite the station main gate – Red House. We were young and inexperienced and enjoyed many a prank with each other. One evening I was upstairs in bed when suddenly bullets were coming through the floor. It was Tony Robson practising pistol firing from the floor below.

We were in Spitfire VBs, which had a flying duration of little more than 90 minutes. The Spit V had a three-bladed prop and, in my opinion, was the most enjoyable of the Marks to fly. The engine made a beautiful sound. In addition to the 2 x 20mm cannon, there were 4 x .303 Browning machine guns. The engine was 40% more powerful than the Spit I, coming in at just under 1500HP. The main difference in performance was an equivalent increase in lift.

Aerial view Kenley April 1995. Runway still in original layout

WINE, WOMEN AND SONG

Kenley
28 November 1941

On arrival we first went to the orderly room for the usual briefing and then were shown to our billets. 'G'day Cock' and such like greeted us, and 'Must come to the hop tonight.' I knew a couple of the lads here, Jack Rae who Bob Gyllies will know, John Palmer who was at Collegiate, Norm Holmes[31] who was at Levin and David Clouston who was at Varsity with me, as well as Andy Kronfeld who I knew in the rugby circles. We soon got to know the rest. The billets are great and with cupboards! We can at last get our gear unpacked. The fire is looked after by our orderly, who also makes our beds and looks after the place. The mess is good and the food is excellent, served and cooked by WAAFs who are a jolly sight – better than the men.

The party put on by the NZ Squadron was a great show and it was there we met our CO S/L Wells, DFC and bar – an NZ volunteer who has done well. It was like this (a Zane Grey start anyway): He bowled up to those of us who were knocking a beer back and said, 'I'm Bill Wells, who are you? Have a beer!' Typically NZ. We also met the adjutant in similar manner. A great mob of chaps, no boloney, do anything for you, eager to fight for the cause and never let you down – there is no distinction between sergeants and the officers, they are all Bill, Tom, Dick, etc. I don't think I can pass the censor with much more about the place except that we are flying Spitfire VBs, the fastest type, and they do a fine job. Another bonus, walking is over. You pick up the phone and ask for the van and over it comes driven by Waffles – A WAAF!

We went to London the other night and first stop NZ House. I ran into Toby Webster at the door and had a long chat to him. He is very fed up – nine weeks OTU and about nine hours flying and they get treated like kids. Thank goodness I dodged bombers as they will still be here training at the end of the war at the rate they are going. I went upstairs to give in a change of address and I saw a P/O talking with his back to me, and he turned round and who do you think it was? Paul Hayward who was at Wanganui Collegiate with me. He trained as a fighter pilot and he is itching to get Spits.

Well, must close for now as I have to be 'at readiness' at dawn tomorrow for some harmless show! Probably nothing at all.

---

31 Norm Holmes was killed in June 1943 flying Hurricanes in North Africa.

Kenley
Wednesday, 9 December 1941

Nothing happened today. It was not very good as far as the weather was concerned and I sat on my seat all morning 'at readiness' hoping something would happen to brighten up life. This afternoon we had a bit of formation for about an hour, which was quite enjoyable though very bumpy.

A couple of the boys were in London yesterday and were told the Trans Pacific airmail service may be discontinued. It may mean you will not receive any mail from me for a fair time and vice versa. I'll hold this till I get some leave, and inquire into the situation.

In our billet Red House, there are two or three to a room, plenty of hot water and a kitchen with a gas stove. Toast is the specialty with cheese, honey or anything going. Last night after a couple at the Golden Lion – a pub along the road – we had toast, sardines and spaghetti and we were just on our way to bed when a few boys who had been to a local hop came in with some WAAFs and we had a party. I wandered about in my pyjamas, Irvine jacket (fleece-lined leather jacket), flying boots and WAAF's hat and looked the latest from Paris.

My only worry in this outfit is what I am going to do when I do get back to NZ? I hope I'll be able to take to farming but I can't tell at all yet.

Always thinking of you,

Doug

Kenley
Tuesday, 16 December 1941

Dear Mum, Dad and Girls,

Ten more days and Xmas will be over and you will be enjoying the sun at Manly beach. I hope I will be there next year and see the New Year for 1943 on the tennis court to the tune of Auld Lang Syne and Scottish Customs – you can never tell!

The first letter I wrote to you from here I sent ordinary mail. It is a great pity the mail has become so disorganised. Before it was great to get news from you about 14 to 16 days old and I expect you found the same. I sincerely hope that when it settles down they will continue the Clipper Air service – though I doubt it as Pan American Airways will not be over-anxious in losing one of those Clippers, which must cost a few quid each![32]

Sunday, 21 December 1941

I received the biggest knock-out blow in this outfit so far when I heard John Grierson had been killed. John's death is the first that has affected me. It doesn't pay to worry in this racket, as Dad will know from the last lot. John was a great pal to me and I was with him for a long time. When I first heard the rumour he had been killed I wrote to the Adjutant of Moreton-in-Marsh, a Wellington bomber base. I received a letter in reply, a copy of which I'll give you. Incidentally I have just written to John's family and I also gave them a copy of it. I know the letter will revive old memories but I'm sure they will appreciate it. Here is a copy word-for-word excluding the reference addresses and date.

<u>P/O JA Grierson</u>

In reply to your letter of 16 December, I regret to inform you that the above named Officer was killed whilst on a night training flight on the night of Sunday, 7 December 1941.

The funeral took place at Benson on Thursday, 11 December 1941, and full service honours were accorded.

Photographs were taken at the time of the funeral and these have been forwarded to the proper quarters for onward transmission to the next of kin.

> WJ Kidley F/O
> For Group Captain Commanding
> RAF Station
> Moreton-in-Marsh

---

32   The Clipper Air Mail Service was suspended on 19 November 1941 shortly after the US joined the war.

I wrote and asked for all he could tell me about the crash. John's death will be a very bitter blow to the family, especially as they have Don over here flying the same type of aircraft. The last I heard from John he wanted to get on the same squadron as Don and hoped to arrange to meet me when I was on leave. He saw some of the other lads at the Sussex during the week that I was in Carlisle. Our last night together was such a do and it will always remain in my memory.

Last Wednesday I had my first game of rugby in England and played for Kenley against the Grenadier Guards whom we were very lucky to beat 6–3. It was a very hard game and nearly killed me as I am not what you would call in condition and the Guards were very fit and, as you know, none of them under six foot. We have got quite a fair team here and have only lost once so far against Roslyn Park. I don't know why they call it the Kenley team as it consists of 12 NZ boys, two Aussies and a Canadian. The skipper Alan Deere, DFC and bar, you have no doubt heard about is CO of the English squadron. He plays quite a fair game. Marty Hume was in a provincial NZ rugby team so our opposition may have their work cut out.

On Thursday we were on the job at dawn and took off in the dark. The next I knew we landed at Martlesham Heath on the coast north from here. We operated from there and patrolled a few boats and expected trouble but it did not eventuate. On landing with my section I crashed . . .

My first operation on 18 December 1941 was nearly my last. Our function was to escort minesweepers in the Channel – due to the fog we didn't even see them. We did not have enough fuel to return to base so we were diverted to Martlesham Heath. The weather was appalling but the Flight Commander instructed our flight of four to land in formation. I was No 4 and I thought our flight leader was bringing us in too fast. Instead of coming in at 90 mph I was going 100. Being on the outside I had too much speed on and barely touched down by the middle of the drome. I didn't have enough experience to follow the rule: When in trouble landing, open the throttle and go around again. I didn't have enough space to stop before the boundary fence which was approaching fast!

I was thinking this was the end of the war for me, and indeed my life, as I was heading at speed directly for a petrol tanker refuelling aircraft. The drome had been bombed by the Huns the previous night and by good fortune I ran into one of the bomb craters. The undercarriage broke away, the prop broke and after much noise and a completely destroyed aircraft I emerged uninjured to live another day. It was all over so quickly I had no time to fear the end was nigh.

Bill Wells, our CO, was also at Martlesham Heath at the time. He was going by train to London for a night out. He drew me aside asked me to fly his aircraft back to Kenley as a confidence booster when the weather lifted.

Also on this trip John Palmer was shot down by an Me109. He parachuted into the Channel and was picked up by one of the minesweepers.

Before a trip we would go to the ops room and the Intelligence Officer would detail the Operation Plan, whether we would do high, medium or low cover, or go on our own or in a wing as a circus. Then the W/C would give his overview and provide the take off detail. The CO would say his bit and most pilots would feel some tension prior to take off. Once in the air you generally never thought any more of it as there was a job to do. When we finished we would have a couple of cigarettes and then might pee on the wheel and come in!

Some should never have made it to pilot. We had heard cases of pilots in other squadrons repeatedly reporting fault with their R/T or their engine and returning to base and those that simply vanished from the combat scene but miraculously rejoined their squadron on the run back to base. There was an NZ chap who had done seven bomber missions and then he could not get into the bomber as his nerves were shot. Normally they had their wings and commission removed but he went down to work with Bill Jordan who was a wonderful High Commissioner.

In The Great War they were shot for desertion. In our war the propaganda was that they were 'moral fibre' cases. We had one, an Australian, we kept on in the squadron for other duties as we did not want him to be declared. He never flew on operations so we had to carry him. The hierarchy were displeased and it probably cost us promotion. The doctors also had little say in these situations or in sending us to hospital as there was always someone in the squadron who could out-rank them.

We would regularly take off on a dawn show in good conditions and come back to find it all fogged in. The advantage with England was there were many alternate dromes to land. On one occasion when we couldn't land at Kenley we came into Gatwick which was clear and only 30 miles south. It had a metal strip for landing and I remember the chap behind me had a problem where the strip fell apart, rolled behind him in a coil and eventually caught up with him and ruined the tail end of the plane.

[Letter continues]

. . . As it was, the plane was a complete wreck and all I had to do was undo the straps and climb out. I did not get the best of receptions from the Flight Commander, though he was jolly decent about it, and the CO said little though it was his duty to do so. A report will go to Group but I hope I don't have to go before AOC as I believe he goes rather crook! The CO is of the opinion I will get out of it OK due to inexperience and my good assessment and report on flying from OTU. I hope so. I believe the worst I'll get is an endorsement. I thought it was merely bad luck but they have different ideas.

The weather came down on Thursday and we only managed to get back to Kenley today not long after lunch. We were lucky as the fog was down all morning and just cleared enough to let us off. All the way down was fog. We flew well above it and not long after we landed it came down again over Kenley. Today is terribly foggy again.

The first night we were away we struck a sergeant's dance and jogged around in flying boots and battle dress. It was a very good night. Next day we went into Ipswich and had a shave. We looked real cards wandering around the town as all we had to wear was flying attire. After the barber we went to a place for a feed, then a show, a couple of beers and back to bed. On Saturday we were at readiness but due to fog we were soon free and played snooker all day. At night the Winco – a Scotchman, Finlay Boyd, DFC and Bar, and a great chap who likes his beer and has an unending supply of yarns – organised a party at the Black Bull, a pub which had a dance going. The Winco got transport and the Aussie squadron and our lot had a great night. At Martlesham there was an Eagle Squadron (USA), a Canadian Squadron, an English Squadron, Aussie and our squadron, a League of Nations. By the time we left we had just about had enough as life was a bit hectic, and our clothes were showing signs of dirt and smell! We flew home as a wing and it must have looked rather good as there were 25 planes in wing formation.

Bruce Wallace is stationed at Ipswich at the moment. I rang him a couple of times on Saturday but I could not contact him.

For Xmas we are having a big feed in the mess of turkey, goose and chicken – sounds good and it will no doubt eat well. They had a Xmas draw and I was lucky enough to win 50 cigarettes, 'Craven A' too which is not too bad. I expect we will have rather a hectic do. Luckily it looks like the fog will hold and we won't have to do too much flying.

I have sent out my local Xmas cards and did not forget the Leuchs or Uncle Alex, which no doubt you would have imagined I had.

Armourers with anti-gas equipment during exercises at Martlesham Heath. IMPERIAL WAR MUSEUM IMAGE CH003995

I had a letter from Digger today. He is on leave and hoped I would meet him at the Sussex, but I need a few quiet nights and am taking a snappy little WAAF out for the night. I know she has to be in by 11 so I will have no trouble getting to bed myself. If I went up to London I would not get to bed till about two tomorrow morning. I have had a few letters from Mr Beaufort and got a Xmas card from him today. He is apparently a S/L in the RAF and is posted at Sealand near Chester.

Kenley
Saturday, 27 December 1941

Xmas is over and things were very bright down here as there were parties every night for the last week. We had the 'worst' night of the lot last night when we went round to the officers' mess for a few beers – the few beers developed into a few too many and we all ended up at the WAAFs' dance. The Xmas dinner was very good indeed and here is the menu: Alexandra soup, roast turkey, roast pork, roast spuds, mashed potatoes, Brussels sprouts, peas, Xmas pud, brandy sauce, mince pies, sweets various, coffee, cheese and biscuits. All the

403 Squadron RCAF Armourers re-arming cannons and machineguns at Martlesham Heath.
IMPERIAL WAR MUSEUM IMAGE CH004000

accessories were there as well: sausage meat, bread sauce, apple sauce and stuffing. We asked a few WAAFs down and made a night of it in the mess. They brought a really good leg of ham – as a matter of fact it was an NZ ham.

I start a week's leave the day after tomorrow, which will mean I will have New Year's Eve in Carlisle. I'm looking forward to it but I hope they run out of beer as I overdid it last visit. Mrs Rickerby sent down a cake and cigarettes for a Xmas present – very much appreciated, I can tell you. I also received a parcel from you with the socks and wings on-sent from Canada.

The only flying we have done since we returned from Martlesham Heath was an hour yesterday. The weatherman gave us the Xmas present we wanted – wet and misty for the most part! We have got some fresh recruits to the squadron including Bruce Gibbs, Travis Goodlet and Gray Stenborg. It is now a big squadron with 30 all told but it will no doubt be reduced a bit when we get something to do and some cop it.

Well I'll say cheerio for now. Love to all and hope you are all in the best of health.
Love to Nanna also,

Doug

Kenley
Monday, 5 January 1942

Dear Mum, Dad and Girls,

Well, another year started and I hope next year we will be able to celebrate at Manly beach.

Last Sunday was a perfect day and I did my first sweep, the first the Squadron has done since I've been here. We took off and I had trouble with the engine but caught the others up. We climbed to 20,000 feet. You would hardly realise there was a war on, as you could see miles into France and Belgium. It was grand. The engine, which had been giving trouble, packed up again so I yelled over the R/T and headed for the English coast, making sure I could bale out near England. I was jolly lucky in that after what seemed a hell of a time the engine picked up and allowed me about an inch of throttle to play with and gain half speed. To add to the excitement I got lost but I brought her in OK in the end.

Monday was a great day for me as I started a week's leave and headed poste haste for Carlisle to spend New Year's Eve up there. I left Kenley at lunchtime with a few others, five of whom were going to Edinburgh, and Jack Rae and self up the other side. We went to a show at the Plaza which we left at 7 p.m. and after a very good feed at the Quality Inn we went up to the Sussex where we remained till about ten and headed for Euston by taxi. We decided to go first-class and pay the extra on the train and felt absolute cads to see officers standing in the corridor while we slept in peace – the funny thing was our tickets were not collected so we got the trip as first-class passengers for nix. The Rickerbys were jolly glad to see me and after a bath I enjoyed a good feed of eggs and bacon.

In the afternoon I went and saw Mr Askew who had a few parcels for me. I then did a bit of shopping and got a Loewe for you Dad, and a book for you, Mum, called *Fighter Pilot*. Later on I played golf with Tom Gavaghan and Viv walked around with us for the exercise. I enjoyed the golf though I went round in about two hundred. Tom swings quite a crafty club and seemed to know a bit about the game. Tom runs the local division of the Home Guard up at Harraby. He is probably the only one amongst them who is commissioned. He keeps them well fed with his hams and they spend most of the time at the pub.

Old Year's Day started with cocktails at 11 a.m. We continued through the day and at 3.30 we were at Lady Creighton's. Tom Cavaghan did his annual trick

Sir Keith Park. RNZAF MUSEUM.

Keith Park was born in Thames and initially served with NZ troops in Gallipoli and then transferred to British forces. At the battle of the Somme a shell landed next to him and he was blown off his horse, injured and certified unfit to continue service. Undaunted he joined the RFC and ended WWI a well-decorated pilot, having shot down a number of his opposition.

He ran Fighter Command during the Dunkerque evacuation and the Battle of Britain. This comprised the stations south and east of London, including 11 Group and Leigh-Mallory, who ran 12 Group, under him. There was extreme jealousy between the two. Initially the German planes bombed the airfields and Park's approach was to release one squadron at a time to meet them. Leigh-Mallory wanted all the aircraft up at once as a 'Big Wing' – the problem being there was nothing in reserve to combat the next wave coming over. At this stage the RAF were outnumbered at least five to one by the Luftwaffe. Park realised that to undertake an offensive role would be suicide and end in defeat.

Leigh-Mallory had Douglas Bader who was also rather Gung Ho fly 12 Group through 11 Group's airspace. Keith Park stuck to his plan and the Germans stopped bombing the dromes with such intensity. The dromes could then be repaired and the aircraft replenished. As aircraft production was good the problem was a shortage of pilots. This led to the squadrons being stocked with inexperienced fliers.

Keith Park was a wonderful man. He had a Hurricane he flew to visit his men in 11 Group. In 1942 he went out to Egypt and Malta and took charge of Air Command. Leigh-Mallory had used his position and the people he knew to undermine Park, much to Park's dismay. My first impression was established while we were at Kenley, when he came to visit us prior to taking command at Malta.

After the war we were both members of the Auckland Rotary Club. We decided we should have a Spitfire on display in NZ. Using his wartime contacts Keith found one and organised delivery by the Navy. It got as far as Sydney and then it got stuck there. I paid to get it shipped from there and it got delivered to the Auckland War Memorial Museum in a crate.

I used to have lunch with him occasionally and coincidentally his son lived opposite us in our first house in Auckland.

ABOVE LEFT Women pilots Cunnison, Rees and Patterson commissioned by Air Transport Authority to ferry planes. GETTYIMAGES.COM REF JD0996-001

ABOVE RIGHT WAAF teleprinter officers outside damaged buildings at Biggin Hill after Luftwaffe attack 1/9/1940 Sgt Mortimer, F/O Henderson, Sgt Turner. IMPERIAL WAR MUSEUM IMAGE CH001550

BELOW LEFT Heinkel 111 crashed during an attack on Biggin Hill, 30 August 1940. GETTYIMAGES.COM REF 3352062

BELOW RIGHT Dornier shot down during the Battle of Britain. GETTYIMAGES.COM REF 53027440

of booking dinner for 40 at the Crown and Mitre Hotel – which no one had any intention of attending. At 6.30 we were at the station to farewell a fellow Grant, a 2nd Lieutenant in the Black Watch Regiment. He was very merry.[33]

New Year's Eve started at Joe's from there to the Grill and we then went out to the golf club's dance. Dick Dias was also a starter and with a few of the boys who were on leave we had a fair do. Lady Creighton was there and had rather a snappy niece, Joan Allan from Newcastle, whom I took over and looked after. The dance finished at midnight and after Auld Lang Syne and Scottish customs, we headed for the 'houses' part of the show.

First stop, Rickerbys', where all 40 turned up. We stayed there an hour and next stop was a place I did not know. We eventually ended up at Cavaghans where all was bright and merry and we made bed just before sunrise. The next morning I was pulled out of bed at midday by Joan and Lady C who were off to Harrisons' for cocktails. Dick, Joe and I instead opted for a quiet lunch and beer, however, before long the mob from Harrisons' arrived very merry and bright. Lady C, on being asked what she wanted to drink, answered 'anything with gin in it.' The party got underway and a reservation made for 20 of us for later that night. The others did not leave till after five, much the worse for wear, and we sat down to a feast of turkey followed up with Xmas pudding, which fixed me properly.

After tea we went out to The Rooking, Scotby, as Joan wanted to change for another do, but when we got there we found the place locked. After a while we figured out how to get in. I climbed onto the garage roof and tumbled through a window that led into Lady Creighton's room. She was dead to the world so I went and let the others in. While Joan changed we helped ourselves to some of the Duke of Scotby's ale. When we got back we found the party had been put off as half of the team was by then incapable of attending anything.

I caught the midday train, which was about an hour and a half late getting in to Carlisle but I got a good first-class seat. I reached London at about 9 p.m. and got a taxi to Charing Cross and as my connecting train did not leave till ten I went up to the Sussex where I met Reg Round, Herbie Duff, and Ivan Stone, among others, and they tried to lead me astray. It was just as well a certain nightclub called the Vintage Club was closed, enabling me to catch the midnight train. I was in bed within the hour.

---

33 It was not until 1984 when Eve and I had dinner with him and his wife at Doug Rickerby's that the remainder of the story was told. He had fallen asleep on the train and omitted to disembark at the correct railway station. Although he was an officer he was arrested and put in prison for desertion.

While I was on leave, Johnny Palmer had some excitement when on convoy patrol. He was having a go at a Hun bomber and got pounced upon. He baled out and used his dinghy and is now with us again, none the worse for wear. It has been foggy all day today and it is now snowing. I tested a kite today and only stayed up 20 minutes as the dirt drifted over from London. I was jolly glad I came down when I did as it settled in. The rest of the day has been spent at Pontoon, which is played very extensively.

Saturday, 10 January 1942

Since I last wrote I have been fog bound at Hornchurch a drome just north of here. We did a rather large-scale sweep on Tuesday and upon returning we could not get down to Kenley due to the weather and so were sent off elsewhere. After playing about for two hours in the air we got down safely but with little gas left. The Air Force was lucky not to lose any aircraft that day. Our stay was very bright and we had four good nights. Max Krebs and self left for home yesterday. We both had u/s aircraft and they did not get mine fixed till late last night. When they did look at it they found the wireless no good so in the end I did not get away till after midday. I was very lucky getting back as I never saw any land at all. With the help of Ops I made it and was pleased to reach base and get on some clean clothes.

I got four parcels today, one from Auntie Mary – gingernuts, which will go well, two from you Mum, and one from the Auckland Golf Club, which was not bad. I had a letter from Gus Taylor sent from Alexandria, Egypt, and he has contacted Colin McGruther, Kel and Nevin Brown, Chas Passmore and Doug Carnahan as well as Don Corbin, Ras Forgie and Johnny Barstow, who were all on the same boat. Gus had had a night out with them. I bet it was a night.

Well, I have done my dash as far as the news goes. I heard from Auntie Eva the other day informing me of Uncle Alex's death so I dropped her a line. We had a bit of snow today and although not enough to cover the ground it is darned cold and I will be jolly glad when the summer arrives. Wish I was with you.

Cheerio for now. Love to all and hope Nanna is OK,

Doug

Kenley
Monday, 19 January 1942

Dear Mum, Dad and Girls,

It is now snowing heavily outside and does not look as if it will stop before morning. It has been snowing most of the week and is fairly thick on the ground. It fell very fast on Tuesday night and I took a WAAF to the local pub the Golden Lion for a quick beer and when I came out there was quite a layer around. Due to the weather, flying – to put it in English words – 'has had it'.

On Monday morning Harvey Sweetman, Mac Ralph, Mick McNeil and self were on early-morning readiness and we had no sooner got settled in our chairs by the stove when we got a scramble from Ops for convoy patrol. It is such a long time since we have had one that when the word came over we looked blank and stared at each other for a minute or two before we realised what was what, then it suddenly dawned on us and away we went. We seemed to be up for hours, the weather closed in and I lost track of my No 2 and got lost properly. More by luck than good management I found the drome and it was so dirty you could not see the runway. I had to make a 'by guess and by God' approach. My first attempt was about 45 degrees out as well as being about halfway down the runway. I made it the second attempt with a nearly dry tank. Most of the rest of the days have been spent in a strong Pontoon school, which has been moderately good to me so far but my luck will take a turn sooner or later and I'll be sorry.

I had to go before the CO 'old Groupy' as a result of my prang at Martlesham a few weeks ago. There were three of us up for interview: Les Scorer was in the English Squadron, which was over there and has since been replaced by the Aussie Squadron. He did something minor and came back with 'Carelessness' in red ink. Another English P/O came back with 'Gross Carelessness' in the good old red so I thought this looked really good, and when my turn came along I went expecting the worst. He read the letter from Air Ministry, which said I was to be punished at his discretion. The CO, a very fine type, talked about the price of Spits as he would the price of fish, and I got off with 'Error of Judgment' in black ink which is the best possible.

I got an entry in my log book which sounds good and typically Air Ministry. One minute they tell us to be careful with Spits and then they go and try and make Spit Squadrons operational in night flying and wonder why

(1)

18.12.41. (i) When landing in formation at Martlesham he noticed another aircraft on the ground ahead of him. He turned slightly & then lost sight of his leader. On touching down he bounced heavily & eventually the undercarriage collapsed.

(ii) ERROR OF JUDGEMENT.

(iii) Admonished.

Guilty.
11 Gp letter 11G/31/67A/7/Tng. dd. 8/1/42.

C. Bouchier
13.1.42.

GROUP CAPTAIN   COMMANDING

R.A.F. STATION, KENLEY,

Endorsement after accident at Martlesham Heath following first operation

they get wiped out. A Spit is a wonderful kite but the landing has to be very carefully watched in daylight, let alone night work. It is their outfit – we just fly for them.

The other day we had a visit from the Mayor of Croydon to have a look at our lounge. The people of Croydon supplied all the furniture and they came to give us the look over. The Groupy was in his usual good humour and introduced the boys by their nicknames. When we were told we could smoke all the boys brought out their rolls including the Groupy who has also taken up the game. He rolled one for the Mayor and his daughter and they said, probably out of politeness, how good NZ rolls were.

I had a 48-hour pass over the weekend and Mick McNeil and I decided to have a big do in London. We had a job booking in at a pub as we had been barred from many of them and ended up at the Mapleton – a lousy show. We dropped our bags and thought we would have a beer in the American Bar there before going on to the Sussex. We had just started our first beer when a dark mop of hair came through the door, none other than Paul Hayward just the same as ever and AWOL – no trouble at all. He is at OTU and is at present flying Hurricanes but he is still keen to make Spits. If he strikes Hurri bombers it will be bad luck as there is no future in that game.

He looked pretty fit nevertheless and wished to be remembered to you all. We left him soon afterwards and ran into Bill Joyce, Wiggy Webster, and a few other lads there and had a beer or six. At nine I went to another pub, the Brasserie, where I met a WAAF I had previously met at Hornchurch. She was with a party and they roped me in. We went on to Murray's Club where I am now an honourable member. It was a good place but I could not stay the distance and left at about 2 a.m. Not being able to get a taxi I set a course for the Mapleton.

I got back before Mick Maskill and Jack Rae so I hit the hay as I was tired. I was woken by a disturbance and sat up to see a girl stumbling over our bags. I exclaimed: 'What the hell do you think you're doing?' Her reply, although not very convincing, was that she was looking for the bathroom. As was the case in these hotels the bathroom was shared between a few guestrooms. With all the commotion Jack and Mick were now well awake. We informed her that the bathrooms were across the hallway and she disappeared. We decided to lock her in one of the bathrooms while we checked our gear and tidied up and got ready to check out. I wasn't entirely satisfied her intentions were innocent but we left her to it.

First stop, something to eat, and Bill Joyce, Jack Rae, Mick and self, made a beeline for the Bower House where we had a cheese salad and sardines on toast. After a bit of a meal we caught a taxi to the Strand Palace and booked in there for the night. I was not feeling the best so I had a jolly good bath and a shave to brighten me up. Mick and Bill decided to go to the Sussex again, but Jack and I piked and went to a show, 'Sergeant York'. After the show we went down to the Quality Inn where we got a very good meal and after that, as it was only about 5.30, we went to another show 'Disney's Dumbo', which I thoroughly enjoyed. When next in London Jack and I plan to see 'Gone with the Wind'. After 'Dumbo' we wandered along to the Sussex where there was a fair mob – all shapes and sizes. Jack and I went down to Charing Cross for a feed and then wandered back to the hotel where Mick and Bill were in the greatest of form. I ran into Wiggy Webster and had a couple of beers with him and Jack and I who were sharing a room got to bed at about midnight. I had just got to sleep when Mick and Bill woke us and wanted to come in. They banged and called out for a while and then there was a terrific crash as if a bomb had exploded.

I found out this morning that Bill and Mick had a 'po'[34] with them and the chap in the room next to ours decided the row was getting a bit hot and asked the boys to stop the racket. He just poked his nose out of the door as Bill threw

---

34 Chamber pot.

the 'po' to Mick who missed it and it crashed at this poor fellow's feet. It had been quite a weekend! We had breakfast and headed back to camp.

The London sirens have just gone but think it must be a false do as I have heard no bombs yet. Dutch Stenborg left us the other day and has gone to III Fighter Squadron.

Saturday, 24 January 1942

The NZ boys have had little mail for weeks now but I did receive your birthday gift of clothes. They were a very acceptable tome.

We had more snow and rain yesterday, the latter clearing away most of the snow. Today we did the first flying for nearly two weeks and I've never enjoyed a flight so much for a long time.

I've had a rotten cold during the past week and have not been out since my 48, but tonight being Saturday I'll probably visit the local.

I had an offer to go to India yesterday but turned it down. Two of the boys are going and I think now they wish they hadn't volunteered. The trouble with overseas postings is the gamble on what type of aircraft you are liable to get. Spits always live here – too precious. I wish to hell they would send our Squadron with Spits out your way. We all worry about the state of the Far East.

Regards to all and hope you are all fit. Tons of love,

Doug

Kenley
Friday, 30 January 1942

Dear Mum, Dad and Girls,

I was jolly glad to receive the first mail for many weeks from you yesterday. I got two from you Dad, dated 5 and 15 Dec, and one from Mum, as well as Shirl, also a parcel containing about 300 cigarettes from Gus Taylor – damn decent of him.

The weather has not been the best during the past few days and tonight it is a combination of heavy snowflakes, rain, lightning and thunder.

Very jolly outside, I must say! Sunday was quite a good day and we did a rather large-scale sweep but had bad luck losing our Flight Commander (B Flight) Jack Strang. He was a grand chap and very understanding of us as new pilots and it came as a big shock, being only my third operational trip. Before we took off he said, 'Christ, I'm cold. Can you lend me your pullover, Brownie?'

His flying became more erratic and started a series of descending loops. I was his No 2 and the three of us followed him down as we are supposed to. When he broke away we were over 20,000 feet and in a full dive. We had a hell of a speed and my nose was spouting a bit of blood due to it. He went into the water like a dart and the plane left no trace on the surface at all. We circled for a while uselessly and returned home. His loss was attributed to failure of the oxygen supply. I lost the beautiful maroon cable-stitch pullover, which he had borrowed. I bought it in Canada for $10. His plane *Southland I* was subscribed from funds from the province.

A Flight Lieutenant direct from Auckland – a New Zealander who received his two bands in NZ, probably flying Tiger Moths – is with our squadron and has got it in his head he is the boy. Billie Compton took over from Jack Strang and is trying to make him 'Arse-End Charlie'. That will knock him! Mick McNeil and I are the usual 'arse-ends' in our flight and believe me the old eyes keep a good lookout. Mick and I had a fly together today and did some good shooting up. We had not flown for a few days and went absolutely mad. This afternoon we went up, five of us, to put on a formation and the weather closed in when we were no more than 200 feet above the drome. There were planes everywhere in the cloud, all lost.

Jack Rae and self have bought a car: it is a beaut, a Morris Ten 1935. It only cost £40 and to hear it going down the road you would think it was a two-ton lorry. At present the generator is out of action and we have to get the battery charged every two days. We do well for gas. We get the usual allowance plus 250 miles each quarter and another 300 miles on top of that, which is quite good. We christened her on Tuesday at a local dance given by the Aussies and she got us home OK.

When we first joined Kenley, transport was readily available. We could call for a car even at 3 a.m. to take us back to our billets. When G/C Victor Beamish arrived, all this changed and we were all issued with bicycles.

The car was previously owned by Vic Hall, a communications expert. Hawk Wells was in charge of the sale and he offered it to us for £40. Jack and I decided to give it a month's trial before we bought it. We got the car and petrol coupons with it and at the end of the month the car was in a very bad state, the back axle out of alignment, clutch not working and the universal had only one bolt. In the end we pushed the car down the bank at Kenley and retrieved our £40 from Hawk. It was then we found out that Vic had only wanted £20 for the car and Hawk was profiteering on the £20 balance. Vic got his £20, we got use of the car and Hawk lost the money he paid Vic.

[Letter continues]

Our old Group Captain has left us and we were sorry to see him go. Our new Groupy is an Irishman, Group Captain Beamish, DSO and Bar, DFC, AFC – not bad – and he flies with us which helps things a lot. He is the brother of George Beamish who played for the British Lions, also a senior RAF officer. We have got some rather good men in our wing: Bill Wells, (our CO) DFC and Bar, Alan Deere (CO of another squadron) DFC and Bar, our Winco W/C Boyd DFC & Bar, and last but not least F/Lt Paddy Finucane (Irish Air Ace) DSO, DFC and two Bars[35] – not bad for a 21-year-old – he is being promoted to S/L and Alan Deere is moving.

7 February 1942

We had a few beers at the Golden Lion last night and celebrated my 23rd, but we were home fairly early. I received a parcel containing whitebait, butter and oysters, which I think must be from you as it has no card in it.

I have done no flying for over a week now and as I go on leave on Monday I don't expect I'll do any for another ten days. It is still snowing quite heavily. Michael and self are going off to spend the night in London, then a few days with Mac Wallace in Derby, and from there to Bournemouth. Quite a travel about. No trouble to us.

The car broke down the other night. Jack Rae, Bill Compton, Dave Clouston and self took old Annie (the car) down to a local dance at the Valley Hotel. We got there OK but when we had to come home something went. The couplings to the main drive shaft gave out and you should have heard the din. We had to push the old dear up the first hill, a matter of about a mile in length and very steep. From the top of the hill

---

35 Paddy Finucane was killed in action, July 1942 – forced down into the sea off Pointe du Touquet when his radiator was hit on a ramrod out of Hornchurch.

to the camp we coasted along at the rattling speed of about two miles per hour.

Our new Groupy is rather fond of regulations and we have had a few of the advantages we had before knocked back somewhat – rather annoying but it can't be helped. As a matter of fact I think we were getting rather slack and the change will probably be for the best. He is organising a dig for victory in the camp so that we can supply our own vegetables. It will require a lot of digging and you can imagine the boys hard at it.

Well I seem to be getting rather low in the page so I'll buzz off.

Tons of love. Cheerio for now,

Doug

On 12 February I was on leave. The squadron participated in an operation following the *Scharnhorst*[36] and other German Naval Vessels. G/C Victor Beamish had taken over as Commander at Kenley from 'Daddy' Bouchier. He was on patrol with Finlay Boyd and sighted the armada off Cherbourg. 485 Squadron did however make contact with the fleet's support and destroyed three Me109s for no losses. F/Lt Compton and Francis awarded DFCs despite the operation being a balls-up right from the start. At that time there was supposed to be a night patrol down to Brest just to check for any movements. It is understood on that night the boys had flu and they did not go down and no replacement patrol was put in place.

While Beamish and Boyd had spotted quite clearly the *Scharnhorst* and other vessels coming up the Channel it was regulation that we weren't allowed to announce anything like that on air. They had to come back and land before anyone could be told.

Due to the resulting delay very few aircraft got to them. The Navy blamed the Air Force and vice versa. By the time they had come further up the Channel

36 The *Scharnhorst* and *Gneisenau* were laid up in Brest after destroying 22 merchant ships in the Atlantic. They were holed up from April 1941 due to intensive Allied bombing. On 11 February 1942 Operation Cerberus launched a dash through the English Channel by the *Scharnhorst*, *Gneisenau*, *Prince Eugen* and support minesweepers and battleships. The Navy was not prepared, Germans had jammed radar, and Fighter Command who had spotted the movement but had live radio communications shut down all combined to let the convoy break through despite minor mine damage. *GNIESENAU never went to sea again*

On return from Channel dash, 12 February 1942 Back (obscured): Mick Shand, Tusker McNeil, Johnnie Checketts / Front: Harvey Sweetman, Dave Clouston, Reg Grant, Bill Wells, Bill Compton, Reg Baker

the weather had packed up. Six Fairey Swordfish biplanes went in and were all shot down. None of their torpedo bombs found their mark. The squadron was supposed to meet up with six Beauforts fitted with torpedos and of course they weren't there. It was amazing we shot any down and were not shot at ourselves. The only damage to the German boats was some mine damage.

Kenley
Monday, 16 February 1942

Dear Mum, Dad and Girls,

Well, here we are again, and the weather during the past week has improved considerably while I was on leave.

Mick McNeil and I left on Monday late as I got stranded at West Malling, Kent, on the Sunday after a scramble escorting bombers. With the weather closing in here Dave Clouston and I went all over the show. I was not sorry when I finally hit the earth but I picked a rotten place as it was well away from any town. Monday was very foggy and when I found I had no show of getting back I arranged for the Spit to be picked up and caught the

ABOVE LEFT Harvey Sweetman, Dave Clouston

ABOVE RIGHT Doug, Max Krebs, Ross Falls in Spitfire

earliest train I could home. We spent Monday night at the Strand and after mucking around London during the morning we caught the 1.30 train for Derby from St Pancras. We reached Derby just after five and Mac Wallace was there to meet us. He has changed a fair bit. I think he has been going at it too hard and is, I think, rather fed up because he can't get into any of the services. Mac directed us to 31 Bromley Street where we stayed over the week. The first night we did a pub crawl and finished up at a local hop which went quite well. On Wednesday we tried to get through Rolls-Royce but it was 'strictly off limits' so spent the day having a look at Derby and playing snooker.

In the evening we booked seats at the theatre. We were in the queue and I heard someone take my name in vain and lo and behold it was Paul Hayward of all chaps spending a week's leave with his folks up there. We arranged to meet him in the bar after the show. We had tea in town – plaice and chips – which was very good. We then went to the show, which was just average, although Alfredo and his orchestra were on and they are very good and brought the standard up a bit. After the show we went to the local hotel and then to another dance.

Snowbound Feb '42: Frank Piercy, Harvey Sweetman, Dave Clouston, Mac Ralph, Griff, Mick McNeil, Doug, Mick Maskill

Thursday evening we went to a Rolls-Royce dance. Paul came along and so altogether we had quite a night. Next day was beautiful and in the morning Mick McNeil and self went on a rather large-sized walk and had a look at the country which is really quite nice. That night we met Mac in town at five and we went out to Adams', his present place of abode for tea. As the lake just below the house was frozen, Mac, Mick, John Adams and self went down and ice-skated till dark. The skating was shambolic so we hobbled off to Mac's local, the Red Cow, and got involved in 'a big school', after which we went to the Adams' for supper and then returned to bed.

Next morning Paul's uncle picked us up and took us to the station where we caught the 9 a.m. for St Pancras, which got in at about 12.30. This gave us an hour to get to Waterloo and board the train for Christchurch near Bournemouth where Mick McNeil and I had to go to a dance with a couple of lasses. We wrote and asked them to book us in a certain hotel down there but when we got there we found no booking. After about seven hours in the train the air was a bit thick though few words were said. However all turned out OK as they had booked us in at another pub. We got to bed fairly early as the dance finished at midnight; the girls had to be at the hospital by 12.15.

We got up at about ten next day and it was glorious to see clear sky and a bit of sun. Mick and I wandered along the river and through the park and it all seemed very peaceful. We met the girls at two and went to the flicks and after supper caught the 6.30 train for London. We reached London at about 9.30, caught a taxi to Strand Palace, booked in and walked up to the Sussex and were there just in time to have a beer, which I thought was pretty good work. After a feed we were not sorry to get to bed and we got back to Kenley not long after eleven.

With the news of the Hun ships coming in and all the kites getting knocked over, I said to Mick that it's more comfortable here in bed and we may get a shirt or two when we get back.[37] Our squadron did well and we were made to hush up all the bloomers made of the whole job. A few of the papers had photos regarding the NZ boys. We got four destroyed and two probable which is pretty good work. The show was a complete muck-up. It was a miracle our wing lost no aircraft.

Those poor chaps in Swordfish didn't have a chance. When they said six failed to return, I said to Mick, I bet only six went out – I was right. The Colonial lads are rather fed up to the teeth over what is going on and I'm afraid I see no future in the way they are going on at present. I was very sorry to hear of Singapore's fall although I expected it and I bet we lost a lot of material there as well as men and a valuable stronghold – I believe it was said to be an impregnable fortress not long ago – funny how these fortresses fall. I only hope to God the war does not descend any further south.

Today was quite a decent day and I had a couple of flips, which were jolly enjoyable, and Mick and I 'shot up' the Leuchs' place at Tadworth. The trouble in a Spit is picking out the house as it is all over so quickly. I think we hit the spot and I hope they were home to see me! I will go down when I get my next 48-hour pass and will take down the tin of whitebait I received the other day. I also received a tin of biscuits from Bycrofts, which have nearly done their dash.

---

37 Traditionally when pilots were shot down there was a rush to get back to base to get first pick of the missing pilot's belongings – a little embarrassing when they turn up a few days later!

R ev. Jimmy Beaufort was headmaster at King's School from 1931–1934 after joining the school in 1928, having been King's College chaplain 1927–1928. He was born in NZ in 1894 and was educated in Ireland, gaining an MA from Trinity College, Dublin, in 1914. In WWI he was in the Army Service Corps and transferred as a Captain to the Royal Flying Corps. He used to delight in telling us as impressionable young boys how and why he joined the church. He would explain that it was during The Great War and his Camel had been hit by flak. As his plane spun earthwards he told himself: 'If I survive this, I will become a bloody parson.'

Subsequently he kept to his word and he was ordained in 1920 in Ireland and returned to NZ in 1922. After King's he became joint headmaster of St Peter's School 1936–1937 and then moved back to England and joined the Air Ministry in April 1941.

It was while I was at Kenley I learnt my prep school headmaster was in the area. I had tremendous respect for him and when I discovered he was at RAF Odiham I telephoned and told him I was flying over. He was adamant that I should not come over as all 'his boys' (as he called his previous students) who had visited had been killed. I told him I would destroy the myth. I took off in bright sunshine but when I reached Odiham, after just a short flight, it was fogbound so I had to turn back.

I tried again a week later but I was told Jimmy Beaufort had arranged a posting to Middle East Command and had left Odiham. I never saw or heard from him again. His Air Ministry Service notes show JM Beaufort as Chaplain RAFVR Squadron Leader and his transfer to South Africa in October 1943. He resigned in August 1944 and died in 1958.

He was a marvellous man and ahead of his time as an educationalist.

ABOVE Rev. J Beaufort, 1931

LEFT Sopwith Camel WWI. Jimmy Beaufort flew a similar plane while in the RFC.
RNZAF MUSEUM

Kenley
21 February 1942

Well here we are again as fit as a fiddle. It has been snowing again today and by the looks of tonight it will freeze over. I had a fly today, non-operational, although I was on readiness from dawn till nine this morning.

We nearly had another do similar to the *Scharnhorst* affair. We were at readiness from early in the morning and finally took off at five but were immediately recalled – bad show and a damn nuisance: kept on pins and needles all day. We have had a bit of activity of late – one of the Aussies getting it and Finucane got hit yesterday but brought the kite and himself back OK.

Cheerio for now. All my love,

Doug

Kenley
Sunday, 1 March 1942

Dear Mum, Dad and Girls,

I have a bit of bad news: Mick McNeil killed himself with Jim Burke. The silly coots were acting the goat in the 'Maggie'[38] and though we don't know exactly what happened, it seems they were doing low-level aerobatics at Three Bridges, Surrey. They hit the ground rather hard and the plane immediately caught fire. Mick as you probably remember came up with me to Derby and was a grand chap. He was really my best cobber on the squadron, mainly because I trained with him in Canada and Grangemouth and I got to know him pretty well. I had the job of getting his personal gear together and sending it with a letter to his people.

I got mail today from Peg and Shirl and Noel Taylor. I got quite a shock to hear Don Corbin and Ras Forgie are missing on *Neptune*. Our boys in the Middle East have had nothing but the rotten end of the stick for a long time now. They must be due for a rest. I was jolly pleased to hear that you were able

38 Miles Magister.

to get enough petrol to get down to Manly OK. The tin of toheroa soup will do its dash tonight.

I returned from a 48 today, which I spent at Glebefield. I got there at about two on Friday and after lunch Mrs Leuch, or Katie as she insists I call her, and I went to have a gaze at that world-famed racecourse Epsom. I was not up with the larks on Saturday morning, though it was before the Leuchs. I had a tour around the garden. The grass is beautifully green after being covered with snow and ice for a period. In the morning Mrs L took me to see a friend of hers who had been complaining because her chimney had nearly been knocked over – by whom? Don't know anything about it – not much! After they had gone we went and visited the Durlachers – I don't know whether you met them – and we had an appetiser gin and vermouth and though I don't like gin, I thought these two made a perfect combination and definitely gave me an appetite, yours truly scoffing a mere five eggs with sausages and bacon. After tea we had to go back and pick up Paul Leuch and I was talked into drinking homemade cherry brandy liqueur, which was the goods. I was up at about nine this morning and had breakfast with Paul who is a very intelligent lad for his age and keeps me on the move. I caught the 10.50 train, and was back in camp by 11.30.

This afternoon I managed to get in a couple of hours flying. The first was a bit of formation and it took the shape of a general 'shoot-up' of all the places of friends we knew, including Glebefield, which we shot to bits. The second trip was an Army co-op effort, which went well, the only trouble being we never found the tanks (our objective) but still it was a good fly.

Our flying last week was restricted and I think I did little more than a couple of flips and they were not enjoyable as it was very bumpy indeed and in weather like that there is very little you can do for practice. We had a squadron dance last Tuesday, which enables us to mix with the ground staff and also to get rid of a bit of cash shouting them. This coming Tuesday is the anniversary of the NZ Fighter Squadron and I have got an idea something will have to be done about it.

Well, I will buzz off for now as I have to get a bit of gear together for the funeral which takes place tomorrow morning.

Saturday, 7 March 1942

You may not believe it but the last four days I've spent in an Army camp. At last over here they are waking up to the fact that we need Army co-op and each pilot goes down to have a look around the Army mob and the Army come up here. Besides giving each service an idea of each other's job it fosters a good spirit.

On Tuesday we had a bit of fun over the channel and we managed to drag the Huns out and got one without loss. On Wednesday morning we set off for the Army camp and though we had only about 50 miles to go it was well on in the afternoon before we got there. I had a good billet with the BSM and sheets which I thought were unknown in the Army, and a batman – we were incidentally at a Canadian unit which makes a hell of a difference.

The first day I was up at 7.15 and after breakfast Dave Clouston and I watched them go through their usual morning parade. We then went off in the Bren Carriers and had a bit of fun as well as getting an idea how and when they are used. In the afternoon we watched an infantry practice attack and they seemed to make a jolly good job of it. After this effort, which finished at about four, Dave and I visited the local town and went to the flicks and then found a pub that sold Scotch Ale and had a pot or two, getting back to camp not long after ten. The next day Friday, we went off on a manoeuvre and did a bit of marching, the first since Levin, and really enjoyed it! When all were at their posts, the Colonel took Dave and self around in his car and gave us the dope on the show. That night was spent quietly in the mess. Saturday was a rotten day and in the morning we watched the machine gunners in action and in the afternoon we were lazy and I spent it reading. The less said about last night the better. Today, according to schedule, we were meant to be picked up at about ten but in usual Air Force style it was nearly three o'clock this afternoon before we left and we missed a couple of shows that came off today however I hope for something tomorrow.

There are four more from the squadron to go out to the Middle or Far East in the near future and I'm afraid I may be called upon. I don't mind in a way but it is pretty tough putting up with an English winter and then missing the summer.

Tons of love to all,

Doug

On occasion we would be advised we would not be flying operations and were on 'release' for the day. Reg Grant decided we should go up to London. We went to a show followed by a session at the Sussex and finished up at Shepherds, as was the routine. We rolled out of the Sussex running late. A US Army Jeep was in the street so we all hopped in. Reg got it started. We took off for Charing Cross Station, bounded along the steps to platform 14 and boarded the train for Kenley – abandoning the Jeep on the platform.

Kenley
Sunday, 15 March 1942

Dear Mum, Dad and Girls,

Last Monday we were on 'readiness' all day and finally got off escorting a few bombers into France. We lost none and got one so did well but the other two squadrons lost one each. Tuesday's weather was duff and so that was that as far as flying was concerned. Being release day, we went to Wimbledon and played the Met Police at rugby, being beaten 6–3 after a jolly hard game. It was my first game for a couple of months and I was jolly stiff the next day. The fog came down so thick that at one part of the game it was impossible to see from one side of the field to the other. We were going to call it off but the fog cleared slightly and we were OK once again. After a hot shower it was afternoon tea and into the bar for a few beers with the troops (in this case the police). The plan was to hit London that night but as we were so stonkered it was onto the bus, back to base, and into bed.

I was on dawn readiness on Thursday. Dawn is getting a few minutes earlier by the day and is currently around six. I was lucky to get a scramble and put up nearly two hours on that flip which was good going. Later in the morning we had an Army co-op practice, which was jolly good fun, and we shot the Army boys to pieces. The afternoon, as far as I was concerned, was dead. On Friday we had another bomber escort job into the middle of France and we came back unscathed though the other two squadrons lost one each. I think the wing accounted for about six Huns that day which was fair enough going. It was a beautiful day and France looked glorious. It would be nice to have a leisurely trip and not have to scour the skies looking for a dirty black cross.

Yesterday we did another bomber escort. We missed the bombers but had fun enough as we ran into Messerschmits and also a few 'flak ships' which two flights of our squadron had a go at. It was the first time I had 'pooped'[39] at any shipping. They certainly slung up some dirt and I saw a nasty flash on the water which was a bit close to be comfortable. Dave Clouston had a bit taken out of his wing. We got no Huns to our credit as far as we know. The Huns wouldn't fight, but they were hovering about five or six thousand feet above like eagles and then down they would come and then up again to repeat their efforts. We climbed after one of these hoverers and were not more than a couple of thousand feet below him when he went for some of the boys below. I'm sure he did not see us – if he had stayed a little longer we would have got him.

Our flight, Billie Compton leading, was last to leave and we had a good 150 miles of sea to go escorting the bombers home. We were attacked by a couple but they had damn all show as they came straight down firing as they went. 'Arse-End Charlie[40]', Johnnie Checketts, got a bullet hole in his wing but that was all. It was a damn good bit of fun. Sunday has not been the best and though there was a show scheduled this morning, dirty weather stopped it – just as well as we had rather a hectic party last night and it was near two when we got to bed. I would have hated to see the take offs at dawn this morning.

I was to have gone on a week's leave last Monday but as the war has brightened up a bit I stayed back. I may take a 48-hour sometime this week and go down to Leuchs' and eat eggs by the dozen. This visiting to Army camps disorganises things a bit and besides that we have quite a number of pilots who are not yet operational, which means hard work for the rest of us. It is too tough to send them on a bomber escort job for their first fly, as it is not exactly safe. They will concentrate as hard as they can and probably lag and then down they go. One of the other squadrons lost one like that the day before yesterday. A few more op hours should see me up for a commission – I hope to get my crown first as I will then get more pay as a P/O.

---

39 Slang for shot.
40 'Arse-end Charlie' is the term applied to the last plane in a section of four flying line astern.

Three families I was fortunate to 'recuperate' with in the UK were the Fergusons in Oxted, Katie Leuch in Tadworth and the Rickerbys up in Carlisle. The Fergusons we first met when Fergie came up to Kenley in his Jag in which he could hardly see over the windscreen. He arrived at the gate at Kenley and the guard stopped him, whereupon he said he wanted to see some of the New Zealanders.

The guard then asked who in particular and Fergie replied, 'the CO.' He was let in and he saw Hawk Wells. Fergie said he was also a New Zealander and had a party planned down at Oxted and wondered if six of the chaps would like to come. But he specified three sergeants and three officers. I was lucky to be one of those picked and had a wonderful time at the party and developed a long friendship with Fergie.

Every couple of weeks they held dances and the whole squadron would go except (usually) those on dawn readiness the next morning. The Fergusons were very hospitable. I visited there a lot and I thoroughly enjoyed it.

I remember on one occasion Tony Robson and I were staying there and Fergie told us he had a VIP visiting the next day who wanted to meet some NZ airmen. The next morning when we were still upstairs in bed there was a loud knock at the door and Fergie's daughter Marion called up to say Mary Churchill was downstairs.

TOP Fergie
ABOVE Fergie's shop, Oxted

ABOVE Hoskins Arms, Oxted. FRANCISFRITH.COM
BELOW The Bell Inn, Oxted. FRANCISFRITH.COM

'Mary, who?' we shouted, so Marion added:

'Winston Churchill's daughter Mary.'

'Send her up!' we replied. It wasn't until later we became aware that Churchill's residence Chartwell House was only a few miles from Oxted.

Fergie was a real character and wore large checked shirts, corduroy trousers and a Tam o'Shanter. He was injured in the Great War and after recuperating he decided to live in England.

After WWII they made a couple of trips to New Zealand, receiving the hospitality of all the boys they had looked after. He was a very modest man and well liked by all, from the most humble to most distinguished. On arranging one of his trips in 1949 he asked: 'For the return journey I want to get back to England cheapest means.'

ABOVE Auckland 1 damaged

LEFT Shows seat of Spitfire cranked up to give better visibility when taxiing

Wednesday, 18 March 1942

I spent a nice 48-hour pass with the Leuchs, comprising mostly rest which funnily enough I found I needed. I felt much better after my stay there, feeding on plenty of eggs, which I reckon are necessary to keep body and soul together. We had a big feed on my last night of whitebait fritters; the whitebait[41] so kindly supplied by Mrs E B Brown. They were quite good, Mum, though not so tasty as the fresh! We cleaned up three tins between three of us and I admit I had more than my share.

Last night we had a pretty snappy party. A New Zealander who lives in a town not far from here – a Mr Ferguson who came from Coromandel and settled here after the last war – came over and took some of us down to a

41 These are quite unlike British whitebait. NZ whitebait are the size of a matchstick. Cooked in flour or a light batter with a dash of lemon and pepper they are quite a delicacy.

Front: Rosie Mackie, Eric Shaw, Dave Clouston with dog / Rear right: Johnny Palmer.
RNZAF MUSEUM

dance. What a do! The dance lasted till one and the bar there was open till 11:30 so all was bright and merry. After the dance we adjourned to Fergie's flat and continued there, singing with great gusto and generally making a noise. We did not get home till after four so one or two of the boys were not exactly 100% this morning. Poor old Tony Robson was on dawn readiness and only managed to get an hour's sleep in. It was quite a party, I can tell you.

I had a letter from Mac Wallace and he asked me to send his regards to you. Bruce is apparently hard at it on the sea patrolling in the vicinity of my port of call[42] on the way to England, poor mug. I bet he gets fed up with that and will be glad of any transfer he may get to warmer waters.
Love to all and hope you are all fit and well as I am.

Cheerio and good luck,

Doug

42 North Atlantic convoy running supplies from Iceland to Russia.

Kenley
Saturday, 28 March 1942

Dear Mum, Dad and Girls,

Well here we are again and we are certainly getting into action and seeing lots of Hun. I have been on two bomber escorts since I last wrote – a week ago – three sweeps and several patrols. Yesterday afternoon I scrambled three times. One circus I missed last Wednesday and the boys had a lot of fun. Bill Compton got two, Rosie Mackie one, Mick Maskill one and Groupy got a couple – good work. Mick Maskill got separated from the rest and had a go with three of them. He got one and received some nice bullet holes but managed to get to a British drome OK. We lost Maxie Krebs on that do but he baled out and will probably be a prisoner of war.

This afternoon's sweep was the real thing. We went over and swept after a raid and got amongst them. I lost the rest and was like a lonely sheep with Huns coming at me like ruddy darts. Luckily they missed and I only had one poop and was nowhere near them. Reg Grant got two and Bill Compton one, and one or two got damaged. Jack Rae and Marty Hume also got amongst it. They came down below the cloud and Jack got a couple and then the fun started when five Jerries got on their tails and they did smart low flying all over France. Marty had a few nice holes but got back OK. Johnny Palmer got nicely peppered and got home early but cursed everyone right and left, I believe, when he could not go up again.

I am sorry to say Group Captain Beamish got shot down and as yet we don't know whether he baled out in the Channel OK or not.[43] We can only hope for the best as he is the type England wants to win a war. The English Squadron got six and lost one, Rudolph, a Czech, who was a very good type. Jack Rae should get a DFM soon and Reg Grant should get a DFC on top of his DFM. This scrapping racket suits me down to the ground, but I have yet to get my first Jerry.

Apart from flying there has been little else doing apart from a dance in the mess on Tuesday night. It proved to be a rather good affair and we all got very bright and merry which told on us next morning. Once in the air all was OK again. The oxygen we get in the Spit cures the worst of hangovers!

43 Both Max Krebs and G/C Beamish were killed on 28 and 29 March respectively.

Winco Victor Beamish in June 1940 after shooting down 2 Me109s over Dunkerque. He was then based at North Weald Essex. IMPERIAL WAR MUSEUM IMAGE CH000490

3 April 1942

I have just completed a 48-hour pass, prior to which we only did minor ops. One day I actually did five trips, though they did not amount to much: a couple of sweeps, a convoy patrol and a couple of section scrambles.

Mick Maskill and self went off to London for a 48 last Wednesday. We did not get there till after five and so by the time we had booked in at the Strand Palace and had a feed at the Quality Inn it was after six. The main reason I went up was to meet Digger Robertson who had written to me and told me he would be up there. He left a note at the Forces Club to say he would meet me at midday at the Sussex, but I was not there in time. As a matter of fact Mick Maskill and I were at a nearby drome in the Maggie trying to get it started. When we did eventually get her to go we were up in a rainstorm and got blown all over the sky.

Mick and I reached the Sussex at about six thirty and met Bill Compton, Dave Russell and Eric Shaw – 485 boys – and started to knock one or two back. I was supping a pint of Youngers Scotch Ale when somebody yelled out my name and there was Dig. I could hardly recognise him as he has gone Navy with a beautiful beard – though of course he's the same old Dig and I was jolly glad to see him. He is at present stationed in Scotland and certainly looked fit and his stock saying is 'Aye Chum' typically Poona. He told me Tubby Graham is going back to NZ among many Navy boys who came over in the ship with Bob Gyllies and Dig. Nookie is stationed in Ceylon and I expect is getting a bit of action. Dig confirmed that Don Corbin, Ras Forgie and Johnny Barstow were drowned. Billy McManemin is now in the Navy and apparently got a very dirty deal when he was kicked out due to a disagreement with his instructors. I can well believe it, as a lot of that sort of thing goes on in the training schools. I saw Pat Larner (was at King's School with me) also in the Sussex. He has been scrubbed from the Fleet Air Arm and is now in the Navy. Dig read me a letter from Graeme Thorburn. He said he was Lance Corporal in some part of the Army and he would probably be able to meet Dig when he got his commission in a year or two's time – typically Graeme!

Well I seem to have not come up to my quota this fortnight but there is little or no news and it is no good babbling on about nothing. I hope you are all well and the Japs are keeping their distance.

Remember me to everyone. Tons of love to you all and hoping you are all fit and well.

Cheerio,

Doug

On 4 April I should have been shot down. The wing carried out a bomber escort to St Omer and on the way back I was lagging behind as No 4 or 'Arse-End Charlie' and reported: 'There's a dozen or so aircraft at seven o'clock above.' Bill Wells was leading and he said: 'Oh well, keep an eye on them.' They were Huns and attacked the Squadron but for some reason didn't attack me – struggling behind.
At that time we flew a line astern formation. With hindsight it was not effective as we were intent on looking at the pilot in front and there was little chance to look behind.

Combat report for 4 April 1942 at 10:30 between St Omer and Calais: : National Archives of the UK

I was flying Blue 4 when we were attacked by 12 FW190s approaching from 8 o'clock and slightly diving. I attacked an E/A which was firing at one of our own A/C with about a second burst quarter deflection. The E/A broke away and dived and I followed him down for about 3000 feet giving the E/A another burst of 1 to 1 ½ seconds and just as I broke away I noticed fragments break away from the E/A which held in its dive. I broke off the attack turning starboard and climbing and continued escorting our bombers. I was unable to find my flight and did not contact any members of my squadron until crossing the Channel at Deal. I claim one FW190 damaged.

Kenley
Saturday, 11 April 1942

Dear Mum, Dad and Girls,

This last week we have only done three shows of any importance, the rest of the time the weather being not the best. I was lucky enough to get a Jerry the other day for which I claimed a 'damaged' and Air Ministry kindly gave it to me. We went in with bombers and a squadron of the Huns came down upon us and went right into the middle of the squadron and did not even poop at me. I had a go at one that was attacking one of our boys and must have put the wind up him for he went over on his back. I went after him, though I was a bit of a fool doing so. However, I gave him a burst and knocked two whopping lumps off him. If he did get home you can bet he would have to send his underpants to the wash. I must have followed him for three or four thousand feet for when I attained my height again all the rabble of Jerries and Spits was a long way off and, believe me, I gave the old kite everything I had to get back up with them – luckily nothing went for me. It was jolly good to let everything go at Jerry and I hope to get many more chances. The trouble is you may go up many times to get among Jerries and not get a shot – there is a lot of luck in this game. We lost two chaps killed that day, Freddie Chandler and a new chap Fox, who should not have gone on the show as he lacked experience and should never have been in 11 Group. John Pattison who joined us in March was shot to bits as was Johnnie Checketts and the 'borer' certainly had a go at their kites that day. Tusker McNeil got a 'probable' and Bill Compton got a 'damaged' as well as me so we were about even.

The other morning we were over the 'other side' not long after dawn but saw nothing apart from a bit of flak on the way out. We generally encounter it on the way in and out over the coast. Those boys over there are getting quite accurate and I feel one could light a cigarette off a burst and say, 'Thanks, Chum!'

We have had one or two parties during the last week. We had a real good 'un in Oxted last Wednesday, which was organised by Fergie. We were called for and taken down not long after eight and danced till one. We again got into cards and went out to an old country house owned by a Mr Soutrow another NZer who turned on a great party. He is a very wealthy chap and has a beautiful old estate and the party was held in what had previously been an old hall. It was ideal and being 500 years old you can imagine what a beautiful spot it was. He was jolly pleased to see us and we are going along to his place for a party in a few days or so. We did not get back till after 5 a.m. and was I glad to see it raining cats and dogs when I woke at about nine – I just turned over and did not wake again till midday. Last night we had a bit of a do over in our billets, the occasion being the departure of Jack Rae who has been posted to Malta.

We now have daylight saving over here and it is light till nearly ten o'clock and dusk readiness lasts till half past nine which is rather boring. It is beautiful at night when the weather is good as it is tonight and I would be flying now if it had not been that the whole squadron is at 15-minute readiness. I had a good trip planned out and the Leuchs' was to be a port of call.

Friday, 17 April 1942

We have had plenty of action the last week doing sweeps or bomber escort about twice a day. As far as Jerry is concerned he is generally there and even though he has the advantage of height, he does not seem to be over keen to mix it. Now and again they venture downwards, but they are easy to dodge so long as you can see them coming, which I found out the other day when three of the cows tried to pounce me, but they had bad luck as I saw them coming. The main thing about this racket is to see everything that is in the sky, so long as you do that you can't go wrong. We are certainly giving old Jerry a bit of work and I think his pilots must be getting jolly tired of being stuck up in the air from dawn to dusk. Hun pilots seem doped as they get up to some very peculiar tactics in the air, such as rolls and other aerobatics when being attacked or even after they have issued attacks – they are really quite comical.

I hope to get up to Carlisle next week to attend Joe Rickerby's wedding but if we are bashing the ball along as much as we have been doing my leave will have had it and I'll have to stay here and 'sweep the vermin from the sky.' We have had about a week of perfect weather, which is rather amazing for England.

Nightlife here has been surprisingly minimal as we have been getting up at dawn and we have had shows from which we do not return till about nine. If we are released in the evening we generally hop down to the local pub and have a pint or two. Beer and cigs have gone up in price, which will knock the boys. The cigarette people must have expected this increase in the past months as cigs have been very thin on the ground but now that the Budget is out and the price set at a bob for them there are plenty to be obtained.

Well, cheerio for now. Tons of love to all,

Doug

90 Warwick Rd
Carlisle
Cumberland

Wednesday, 29 April 1942

Dear Mum, Dad and Girls,

It hardly seems credible that a year ago today the *Awatea* pulled out of Auckland and brought me over here to play aeroplanes.

As you can see from the above I'm in Carlisle again for a week's leave, which finishes tomorrow. The main attraction that took place was Joe's wedding, which went off very well yesterday morning.

Before I came up here we were still visiting France two or three times a day when weather permitted and ever since I left the weather has been perfect and they have been hard at it. Our wing has apparently lost a few fighters and I sincerely hope all our squadron is intact and also my aeroplane *Wine, Women and Song*. We have been pretty lucky of late and only lost two boys last month, which were the first for a long time.

I arrived here last Friday night at about 8 p.m. after quite a good trip up and I was jolly glad to get into bed as the previous night we had a sergeants' mess dance which was quite a success.

On Saturday after breakfast I popped up to the Silver Grill where I met Joe Rickerby and Dick Dias. Dick was also up on leave having got his Second

CLOCKWISE FROM TOP LEFT Carlisle. FRANCISFRITH.COM
Scaur House, Warwick Road, Carlisle
Hannah Dias, Margaret Cavaghan, Ann Rickerby
Tom, Harold, Margaret Cavaghan. Harold was still at school at this time. He was killed aged 19 while serving in the Border regiment on 1 August 1944

Mate's ticket[44]. We had a meal prior to going to Joe's pre-wedding bachelor party. About 14 of us gathered there and Mr Geo Dias picked us up and took us out to Glasson to the Highland Laddie where we picked up Mr Frank Dias. We stayed there till after ten and then proceeded to Frank Dias' place at Port Carlisle where we stayed till about two. The four survivors Dias Bros, self and Joe, whom we would not allow to go to bed, returned to Warwick Rd.

I did not get up frightfully early on Monday but Harold Cavaghan wanted a game of snooker. Then I called in to the bank and saw Mr Askew who is probably being moved to Whitehaven to manage a bank down there. After lunch I bought a wedding present for the new Mr and Mrs Rickerby – a muffin dish, which they seemed to appreciate. It cost a few quid. After that I paid the Cavaghans a visit and met Mr and Mrs Askew and daughter

44 Dick Dias was in the Merchant Navy. He was sunk 2 times in a tanker on his way to Malta. His rescue boat was also torpedoed and just managed to limp into port.

LEFT Doug and Dick Dias at the time of Joe's wedding   RIGHT Mrs Rickerby

Marguerite and at six they kindly drove me down to Keswick. We had a beautiful drive down and had dinner at the Royal Oak and then we set out for the Jobsons', which I picked out from the movie you have of the place. When we got there the maid said they were at a dinner party at the Keswick Hotel. We buzzed down to the hotel and I went inside and yarned to Auntie Sarah[45] and Uncle Dan for about three quarters of an hour, supping rum and milk. We got back to Carlisle at 11, jolly glad to pile into bed.

Tuesday morning, the Great Day, found us all up early as the wedding took place at ten and I had a few jobs which fell my way. The wedding went off well and we had a good breakfast or rather lunch to follow and Mr Gordon, father of the bride, had managed to get a few bottles of Champagne, which helped. It was a very quiet affair and there would be no more than 20 at the breakfast. Dick Dias was best man and did his stuff well and Viv was bridesmaid. They buzzed off at about midday, we found out later, headed for London – the Cumberland Hotel!

In the afternoon Dick and I took Viv and Pat to the flicks after which a party of six of us went to Penrith and had dinner at the George. Mr Jim Dias met us and it was the first time I had ever met him so he was glad to see a Brown offspring. He seemed a jolly nice chap and could not do enough for me. He has not had a drink for two years although shouted us and he had a tankard of water with us. The meal was grand and we got back to Carlisle soon after ten. As for myself I was jolly glad to hop into bed and I'm ashamed to say I did not get up till midday.

I left by the 1 p.m. train on Thursday and there was quite a party of us, including Mr Cavaghan and a man from the factory. We had a compartment to ourselves and we took beer, sandwiches and coffee. We got to London just

45 My godmother.

before seven and as Mr Cav was staying at the Russell I booked in for the night. We had a night out and visited a few pubs in Piccadilly and ended up at the Trocadero – your old haunt – it was my first time there and Mr Cav showed me where you all sat when he had a night out with you. We had a Pimm each at 3/3d a pop and a jolly good meal which Mr Cav kindly shouted me. We got to the Russell at about 11, sat in the lounge and supped a lager till midnight and on the way to bed disturbed Joe Rickerby and had a yarn to him. No doubt he was well-pleased to see us on his honeymoon.

Kenley
Saturday, 2 May 1942

We are now at readiness but it is a miserable foggy day. I doubt we will leave the ground.

I caught an early train yesterday and got back to camp at 11 to get a shock. On 24 April while I was on leave the boys were escorting Hurricane bombers. Jack Liken and 'Goody' Goodlet had been shot down and Johnny Palmer baled out over France and if he doesn't get away will be a prisoner of war.[46] On the 30th, John Pattison baled out in the Channel and was luckily picked up. Mac Ralph got shot to bits and brought his kite back OK with a shot in his heel – he was damn lucky. Bill Compton pranged when his engine cut out and broke a bone in his wrist and cracked his head a beaut – we did manage to knock a few over in spite of our losses and I think we evened up or got a little the better of it. Last evening I went on a do and we took bombers over. The Jerries came down in great style and we were unlucky enough to lose Ross Falls – he baled out over France and will be OK. The other two squadrons in the wing lost one each. We got a few though I didn't have any luck.

We are kept hard at it, not finishing till dark last night and up at dawn to do readiness at 4.30. Tonight, as the weather is duff, I will probably get a good night's sleep, which will put me on my feet again.

Tons of love to all over there. Hope Peg is OK at Varsity and Shirl is flying through Matric.

Goodbye again and tons of love,

Doug

46 Jack Liken was killed, Travis Goodlet and John Palmer became Prisoners of War.

485 Squadron, end April 1942. On plane: Stan Browne, Hec Leckie, Peter Gaskin, Garry Barnett, Tony Robson, John Yeatman, Doc, Dave Clouston, ___, Mick Shand, Doug, ___ Front: Dick Webb, Lindsay Black, _____, Mick Maskill, Reg Grant, Batchy Atcherley, Hawk

Wells, Reg Baker, John Kilian, Bruce Gibbs, John Pattison, Bill Compton, Marty Hume, Hunt – Intelligence Officer, Jack Henry

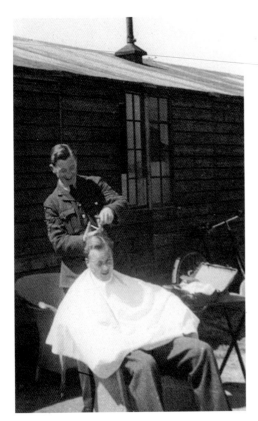

TOP LEFT Ren Hendry gets a haircut

TOP RIGHT Doug at readiness

RIGHT Dave Clouston and three others attempt bike ride

Kenley
Saturday, 9 May 1942

Dear Mum, Dad and Girls,

We have been over to France pretty regularly of late, two or three times a day, and my trips to there are now well in the thirties. I was over this afternoon and we ran into Jerries, a couple of which went for me, but I managed to dodge them and get a squirt into one of them but saw no result. I got a hell of a shock the other day – last Monday to be exact – we got properly pounced on. Mick Maskill got a cannon shell, which peeled all the fabric off the tail, and the same one went for me. I saw him coming and pulled the old kite over and got into a beautiful spin. When I tried to get her out she would not come around and I thought I had been hit but she did eventually straighten up so I went hell for leather into the sun. Johnnie Checketts' plane *Southland II*, the second subscription Spitfire from that province was shot down. He baled out and was picked up in the Channel. Dave Russell did likewise but was not so lucky, dying of exposure. Reg Baker also got a few holes in his aircraft but nothing else. Jerry had a good day!

We have had quite a few promotions of late. Bill Wells has been made Wing Commander Flying. Our old Winco Finlay Boyd pulled out as he had become a nervous wreck.

Bill Crawford-Compton was due to take over as our CO but he was injured when landing after his engine had cut out so Reg Grant took over the squadron. Although the rate of attrition in the Air Force has helped his rapid rise through the ranks, he is the man for the job – and I get on well with Reg! Mick Shand is Flight Commander of our flight and Reg Baker Flight Commander of A Flight which all goes well with the boys. Tusker McNeil has been posted to some gunnery school and 'Griff' Griffith has been posted as Flight Lieutenant to another squadron. Tony Robson, Mick Maskill and self are up for commissions but there is a devil of a lot of tripe to be carved out before we ever see them. I should have my crown through any day now, which means an extra two bob a day and it also carries on when made P/Os.

Early in 1942 Tony Robson had a scheme that we would fly together as No 3 and No 4 and when we were attacked by Huns we would split unnoticed by the No 1 and No 2 and fight the Hun Air Force on our own! I was a poor shot and saw little positive result from these episodes but Tony had done a lot of duck shooting and

ABOVE King George V and Tony Robson

OPPOSITE Film taken by Tony Robson during a 'kill'

was a very good shot. We managed to get away five times until one day I had an
Me109 on my tail and my only hope of evading fire was maintaining a very tight
turn. I heard a hell of a crash and went into a spin – I thought I had been hit as I
had difficulty pulling up. When I got back to Kenley I found that due to the G
forces in the tight turn the radio had come away from its housing. Tony got about
four destroyed and a well-earned DFM from these excursions and I may have got
an odd 'damaged'. After my incident with the spin we decided to discontinue this
activity and maintain contact with the rest of the squadron.

[Letter continues]
    Tony got a wonderful camera film of one he destroyed – the best combat
film of the war, I should think – and it has been released to the news people.
I saw it yesterday on *Pathé Gazette*. The King was down here when I was on
leave and all the news reels in London show the boys up well with the King.

I have got a great photo of Tony and the King, which I dare not risk sending home. There are also photos of the boys in the *Sphere Illustrated News*.

I had a letter from Uncle Hugh.[47] I must reply and tell him I'm still alive and about. He said he is at the Naval Base at Swansea and hopes to get a house as soon as possible. Auntie and Mick are apparently there with him and I expect it is costing him a packet keeping them at the pub. Leave is not the best at present and as I was lucky enough to get a week I don't complain. I will get three days later on in the month and will go down to the Leuchs' and sleep, which will do me the world of good. I don't expect we will be in II Group much longer as we are well overdue for a rest and our list of operational pilots is rather depleted. I think I would rather stay here as I can think of nothing worse than doing convoy patrols all day – they are most annoying and there is no fun in them at all. There was a raid not far from here a couple of nights ago and the searchlights were going full blast. I was too tired to watch the show so turned over and popped off.

I am sorry to hear Don McCullough has 'had it'. It is the first I have heard and I will drop his people a line and express my sympathy. The family couldn't do enough for John Grierson and me when we were on leave crossing Canada.

16 May 1942

I'm glad to say I've been receiving the letters and *Weeklies* the last few days. Today I got one from Mum and Noel Taylor, which contained some great snaps. Thank him for them – they were grand and made me a bit homesick.

The weather during the past few days has been really no good for the sweeps to continue and the first flight I had for a few days was yesterday when two of us 'shot up' Oxted and made a good job of it. We had the police on our tails when we landed but I think it will blow over OK.

Today when we were up, Johnnie Checketts and self decided to have a go. Two Jerries came down on me – I dodged one, had a squirt at him and had to smartly nip out of the line of another who thought he had a bit of meat. I think I diddle the poor Jerry boys as I occupy too much sky for them and do not do the right thing at the right time – secret of success in my opinion. I saw no results on the chap I fired at but the film came out well and I would not be surprised if he got a bullet or two in his fuselage. We had

47 Ted Brown's stepbrother born Cumberland 1886. Mick, is Hugh's daughter.

On Spitfire: Dave Clouston, John Liken, Tony Robson, Peter Gaskin, John Palmer. Middle: Eric Shaw, Rosie Mackie, Tusker McNeil, Bill Compton, Marty Hume, John Pattison, Jack Rae, John Kilian, Intelligence Officer, Bill Wells, Bruce Gibbs, Dave Russell, Mick Shand. Front: Doug, Johnnie Checketts, Stan Browne, Hec Leckie

reporters down here again yesterday and we had photos taken. Hawk Wells gave a broadcast over BBC the other day but it apparently did not come out well as it was re-read by the announcer.

We had another grand party at Oxted last Wednesday and did not hit the hay till nearly five. Next day, thank goodness, was lousy and I slept well till midday. I get three days leave next week and will visit the Leuchs, which will not be before time as my last visit was a long while ago. The trouble is we cannot afford to take too much leave as we have not got the pilots.

Cheerio for now,

Love, Doug

Jack Rae, Eric Shaw, Dave Russell, Peter Gaskin, Bill Compton, Rosie Mackie. In front: Doug, Dave Clouston

WINE, WOMEN AND SONG

Kenley
Saturday, 23 May 1942

Dear Mum, Dad and Girls,

The weather has been fairly duff and we have only done a couple of sweeps this week and nothing of note happened. The other day Johnnie Checketts and I did what we call a 'rhubarb'. This operation is carried out in rotten weather when the cloud is right down so that two or four of you can cross the Channel just above the water and with plenty of cover. We went to a place between Dieppe and Le Havre[48] – can't say where, as you know! – and shot up various things – a few train trucks, a signal box, which I set alight, an engine shed, which got it pretty badly, and a barge or two – as we came out. It is quite dangerous in that if you happen to run into Jerries you have had it and there is also fire from the ground to cope with. The film was a beauty and the camera chap told me tonight it may be shown on the screen in the news reels.

Tony Robson got the DFM and he damn well deserved it. Tony, Mick Maskill and self will be paying Groupy a visit on Monday regarding possible commissions. He will put us up and then we will visit the AOC and some months later we will be informed we are officers – maybe! We should all get them as we all have around 70 hours of ops. However, the old cock is a bit finicky so we can only wait and see what he decides. My crown is only four months overdue!

I had a three-day pass this week though I didn't miss any flying. I stayed in Oxted the first night with Fergie and took a girlfriend of mine out for a stroll. Fergie has got a wonderful wireless set with which he gets NZ. We played around with it from midnight till nearly two and America came through as clear as the BBC. The contraption has 12 valves and some power. I left Oxted that afternoon and tripped off to Tadworth to visit the Leuchs, they are all fit there and send their regards. Paul has just started boarding school and it seems to suit him down to the ground, judging from his first letter home. Katie Leuch has got a white linen tablecloth on which she gets everyone to sign their names and then the signature is embroidered in red – quite effective and there are many notable names upon it, including mine! That night for dinner I had a couple of large plates full of fresh asparagus with melted butter on them. Were they good? I'll say.

48 St Valery en Caux

The war seems to have been progressing quite well during the past few weeks and I hope the Russians keep up the good work. If they keep going as they are, I think this war will not last so long as anticipated. I am looking forward to the day when we go into France and I will certainly be able to use my guns to good effect. I only hope the Russians get to Berlin or into Germany before the British as they will make a mess whereas our mob will no doubt shake hands and say 'Nice day' or some such foolish remark.

Well, I'll buzz off now as I'm on dawn in the morning.

May was a typical month with over 27 operational hours, including six circuses, six rodeos, two scrambles, two rhubarbs, patrol, drill, ramrod and sweep.

On 2 May, circus Marquise-Desvres. Ross Falls was shot down and baled out over France and ended up a POW. I was commissioned at this time and took Ross' hat, which I still have today. In a circus we would go in close escort to bombers as a wing with the intent of bringing German fighters into battle. On another circus on 9 May, I fired at an FW190. Saw aircraft and chute fall into sea east of Mardyck (near Dunkerque).

A scramble was a call to air with some urgency.

A sweep was a conventional formation of fighters not acting as bomber escort but with the intent of drawing enemy fighters up.

On 5 May rodeo (fighter sweep without bombers) to St Omer, which was considered to be a formality but we were bounced. F/Sgt David Russell shot down and killed and Johnnie Checketts baled out in the Channel. He was collected and claimed an FW190 damaged.

Ramrod was a bomber strike with fighters in proximity but not in close escort.

On 16 May, carried out a rhubarb – low-level attack usually carried out in pairs when cloud base low and German Aircraft unlikely to be airborne. Damaged two locomotives – bags of steam! These opportunistic sorties were extremely dangerous and the targets were often booby trapped. Conversely an anti-rhubarb was our response to enemy rhubarbs over British defences.

By May 1942, all of the founding members of 485 Squadron had been killed or transferred out.

Saturday, 30 May 1942

I have had a rotten cold for the last week, right in the middle of the chest, and have been off flying but seem better today and hoped tonight to get on a show

Year: 1942		Aircraft.		Pilot, or 1st Pilot.	2nd Pilot, Pupil, or Passenger.	Duty (Including Results and Remarks).
Month.	Date.	Type.	No.			
—	—	—	—	—	—	— Totals Brought Forward
MAY	1	SPITFIRE VB	Q	SELF		(20) CIRCUS 150. LE TOUQUET - GRIS NEZ.
"	3	"	Q	"		(21) CIRCUS 145 - MARQUISE - DESVRES
"	3	"	Q	"		(22) RODEO - LE TOUQUET - MARQUISE
"	4	"	Q	"		SCRAMBLE - AIR SEA RESCUE
"	4	"	Q	"		(23) RODEO 18. HARDELOT - SANGATTE
"	5	"	Q	"		(24) RODEO 19 - ST OMER
"	6	"	Q	"		(25) CIRCUS 159 - TO CAIN.
"	6	"	T	"		(26) CIRCUS 160 - CALAIS VIA LE TOUQUET
"	7	"	V	"		SCRAMBLE - BEACHY HEAD + OUT TO SEA
"	8	"	Q	"		(27) CIRCUS 166 - 6 BOSTONS TO DIEPPE. AS CLOSE ESCORT
"	9	"	T	"		(28) CIRCUS 168 - 6 BOSTONS TO HAZEBROUCK K
"	10	"	Q	"		CONVOY PATROL - SOUTH NEW HAVEN
"	15	"	Q	"		COMBAT TRIM
"	16	"	Y	"		(38) RHUBARB - ST VALÉRY EN CAUX
"	17	"	Y	"		(29) RAMROD 33 - BOULOGNE
"	18	"	P	"		(30) CHANNEL SWEEP - BOULOGNE - DUNKERQUE
"	23	"	Y	"		TO FARNBOROUGH + RETURN
"	24	"	Q	"		(31) RODEO HARDELOT - ST OMER - GRAVELINES.
"	30	"	Q	"		(32) RODEO - ST OMER
"	31	"	Q	"		ANTI - RHUBARB - HASTINGS - SHOREHAM
"	31	"	Q	"		(33) RODEO - ABBEVILLE

GRAND TOTAL [Cols. (1) to (10)].
284 Hrs. 50 Mins.

Extract from Flight Log May 1942, showing a range of sorties, including: circus, rodeo, ramrod, and rhubarb if there was one. They worked it well for me – Mick Shand suggesting I go and have tea and not long after the whole squadron took off – nicely worked and I'll have something to say to Mick when they get down.

We now have the proofs from the photo shoot. There is a war correspondent called Mitchell who is sending some over to NZ. I expect they will appear in the *Weekly* or some such. I hope he does not 'shoot a line' as I'm afraid he knows one or two of our escapades and knowing the press if the same are printed they will be enlarged to a fair extent.

Dave Waters is also missing and will have 'bought it'[49]. From what I've heard he was on a rhubarb and on the way over he collected the sea. In some conditions when flying fast and low over the sea it is difficult to judge the surface. He was stationed not far from us flying Spits and had previously been shot up once or twice.

I was in the Sussex the other night and met a fellow, Harold Mace, who said he knew Peg and was on the ship with Bruce Wallace. Their last trip on the way over – convoy work up north – they were bombed by planes and then attacked by three Hun destroyers, two of which they sank and damaged the third. Unluckily they were smacked by a torpedo but struggled into a port where they remained for about seven weeks, most of the repairs being done by women. On the way back one day they were bombed by 40 Ju88, ten dive bombers and five torpedo bombers as well as half a dozen subs so you can appreciate them being knocked over. They were lucky to be picked up and not have to go in the water. Bruce is at present with Mac on leave and expecting an interview or 'board' as they call it here prior to getting his commission. With any luck I'll see the old rough again soon.

During the last few days of bad weather we have been snapping up a few new pilots, including two Wellington boys, Lindsay Black and Garry Barnett. It will enable us to get a bit more leave and if we get another bad run like we did a few weeks back the new recruits will be hard at it.

Tons of love to all. Cheerio for now,

Doug

49 Dave Waters was killed on operations 9 May 1942

Garry Barnett, John Pattison, Doc, Bruce Gibbs, Tony Robson

Kenley
Sunday, 7 June 1942

Dear Mum, Dad and Girls,

Well today is the first day we have had any peace for a full week or more, the weather being fine and very hot and as a result we have had two or three shows a day which are damn tiring. We only had one day when we ran into much and that was at the beginning of the week. We were over France and the first sign I saw of the Hun was a Spit spinning down from above us and then there they were right on our tail. Tony Robson and I broke and there we were with about eight or more of the Jerries – I thought we had had it. I had a poop at one chap and think I missed him but the film did not come out so I couldn't tell how far away I was from target. Tony fired off a fair bit of film and thought he got one. A Hun got on my tail firing furiously and I spun down a bit but some shrewd Jerry was waiting for me and all I could do was dive for cloud some 10,000 feet below with him pooping at me – believe me I was using plenty of skid. When I made the cloud I had to smartly get out again as all my instruments went haywire. I lost that fellow and only met one other coming the other way. I was

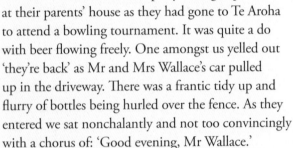

Mac and Bruce Wallace were friends I had made in tennis circles in Auckland. They both used to come up to Manly, Mac in his Model T Ford and Bruce arrived once on his bike. Given that in those days it was a 30-mile metal road, this was quite a feat. I recall there was a party arranged pre-war at their parents' house as they had gone to Te Aroha to attend a bowling tournament. It was quite a do with beer flowing freely. One amongst us yelled out 'they're back' as Mr and Mrs Wallace's car pulled up in the driveway. There was a frantic tidy up and flurry of bottles being hurled over the fence. As they entered we sat nonchalantly and not too convincingly with a chorus of: 'Good evening, Mr Wallace.'

Mac gained an engineering scholarship to England before war broke out. He was for the duration at the Rolls-Royce plant in Derby and worked on Merlin engines that were fitted on the Spitfire and other aircraft.

Bruce joined the Navy and in March 1942 he was on the ill-fated HMS *Trinidad* doing escort on Russian Convoy PQ13. En route the weather was atrocious and on engaging German destroyers, the Trinidad was hit by one of its own torpedoes and lost 30 crew. The Trinidad limped into Murmansk and undertook repairs. On the return journey in May she was hit by a Ju88 bomb and scuttled with the loss of a further 60 crew.

TOP AND ABOVE Rolls-Royce Merlin 45 1470HP engine used on Spitfire MkVB, which achieved a height of 35,000 feet; Rolls-Royce Griffon 65 2050HP engine used on Spitfire MkXIVB, which achieved a height of 43,000 feet. ROLLS-ROYCE HERITAGE TRUST

ABOVE LEFT British Fiji Class Cruiser *HMS Trinidad* at Hvalfjord, Iceland, February 1942. IMPERIAL WAR MUSEUM IMAGE A007683

ABOVE RIGHT *HMS Fury* refuels from *HMS Trinidad* in heavy Atlantic seas and falling snow, March 1942. IMPERIAL WAR MUSEUM IMAGE A007931

in no mood for a scrap and neither was he so I headed smartly for the sea and came home on the deck with no holes at all. I was worried about Tony as I left him with six Jerries and I was jolly glad when he got back though he had a few holes in the plane. We lost Garry Barnett and Junior Browne and were jolly lucky to get off so lightly. G/C Atcherley got shot down in the Channel a week or so ago and returned yesterday none the worse for his experience apart from his arm in a sling.

As the weather is now a bit duff we go on release till tomorrow which will enable us to get in a few sleeping hours. Last night the WAAFs at Ops had a dance and all our boys made a real night of it. As a result I do not feel absolutely in peak health this morning but will no doubt see the day out.

Garry Barnett and Stan Browne had only been with us a short time when they were both shot down on 31 May 1942 on a rodeo to Abbeville. Garry baled out near Amiens and Stan force landed as his engine had been hit and was overheating. They made their separate ways for the south of France where they were caught by the Vichy Government and incarcerated in a castle. They escaped through a sewer pipe, quite a feat as neither were the most slender squadron members, and headed for Marseilles. A number of escapees had congregated there and were picked up by submarine and delivered to Gibraltar for transit to England.

Saturday, 13 June 1942

This past week has not been the best as far as flying is concerned and I have only done one sweep, which did not amount to much. We did an air-sea rescue a few days ago, which was rather amusing. We had two sections of three: Dave Clouston leading one and myself the other. We located the boats OK and managed to get a couple of chaps picked up by the rescue team. When we turned for home Dave Clouston who was the flight leader set course and I saw a coast approaching. I thought that it did not look like good old England but I did not worry much as all my instruments – speedo, altimeter, etc. were up the shoot. Then a town came in sight and I was damn sure I had never seen it before so I called up Dave and asked where we were, the answer being, 'you tell me!' Suddenly we realised we were over France so we turned tail and headed for home. Dave was lost and I had a rough idea where we were so I took us towards Dover. As my speedo was shot Dave took us home to base from the coast.

Marty Hume, Mick Shand, Bruce Gibbs, Stan Browne, Hec Leckie

Tony Robson, Mick Maskill and self had interviews with AVM Leigh-Mallory re commissions early on Tuesday morning so we decided to make a night of it in London on Monday. We were very lucky and only had to wait for the old bugger a couple of hours! We went through the usual question and answer sessions and now have to wait for officialdom to come through. What annoys me most is that my 'crown' has not come through, a mere four and a half months overdue. It means a few bob extra a day, so I hope the blighters give us the back pay we are expecting.

I had a 48-hour this week, which I spent on the camp. I slept round the clock both nights, lazed during the day and saw a couple of flicks.

Mr Askew wrote to tell me he is not going to Whitehaven but has a promotion to Lancaster. He is jolly proud and says he will have a staff of 40 under him.

We had it confirmed that Johnny Palmer, Ross Falls and Trevor Goodlet are prisoners of war and OK. We thought Goody had had it as the last sight of him was heading for earth with about 20 feet of flame following him. He appears to have been slightly burnt but the quacks over there apparently patched him up.

Rosie Mackie and Marty Hume got shot up a bit today on a rhubarb. They went a bit near some heavy flak, which put a few holes in their planes. They made a drome in England OK though their planes will be off the flying list for a while – poor old Spitty, he gets it every time.

I expect you often worry as to whether I'm included in the list when we do sweeps and lose a fair number. You needn't worry. Even if posted as missing there is a very slim chance of me biting the dust. Most of the kites lost are hit in the engine. I have got out of a lot of narrow squeaks now and provided they do not surprise me they have got no show. If the worst does happen we have a damn good parachute to use.

We have recently imported some new pilots, mostly sergeants. We are not sorry to see them and they all seem to be doing well for themselves.

On Monday the squadron is going away for a week to have a rest and some training. One thing we may be sure of is regular hours for a change, which will be beneficial to all concerned.

Cheerio again. Tons of love,

Doug

Kenley
Thursday, 25 June 1942

Dear Mum, Dad and Girls,

We had a week in Ipswich getting back to Kenley last Monday. The previous Monday the weather was rotten. We ran into pretty thick weather most of the way up, though round about Ipswich was fairly clear and we got down OK. The idea was to improve our shooting by firing at a drogue.

The first night all the boys had a pretty hectic party. We ran into Alan Deere who was leaving the following day and something had to be done about it. We had a night at The Great White Horse. The billet for the officers was a house, which belonged to some Marquis. The sergeants were billeted in private houses not far from the camp. We did not see much of them as we mealed at the camp, and when off duty they were out most of the time. We were due to start our air firing on the Tuesday morning but as the weather was still off we held a big pistol shooting tourney, sixpence in. I did not collect at any time but it was jolly good fun.

On Wednesday afternoon I had a poop at the drogue and after that slept in the sun. That night we had another rather large-sized party at a hotel called

The Bull a fair way from Ipswich. Thursday morning I took three of the new fellows for a practice fly – weaving formation – after which Mick Maskill and I went on a shooting expedition and I got a bunny – blew its head off – a crow and a partridge – I'm getting pretty hot with the shotgun now, so keep that gun of yours under lock and key, Dad. In the afternoon we went to the flicks and had a few beers to follow, getting home fairly early but it did not deter a good sleep in on Friday morning. On Friday afternoon we had a general shoot-up of the drogue and Spits were coming at it from all directions. I think the ground crews enjoyed the entertainment. I also paid a visit to Harvey Sweetman who used to be with us. He is now a Flight Lieutenant at a night fighting squadron about half an hour's fly from Ipswich. He was jolly fit and damn well fed up with his night flying in Hurricanes. That night we went to the local Vaudeville show instead of the flicks. On Saturday morning I had another poop at the drogue and went on another shooting expedition but only got a rabbit. That night we went to a local hop and put over a bit of the Clark Gable with the local lassies.

Sunday morning, the programme was plenty of sleep and in the afternoon Mick Maskill, Tony and self spent the afternoon at the officers' billet. As it was sunny we stripped off and mixed a bit of deck tennis with a few beers and a fair afternoon tea. The Marquis has about an acre of vegetables including strawberries completely wired in with netting. One of the new lads, Jack Henry, and I carefully withdrew a few staples and ripped in and tried the strawberries of old England – they were pretty good – the difficult part was replacing the wire so that no one would notice we had entered. Later in the afternoon Tony and I were prancing around with the shotgun looking for an odd crow when we discovered some nectarines in a glass house which was very well locked up, but undaunted we found a place Tony could just squeeze through. After much struggling he made it and handed me out half a dozen of the Fruit of Eden when lo and behold the big-shot gardener arrived on the scene in a rather irate mood. He said he would have to report us. When Tony had been let out we changed our line of talk to how well he managed the garden with so little help and by so doing managed to talk him out of the evil intentions he previously had. The only snag was he took back the nectarines. It reminded me of the days at Manly we used to pay old man Hobbs a friendly visit and relieve him of his peaches. On Monday we got back to Kenley OK and the boys reckoned we had returned to operations for a rest!

I was to have had five days' leave but we only have eight experienced pilots capable of leading sections so yours truly being one of the 'honoured' ones with experience can only take a 48 and I must be within easy reach of home. Johnnie Checketts has been posted, as has Johnny Pattison, as a Flight Lieutenant.

Dave Clouston will be out of action for a few months as he did a bit of sleepwalking one night and fell from the top floor of the mess some three stories and broke one arm in 11 places and the other in four as well as breaking his jaw – he is damn lucky to be alive. I went and saw him a couple of days ago. He is very miserable with both arms in plaster and his mouth all done up in a network of wires to keep his jaw in position. It is such that all he can consume is milk and soup through a straw. I offered him a beer, which he had no inclination for, proving he must be not so good.

I had a jolly interesting letter from Gus Taylor last week and he appears to be getting over a fair amount of the sandy wastes of Libya, Egypt, Palestine, and Syria and appeared to be in pretty good nick. He had had a bit of a party with Hal Thomas who used to be with this squadron and is now an instructor in Aden. He had lately seen Jackie Lees, Colin McGruther, Kel Brown who 'had up some Greek ribbon' as Gus put it.

Bruce Wallace rang me up the other night from London. Tell Mrs Wallace he sounds jolly fit in spite of his experiences. I could not get in to see him and it was a thrill to hear his voice for the first time since I left NZ too long ago.

Remember me to everyone and tons of love to the family. I hope Nanna understands that I don't get the time to write to her personally – I know these letters are in easy reach of her.

Well love to you all. Hope Peg had a good birthday – I sent a cable.

Cheerio for now,

Doug

Kenley
Monday, 6 July 1942

Dear Mum, Dad and Girls,

Life as an RAF officer is jolly good. We have a grand mess like a first-rate hotel, the meals better than in a pub. Expenses may get a bit of a knock for a while until my crown comes through, anyway when I get that I will get 20 quid back pay and an extra bob or so a day as a P/O.

There was only one sweep last week but the convoy patrols give us a bit of flying. I have done a bit extra in the flying line training the new fellows. We now have an A1 squadron as far as personnel go but very few experienced pilots. No doubt we will have a packet of fun stored up for us and many will fall by the wayside.

I had a jolly pleasant time at the Leuchs' – ate plenty and had plenty of sleep. On the Friday I decided to mow a few lawns. It was a beautiful day so I set to work until some poor inoffensive bee took rather a poor view of me and injected his string into the bottom of my foot. Katie was in London so I brought my mind back to when Mother used to rush me to the washhouse and smartly apply Ricketts Blue. That night we had a grand feed of strawberries and cream. On Saturday morning I had a good feed of scrambled eggs to help me on my way to camp.

This week I have been popping into London to have a fitting for my gear. The weather has been good enough for swimming in the pool, which is situated in the WAAF officers' mess. On Tuesday we had our first party for a while at Oxted. It consisted purely of the NZ squadron and Aussies and the dancing was carried out in the old barn, which is specially rigged out for that purpose. Close to the barn Soutrow has a very large swimming pool surrounded by lawns, which provide an ideal drinking spot until black out. The pool proved rather disastrous for Mick Shand and me. We were acting the goat rather near to the edge when someone of ill repute who still remains unknown gave us a push. The whole show caused much amusement. Mick then hopped out and removed everything except his underpants, which he promptly lost when he dived in again. Soutrow took us up to his place and gave us some dry clothes. It was a jolly good night and next morning as luck would have it was nice and foggy.

We officially entered the mess as officers last Friday with all the boys waiting for us at the bar with their tongues hanging out. We had to do the customary shout, which caused a great shock to our wine accounts.

On Saturday we had a release early in the afternoon and Reg Grant, Mick Shand, Bruce Gibbs, Tony Robson, Marty Hume, Jack Henry and self caught the earliest train for London. We visited the Forces Club where I did not see anyone I knew and then we went to a show, which had about 40 minutes of Ambrose and his Orchestra with Dorothy Carlos and a few other good singers.

We are stonkered for hotel options in London now following my last visit with Mick Shand to the Strand Palace and being banished from many others. We were at the top floor where a spiral staircase led all the way from the ground floor out onto the landing. Mick said 'Brownie, do you want to hear and see a bomb go off?' He grabbed a large aspidistra pot plant and nonchalantly dropped it over the edge whereupon it drifted from view, almost in slow motion and then exploded radially when it struck the tiled entrance nine floors below.

I will have to go now as I have suddenly been called to readiness.

Cheerio for now.

Sunday, 12 July 1942

On Tuesday evening a notice came through telling us that the whole squadron was to move next day out of 11 Group for a rest. There was much moaning and wailing to be heard among the boys as we had been pretty slack over the last month or so and ready for more work – however, to put it in Air Force lingo 'we had had it!' Tuesday night coincided with the first Tuesday of the month, which meant free beer in the mess. The AOC also paid a visit, which meant the usual spit and polish tea. This did not deter the boys and they were going well by the time dinner was served and the formal setting was somewhat upset by the regular visits to the lav. After dinner the party proceeded with great gusto – it was a buck party and dirty songs were the mainstay of the evening for quite a while and the band in turn did their stuff. The end of the evening was rather a shambles. There were many sad faces and rotten heads next morning. We were up fairly early in order to get our gear ready for transit. As we were not 'sailing' till about two I buzzed off to see my various girlfriends of ill fame and wished them a merry goodbye. I left the best till last. We talked away an hour over a few noggins consisting of tonic water followed by a couple of aspirins, for my part!

When I got back to the mess a few of the boys had got going again and booze was flowing. Mick Shand, dressed up in full waiter's kit, was dishing out beers on the house and making a nuisance. We must have made a fair impression there as we had most of the station and WAAFs to bid us farewell and I really believe they were sorry to see us go!

Kings Cliffe

*

Kings Cliffe Command: G/C Basil Embry. W/C Jamie Jameson.
CO Reg Grant. Flight Commanders Mick Shand and Reg 'Baldy' Baker.

Our 485 farewell at Kenley coincided with a send-off for Hawk Wells. Everyone got very merry and there were also a few girls along. On this particular occasion later in the night Mick Shand was wandering around with only a belt on and a dahlia flower covering his private parts. Hawk Wells decided to push him into the kitchen staffed by WAAFs.

The next morning the 'Queen Bee' reported this to our Kenley G/C Batchy Atcherley. Mick was in trouble already and that morning decided to have a few drinks to follow on from the night before. At lunch in the officers' mess Batchy Atcherley, our Group Captain, had invited a couple of the Top Brass from Group including Leigh-Mallory to join us. Mick was behind the bar in a beige apron serving the drinks and also having a few. Pointing at Mick, Batchy shouted 'Get that man out of here!' Of course Mick was in no condition to fly his Spit. We all flew to Kings Cliffe, Cambridgeshire, except Mick who came in the transport with the rest of the baggage.

A couple of months prior Mick Shand and Reg Grant had been to an official dinner. Mick was seated beside an Air Vice Marshall's wife and picked a large flower from a bowl in the centre of the table, sprinkled salt and pepper on it

OU-S being pushed backwards at Kings Cliffe. RNZAF MUSEUM

and slowly ate it. The AVM's wife was somewhat aghast. Mick selected another from the bowl, sprinkled salt and pepper on that, and delicately offered to his neighbour: 'They're very good, Madam, would you like to try one.'

The posting to Kings Cliffe and 12 Group was to give the squadron some 'rest time' and the opportunity to rebuild with new pilots replacing those lost at Kenley, and for the existing pilots to regroup and recuperate. Although it was supposed to be light duties, four pilots were shot down and killed and Mick Shand joined Stalag Luft III as a prisoner or war.

In a Fighter Squadron the pilot content was nominally 24 pilots, of which odd ones would be on leave, and when pilots went missing it took time for new boys to gain the necessary experience for operations.

We were involved in squadron operations once or twice each week. In addition, we had regular patrol areas to cover with a section of two aircraft and also carried out rhubarbs.

Kings Cliffe was a wartime station and big enough for only one squadron. Our W/C Pat Jameson was stationed at Wittering. The temporary buildings were basic and the food was not that great but we were included in monthly parties at Wittering where the food was fabulous. After the first party Mick loaded the bus with leftovers, such as lobster and roast beef. There was far too much and most went bad.

Basil Embry had four DSOs. He had escaped from France and taken out a couple of Germans in his travels. He was made Air Commodore Group HQ and had been ordered not to fly on operations again. For six weeks he just put his feet on the desk until the hierarchy relented and gave him his station back, with him as Group Captain. When we arrived he said he wanted us to help with a job bombing a prison down in Nantes. He flew under a fictitious name 'Winco Smith' as he was supposed to be 'non-flying'. He took a precautionary cyanide pill with him as he knew he would be a marked man if captured by the Hun. A great guy! Basil Embry ended up as Air Chief Marshall Head of the Air Force. He had a dislike for political interference, which came with the job. Consequently he only had the post for a couple of years and retired early. He wanted to buy a farm so Jack Seabrook offered him a loan to get him going. Basil was a very proud fellow so he turned the offer down. He and Hope settled in Western Australia and farmed an outback property about 200 miles in from Perth. He suffered a stroke and was confined to a wheel chair. It was a desolate existence and a sad end.

Kings Cliffe
Cambridgeshire
Sunday, 12 July 1942 continued

We arrived here at Kings Cliffe, a satellite of Wittering, and we are certainly in no-man's land. As we orbited prior to landing I only noticed a couple of houses for miles around. Now that we are settled I think we will be able to arrange quite a bit of fun. We should have plenty of leave – about a week in every four – which will be welcome as I have not had any leave bar a couple of 48s since I was last in Carlisle for Joe's wedding. We do continuous readiness a section of two on all day and two sections or a flight on at other times. Though it sounds a lot it is not bad as we have little work to do. All the flying I've done is stooge and the countryside looks rather good round about the sector.

The mess and the billets are not the best and nowhere in the same street as the Kenley mess. We are hot on the trail however and I think that in a week or so we will be able to have a considerable improvement in the food and liven things up a bit. We are trying to arrange a dinner for the Wincos and Group Captain of our parent station and as we have got a lot of tins of toheroa soup between us and a lot of oysters (we had a case sent to us from the Ozona Factory) we should create a fair impression.

Last night happened to be a big night for our parent station and we all popped over. Drink of all kinds was free. Nevertheless, I still drink beer and there was plenty of it. To see the supper you would little realise there was a war on. I will endeavour to explain what was on the spread. It was laid out buffet style and consisted of hors d'oeuvres of potato, hot peas, curried and stuffed eggs, caviar, sardines, whitebait, whale roe, tomatoes, mushrooms, olives and so on. At the centre section there were salmon and flounder done up like an iced Christmas cake in sauce which was the art of a master and hundreds of lobsters and crab. At the other table there were strawberries, gooseberries, raspberries, black and red currants and savories of all manner and kind. It was an amazing spread and I must say I did it justice. Who would have thought there was a war on? On occasions like this you appreciate how well off we are compared to the Army and Navy boys.

We will get some experience night flying up here and then go on night ops so that we may be able to bag an odd Jerry who strays over this way. Apart from that we will do a fair number of rhubarbs so that 485 Squadron will still be doing some offensive work – the sooner we get back to plenty of action the better.

Cheerio for now,

Love, Doug

Kings Cliffe
Friday, 24 July 1942

Dear Mum, Dad and Girls,

I returned at midday by the Flying Scotsman after seven days leave spent mainly in the county of Surrey. Marty Hume and self set off together last week and reached London on Friday afternoon. I went up to the tailor and got the rest of my gear and then went to the Forces Club where I saw damn all except for young Johns who has done six or seven weeks of ops and appeared to be very fit and was doing 'a big line' with a rather snappy WAAF. After that Marty and I booked a room for the following night and proceeded to the Chez Moi where we had a couple of beers and rang the Leuchs.

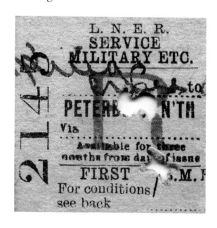

During the week we were mainly at the Leuchs' and Fergie's catching up with rest and doing a few odd jobs. We returned the clothes we had borrowed from Soutrow after the episode in his pool. Fergie took us to see Dave Clouston at East Grinstead Hospital but he had buzzed off so we went round to a Captain Thorpe's place (friend of Fergie). It is one of the grandest houses I've seen over here. We played croquet and drank a few beers with him and altogether had quite a bit of fun. We visited a few pubs and caught up with some WAAFs but that was about it.

Thanks for the £30, which arrived today. I also had a letter from Uncle Hugh and one from Mr Askew. I received a bundle of cigarettes enclosed with the parcels you sent me the other day but HM Customs got nasty and decided to make me pay duty of 8/9d on 40 cigarettes and a tin of Greys which was a bit hot!

The week before leave we were supposed to be 24 hours on and 24 off but it did not work out that way. The Army decided they wanted some practice so we had to go up three or four times a day to give them a thrill.

We imported six new sergeants. The boys have been doing rhubarbs over France and P/O Harrison failed to come back one day. However, since we have been up here we have knocked over about a dozen trains. Night-flying exercises continue. There were quite a few bombers over last night and Harvey Sweetman, now with 486 Squadron, got one. One of the boys had a letter from 'Dutch' Stenborg who is now in Malta and says he got two down there.

Last week also we flew down to Kenley to attend a farewell to Hawk Wells who is going for a trip to NZ – lucky man. We took a Miles Master so that we could bring the Doc along with us and also Harvey Sweetman came in his Hurricane. It was a mongrel mob so we called it Dumbo's circus. The only trouble with the 'do' was we had to return at seven next morning and there were many bleary-eyed fellows who sat down to breakfast. When we arrived back here Mick Shand and Bruce Gibbs pranged and are both lucky to be alive as they made quite a mess of the two kites. Gibby came in too close behind and before Mick had got off the runway he ran up the back of him. The propeller took the tail, then the fuselage and just stopped short of Mick's head.

We are getting a bit better organised now and we have flicks as well as a dance in the camp once a week – the troops enjoy it, which is the main thing. The food is improving and after we have been here a while we should have everything in ship-shape condition.

Cheerio for now. Love to all,

Doug

Reg Grant assured Group we were all qualified and proficient night-operational pilots. I was the first to be sent on this exercise – and I do not recall any other 485 night patrols in Spitfires at this time, July 1942.

In wartime the whole country was 'blacked out' and on nights with bad weather one would be fully reliant on radio. I took off and could see nothing, little knowing that I was flying in cloud. My radio packed up but as I had flown on a compass course I turned on reciprocal. I was short on gas but by good fortune the cloud cleared and I picked out the stream near Peterborough and from this position flew to Wittering. I dropped to 300 feet and luckily saw the 'Glim Lights' on the runway which could not be seen above 350 feet.

Kings Cliffe
Monday, 3 August 1942

Dear Mum, Dad and Girls,

During the past week we have done our 'readiness' with little of note and have now got ourselves night operational. We were unlucky that both nights there was any action 'A' Flight got off and though they did not make contact with Jerry, they saw the bombs find their mark. Apparently it was a wonderful sight with flak fires and other incendiary action. We had Jerries flying low over our area and they let loose a bomb or two and the ack-ack enlivened proceedings somewhat. A Ju88 flew so low over the drome that a few miles away it collected high tension wires and a few Huns bit the dust. Tony Robson and I thought we would be shrewd one very dirty morning and did a patrol in the Wash and blow me down about half an hour after we left the place two bombers came in and raided a drome. We would have been nicely situated to have a pop at them if we had been there at the same time – better luck next time!

Reg Grant, Batchy Atcherley
offers a cigarette to Hawk Wells

The rhubarbs were dangerous operations and some 50% of those who participated did not return. We tended to do rhubarbs in pairs when the cloud is down and at sea level across the Channel to avoid the radar. The danger with the rhubarbs was the flak. When flying so low it was just a matter of luck if we struck a flak path. It was great fun but could be costly in terms of lives lost.

[Letter continues]

Someone's God was on my side yesterday. Four of us decided to do a rhubarb in the Ostend area after train engines primarily. I led one section and Mick Maskill the other and we split when we hit the French coast. I took my No 2 in a south-easterly direction and the first shot I got was at a few barges in a canal. We went a fair way further south – too far really – and finally I came across a few trucks and pooped at them. The trucks were about a mile in front of a village in which an old girl was wandering. I felt sorry for her as she did not know what to do, whether to fall down or make for a ditch and the result was jolly amusing. Further on we had a go at a signal box, blowing some nice

Dornier shot down by Lindsay Black leaves a large hole in a potato patch

holes in the walls, and made a general mess. On a bit more we had a bit of luck. We came near a town, which I skirted and noticed a train in a station with the engine poking out nicely. I was in a beautiful position and sent him for a six. The station, train and engine being enveloped in steam – a certain destroyed, which was so good. I went back and took a photo. At this stage I did not know where in the hell I was – somewhere in France – so I steered my reciprocal as near as I could reckon. I headed north, passing south of Bruges and managed to get somewhere near where I came in . . .

Got to lay off my news for a minute: great excitement! Ops have just rung through and told me Lindsay Black and Mick Maskill have shot down a Hun about 20 miles away!

Got the real dope on the Jerry, a big bomber, a Dornier. Mick and Lindsay got vectored on to it and they thought it was a usual 'no show' but they passed over a town which had just been bombed and that raised their hopes. When they finally got on it Lindsay was in the best position and fired chasing it into cloud and Mick thought he would be shrewd and wait underneath and consequently never had a shot. The next sight was the Hun dipping out of the cloud in a steep dive and hitting the middle of a field of potatoes. It blew up rather nicely – fried Hun and roast spuds! When they got back we grabbed what transport we could and ripped smartly down and viewed the remains of the Hun kite. All we could see was a raging inferno. The crew of the Dornier was all stewed. We got a prop blade and ammo and we hope to get a fin of the tail unit, which is more or less in the one piece. Really good work and all we can do is hope for more.

. . . I will now return to my line. I think I had just shot up the engine and was heading more or less north-west. All went well till I came to a canal and noticed tracers getting a bit close and naturally thought there was a Jerry on my tail. I thought I had lost No 2. I climbed a bit to have a look and if I was in trouble I hoped to get some cloud cover when there was a hell of clatter. I had been hit. My tail unit had had it, knocking off most of my rudder and making a tangled mess of my right-hand tail plane and all the rear part of the fuselage was full of holes. The luckiest part as far as I was concerned was a piece of shrapnel, which missed me when it came in through the Perspex behind my head. It knocked a whacking great hole in my hood, which flew back and waved in the breeze. I was, to put it plainly, bloody lucky! To get on, when I was hit the thump cut out my engine and I thought the engine had caught a packet as well but it picked up and I went to the deck. The next thing for me was to get out very quickly so I headed for the coast near Ostend. When I approached the coast I noticed whopping pillboxes and then tracer and flashes and the burst of the big guns – they missed us except for a few .303 bullets in the wings. When I got onto the sea I thought I had better climb in case I needed to bale out but the whole way across the channel I only made up 3000 feet. It seemed to take hours to get over. I called up and got vectored to the coastal drome Martlesham Heath and prepared to land. The wheels were OK and the only trouble I had was lack of rudder and elevator control. I've never landed a bomber in my life but I should think that landing of mine was carried out in a similar manner, as I had to heave back on the stick to get the tail down and reduce speed.

When I got out I nearly cried as my Spitfire, poor old 'Q', had seen her day. By Jove she had served me well and got me out of a squeak or two. I hope the photographic section will take photos of the damage and I will be able to post a snap on to you. I was picked up in the Maggie and glad to get back here and have a good feed. I've got a new kite which is getting the general look over now and I hope to give her a first flip tomorrow. In all probability it will take a week or two of tests to get her in ship-shape condition.

Tomorrow the Hon. Wally Nash,[50] number one public binder and bull artist will be dining with us and we are all going to be very polite to him and

---

50 Then Labour MP for Hutt Valley, Wellington, and later NZ Prime Minister. I have never been a labour party supporter, consequently my opinion of Walter Nash is somewhat biased!

give a good impression so that we may be able to get some money out of him for the squadron. We intend to send the squadron up to escort him a bit of the way here – he is flying up, and I bet many of the boys would just love to squirt a bit of lead into his plane.

I hope I don't have to have an experience such as I had last Sunday even though it meant I could give you a good story!

Love, Doug

A retrospective review of the same operation:

Murray Metcalfe was only 18 and had little operational experience but was insistent in being my No 2 for the trip. In a rhubarb it is important to know the position of the No 2. Regretfully he had lagged behind and when I did a climbing turn to check he was OK I was hit by a 40mm Bofor. I was down low at about 100 feet but I managed to maintain some control and headed for the coast. I didn't know the damage incurred and I found my speed was limited to 150 mph while normal speed for the throttle setting would have been 250 or more. I crossed the Channel and instructed Murray to lead me to Martlesham Heath with about 100 miles of sea to fly over. He had no doubt panicked and headed south, leaving me on my own – rather an uncomfortable situation to be in. It was difficult to gain height and in the 100 miles only managed 3000 feet. I reached my destination with a reception committee comprising fire engine and ambulance.

I expected to crash land. I decided to carry out a normal wheels-down landing and fortunately all went well. The plane, however, was a write off. The rudder had been destroyed and starboard tail plane shattered. Shrapnel holes were along the port side and my hood was also destroyed with the initial flak impact. Luckily none of the control cables were hit, nor the engine damaged when under fire. My course was mainly straight for Martlesham Heath and, as a consequence, I wasn't doing much turning so I got back in one piece.

I only landed at Martlesham Heath twice and on both occasions my aircraft was a write off. You never get any sympathy when you crash – it was business as usual. At that time Reg Grant was our CO. I called him up and all he said was: 'Good God, you're alive. We'll send someone over to pick you up.'

Sergeant Langlands did not return.

7th August, 1942.

Dear Mr. Brown,

When visiting the New Zealanders at the various airfields in England yesterday, I met your son Douglas Gordon Brown, and I am sending this note to say that he looked well and strong and was keen on his job.

With the other men from New Zealand he has done splendid work to help to defend England and to remove the menace that is now facing the world.

I hope that his work will continue and that later he will come back to you in good health.

Yours sincerely,

Nash

Mr. Brown,
7 Bourne Street,
Mt. Eden,
AUCKLAND.

Letter from Walter Nash

TOP My Spitfire, OUQ damaged from German ack-ack near Bruges, 2 August 1942

ABOVE LEFT OUQ damage – shrapnel hole between O and U

ABOVE RIGHT OUQ canopy damage

WINE, WOMEN AND SONG

Officers' Mess
RAF Station
West Malling
Kent

Thursday, 20 August 1942

Dear Mum, Dad and Girls,

As W/C Wells – Hawk Eye – is on his way over to your fair isle, he is going to take this and post it over there and you should get it in a couple of weeks or so.

As you can see from the address, we are south again but only temporarily I think. I had a lot of fun yesterday in the Dieppe show and I saw my fair share of Jerries but did not get a poop. They did most of the damage, but I managed to dodge trouble. It was a long day as we got up at 2.30 a.m. and did not get down from the last flip till about 7.30. It was good fun nevertheless. The only decent show I had was to follow a Jerry bomber which I chased but he was a bit too tough and I could not overtake him.

The weather has been grand the last week and this morning I had a swim before breakfast in a nearby pool and it was remarkably warm. The fruit is beginning to ripen now and I have been knocking back a plum or two during the past few days.

I am fit and well. Regards to everyone. Tons of love,

Doug

Kings Cliffe
Wednesday, 26 August 1942

Dear Mum, Dad and Girls,

The week after I last wrote – the quick note Hawk Wells has taken to NZ – was fairly uneventful and as far as flying we did the usual stooging and playing about. On the Thursday, Jack Henry and I went off to London with Arch Riley – a new sergeant – and intended to meet Marty Hume there.

Thursday night was rather hectic and Arch Riley and self buzzed around with a couple of WAAFs, who were very successful in taking us for a ride and helped me spend a little money. On Friday Jack and I met Reg Grant at about ten and went to a jolly good show called 'Holiday Sun', with Fred Astaire and Bing Crosby. On Friday night, Jack Henry, Reg Grant and self all met at the Chez Moi and knocked back a few noggins to the tune of three lovely lobsters kindly paid for by the boss which we appreciated and no doubt cost him a princely sum. In appreciation the three of us took him to dinner, after which we returned to the Chez Moi and I met a rather snappy lass – a good type – Judy Allen by name. I did the decent thing and saw her home in a taxi!

Next morning Jack and I did not get up with the sparrows. We headed for the Forces Club and carried out a hunt for Marty Hume. I bought a pair of shoes, which cost £3-6-0. Jolly good ones, especially for the winter. Then we went to a show, which you would really enjoy – 'Twin Beds' by name and the acting of Mischa Auer was very good and amusing. I remembered there was a telegram for yours truly and with Marty's non-appearance I realised a recall was probably afoot. We nipped smartly down again after the show to find the awful truth. We put on a bit of speed and had a meal, went to the pub and packed our bags, caught a taxi and were on the train in 40 minutes.

We got back to Peterborough about six and the CO came and picked us up. Next day, Sunday, we flew down to West Malling, not far from our old base in 11 Group. On Monday, we did a bit of a sweep over France and a rather funny incident occurred. After the briefing we only had five minutes to get everything ready, so we all piled into the two small transports we had and away down the perimeter track we went. We had not gone far when a back wheel flew off the first car and she did a couple of rolls – what a panic! Three of the boys were temporarily outski and most of them had bumps and bruises. Our force of fit pilots was somewhat reduced so the rest of us flew most of the remaining Dieppe trips.

On Tuesday the 18th there was another piddly sweep which I did not go on but flew up to Kings Cliffe in a Tiger Moth taking Sgt Metcalfe with me to bring it back while I returned with the Magister. It seemed odd back in the Moth doing about 75 mph and getting very fed up and tired with the length of the journey. However, we made it with my expert navigation – following all the railway lines!

That night we were all to be in the wing's pilot room and we were given the dope on the Dieppe show, which was to come off next morning at dawn.

We were at readiness at 3.40 a.m. and though we expected to get off early we missed out on the early action. We got off at about eight as 'cover' and ran into a bit of a hornet's nest, which comprised FW190s.

There were four squadrons of us that day. I do not know the losses of one of the squadrons with us. The other two squadrons included in our wing lost two and three pilots respectively as well as a couple damaged. Our squadron was lucky in that we had all experienced fellows with us and I must say they flew well and kept their eyes open. My No 2 got a bullet hole in his tail. I had yelled out a warning on the R/T and he just managed to save himself from serious mishap. We spent half an hour dodging the cows. Jamie Jameson, the NZ Winco leading us, destroyed one, as did Mick Maskill and Lindsay Black, and Reg Baker got a damaged. I didn't fire my guns. I only had one chance of doing so and thought better of it as my foe had a friend!

The next show our squadron did I was not on. It was the withdrawal which was carried out according to schedule and the boys only saw four Hun bombers which were pounced on by a couple of squadrons of Spits and were blown to bits, poor beggars. The next one was carried out soon after the return and I missed it as I thought I would sneak in a lunch and a bath at the mess. I went on the last one and there was a bit of excitement as a few Dorniers were trying to squeeze through and drop a bomb or two and then buzz smartly off. Our section saw one and I opened out in full pursuit but he got into the cloud and there were a few Spits in a better position than me. The poor fellow was in for a reception when he got to the other end of the cloud as I should say there were 16 Spits in pursuit, some on top of the cloud, some underneath and some in the middle. Reg Baker, leading yellow section, was first there and used all his ammunition and claimed a damaged. He won't have got far as Reg said there was a queue of Spits waiting for a shot!

So much for Dieppe.

The combined Dieppe operation was made by Army, Navy and Air Force. This exercise was carried out to test the German defences in the Calais area and their reaction. It was not a great success as there was significant Army loss, particularly Canadians, but no doubt many lessons were learnt. More than half of the 6000-odd troops were killed, injured or became POWs. The tanks they took ashore had great difficulty with the beach, which was of pebble formation. Standard tank tracks had no grip and proved unusable. Over 100 RAF aircraft were shot down – more than twice the German losses. We had little action as top cover.

YEAR: 1942		AIRCRAFT.		PILOT, OR 1ST PILOT.	2ND PILOT, PUPIL, OR PASSENGER.	DUTY (INCLUDING RESULTS AND REMARKS).
MONTH.	DATE.	Type.	No.			
—	—	—	—	—	—	— TOTALS BROUGHT FORWARD
AUGUST	18	SPITFIRE VB	Q	SELF		WING PRACTICE
"	18	TIGER MOTH		"	S/O METCALFE	W. MALLING TO WANSFORD
"	18	MAEKSTER	R1892	"		WANSFORD TO W. MALLING
"	18	SPITFIRE VB	Q	"		AIR TEST
"	19	"	U	"		(a) FIGHTER COVER AT DIEPPE
"	19	"	Q	"		(b) WITHDRAWAL COVER FROM DIEPPE
"	21	"	Q	"		W. MALLING TO WANSFORD
"	27	"	Q	"		LOCAL
"	28	"	Q	"		COMBAT DRILL
"	20	"	Q	"		TO MARTLESHAM HEATH.
"	29	"	Q	"		(b) CLOSE ESCORT BOSTONS TO OSTEND
"	29	"	Q	"		MARTLESHAM TO WANSFORD

Section of log book during Dieppe raid

[Letter continues]

We did another show on the Thursday and returned to Kings Cliffe
on Friday. We had one or two binges while we were there and really had
a thoroughly good few days. On Saturday Marty Hume, Eric Shaw and I
started off for a few more days' leave. The first and second nights we had in
London. Originally we only intended to have one night in London but on
Sunday afternoon we ran into Jack Rae who you remember used to be with us
at Kenley and had just returned from four months at Malta. He certainly had
some experiences but nevertheless seemed full of beans. He was shot down
on his second trip and still has his leg bound up. Funnily enough the chap
who shot him down was himself shot down not long afterwards and Jack had
quite a yarn with him as they were together in the same hospital. The chap
who shot him down was a Czech. Jack said he will always remember one lot
of Italians who were shot down. When they crash landed they rushed about
cheering loudly: 'Been shot down by Spitfire, jolly good!' He reckons the
Maltese themselves are not particularly battle hungry, but if they get a Hun
who has baled out it is the last the authorities see of the Hun. We had quite a
night together and he certainly told me some stories – he was damn glad to be

back. The next day I met Russell Dickson who trained in Canada with me and he had also just returned from Malta after having been shot down by our flak. It was not the ground gunner's fault but Russ was in hot pursuit of a Ju88 and could not resist the temptation, and caught it. He baled out OK with a bang in the knee.

Who should I also run into but Toby Webster – you will remember I often mentioned him in the Canadian days. He is still the same and has had a lot of fun flying planes out to the East. He is connected with the Cooks Travel Agency, having seen most of the Mediterranean and all of Africa and he even got stranded in Malta for four weeks where he was duty pilot. He told me an amusing yarn.

One day he was on the job when the sirens went and after all the boys had gone down the 'hole' and he had seen the Spits off, he went down. After about ten minutes of bombing he poked his nose out but went smartly back again as the shrapnel was coming down like hail. When things became quiet he got back to his office and there was a ring on the phone – the CO asking how many planes there were and how many bombs were dropped, to which Toby said 'I dunno' and hung up. A minute or so later the Intelligence Officer rang up with the same request and Toby hung up with the same 'dunno' as his answer. When the phone rang again with the Engineering Officer on the other end wanting to know the same dope, it was too much for Toby and in his usual way he said, 'I don't know what sort of a bloody fool you think I am, but if you want to bloody well sit out in the middle of the airfield and count each plane as it flies over and each bomb as it drops you bloody well can!' Good old Toby.

Cheerio,

Doug

Kings Cliffe
Monday, 7 September 1942

Dear Mum, Dad and Girls,

We haven't done much except stooge flying and a couple of shows. Marty and I went up to London for a final fling at the end of our last leave and had lunch with Esmond Durlacher a stockbroker, a friend of the Leuchs and a jolly good fellow. He took us to some tonky place and we had a good feed of lobsters. We yarned with him for a fair part of the afternoon and then I went to the Chez Moi for about half an hour and then took a lass to the pictures: 'The First of the Few' with Leslie Howard and David Niven, which outlines the life of Mitchell who designed the Spitfire and the Schneider Trophy Machines. Despite a late night Marty and I managed to catch the Flying Scotsman the next morning for Peterborough. The weather was grand when I got back and we had three perfect days which we made as much use of as flying would allow and also went swimming in the river. We went to Lord Burghley's place one afternoon where he has got a lake especially equipped for swimming and lazing around, and quite a happy afternoon was spent. On Sunday we were up early and went to Martlesham Heath on the coast to escort a dozen Bostons to Ostend docks. It was an accurate raid and we saw no opposition apart from some flak. We were in and out and the poor old Hun had no chance.

One day last week the pilots in our flight got together a soccer team to play the ground crew. Most of our boys hardly knew what a soccer ball looked like and they whacked us properly. After the game Tony Robson, Marty Hume and self went shooting with a chap Bill Tomkins, a local farmer who has got a large place not far distant. We were not very lucky and only got a couple of pigeons and a cock pheasant. Yesterday Tony, Bill Tomkins and I had another go shooting. Bill has got a .22 with a telescopic sight and we went over to his place in the car in the hope of getting some rabbits but they kept well hidden. We had shots at partridge at about 200 yards. I managed to get one by luck and altogether we got half a dozen. The trouble with shooting like that is that there is damn all of the bird left. While we were there a wily fox poked his nose out of the wheat but he did not stay long enough for us to focus the sights – lucky for him. We had some supper before we left – pheasant sandwiches – very tasty too.

We did another show the day before yesterday where we took 36 Fortresses to Rouen, which was not particularly successful. We were too high and I had a tummy ache, which put me off somewhat. As far as Jerries were concerned I only saw a couple and they were not in my vicinity. However it gave the boys some life.

On 1 September we were unlucky to loose Arch Riley on a rhubarb – he apparently caught a packet as I did, only he got it in the wrong place. He called out and said he was hit so if the swines did not keep firing at him he may have made the ground OK. I hope so as he was a decent chap and too good a fellow to lose as he was just getting the hang of things.[51] We have had two new officers posted to us, the first for quite a time, a P/O and a Squadron Leader, Pheloung, who seems to be a jolly decent chap. He has been in the RAF for five years or more, coming from good old NZ for a short service commission, and has been on the instructing racket ever since the war started. This is the first time he has been lucky enough to get to an operational squadron. I expect he will be with us for a time and then will take over a squadron of his own. If he picks it up as well and as quickly as John Kilian he won't be with us long: John has now got a squadron down south and is doing well. Johnny Pattison, who Peg mentioned as knowing his sister, is now a Flight Lieutenant attached to the Yanks, giving them the 'gen' on how, when, where and why to fly Spits and fighters generally on ops. He is a great lad, John, and came to see us about a week ago – he was very fit and very fed up with lack of activity.

Last night the pilots put on a show for all the ground crew and they did well in consuming 90 gallons of beer. To put it in Reg Grant's words we put it on 'to show our appreciation for the good job they did when we were on the Dieppe show and for the many other times they have worked hard and got bugger all thanks for it.' Our ground crew is a great team and they work long hours keeping our kites airworthy.

Tons of love,

Doug

At Kings Cliffe the mess and residential buildings were set among trees and the locals paid for shooting rights even in wartime. The season opened 1 October but we had shot most of the pheasant beforehand. Tony and I went on a shoot with Bill Tomkins, a local farmer the squadron befriended, and we shot 94 pheasant in one morning.

Subsequently we entertained Bill Jordan, the NZ High Commissioner in the UK, to a game dinner.

Tony Robson and I were detailed to go with the owner on his annual shoot. He was very surprised when he only got two birds when his usual take was in excess of 50.

---

51 Riley became a POW.

Kings Cliffe
Friday, 25 September 1942

Dear Mum Dad and Girls,

We had a really big party, which had cause to be held! Reg Grant, Mick Shand and Reg Baker were awarded a DFC all at once. T A Barrow, the Secretary of State for Air in NZ with whom I had all the correspondence in the days before I actually went to Levin, paid us a visit and had lunch after which a few of us went up and shot the drome up for him and did a few low-down aerobatics. He left us at about 1.30. When he went, Reg Baker tried to buzz off on leave so we decided to have a party there and then. All the lads who had received awards produced a bottle of gin and a bottle of vermouth each as the order was put forward by Reg Grant that nothing but spirits must be drunk – what a prospect! By seven o'clock a dozen of us had got through 11 bottles of gin, three bottles of vermouth and a bottle of whiskey – half a dozen of the lads popped off for a sleep and came back at odd intervals. After that we started on beer. Mick Maskill had a few too many and left early and Reg Grant and I took him up to the billets at about five. I went back to see if he was OK at about six and he was flat out in a patch of cabbages near the billet. I thought we had seen the last of him for the night.

At about ten o'clock we had a ring from Wittering to say Mick Maskill was over there, and we had to go over and get him. Although he does not remember a thing, apparently what happened was that Mick Shand who was a bit the worse for wear took the CO's car up to the billets to have a doze and Mick Maskill discovered it. He apparently drove as far as Wansford, a village about three miles away on the Main North Road and was turning violent circles in it. An Army colonel stopped him and said, 'You can't do that round here' and Mick jumped out minus tie, hat and false teeth and said, 'What do you bloody well think I'm doing then?' There were a couple of captains with the colonel, one a padre attached to Wittering, who is a jolly good chap and kept very quiet, and another who as soon as they arrived at Wittering clicked his heels in SS fashion and said he wanted this man under arrest for insulting his colonel. The entrance must have been funny. When Mick has had a few beers he always has the stub of a cigarette in his mouth, which he periodically tries to light with little success. He was attempting to light the same when they entered and of course went flat on his face and skinned it rather well. This did not deter him and he went on attempting to light it in the prone position. The Army padre said never in all his life has he laughed so much.

NEW ZEALAND GOVERNMENT OFFICES,
415, STRAND,
LONDON, W.C.2.

2nd September, 1942.

Dear Mr. and Mrs. Brown,

I write to say that I have recently had the pleasure of visiting our R.A.F. Squadron and that I there met your son Doug. I happened to be there the day after the great exploit in which he took part and of which he has probably told you. Our Squadron went to the battle four times, brought down three German machines, and returned finally to its base without the loss of either a man or a 'plane. The officer who led the Squadron was Reg Grant of Ponsonby, whose father's address is P.O. Box 16, Ponsonby. I thought, maybe, you would both find pleasure in meeting as your sons took part, side by side, in the great battle of Dieppe.

It was a great pleasure to hear Doug speak of Mr. Malcolm Robb, whom I know so well. My hearty greetings to him.

Doug is held in the highest esteem by his fellow members of the Squadron. They are indeed a happy family and it is a great pleasure to visit them at any time.

I trust you will not be unduly anxious concerning your son, as he is very well and happy, and he assured me that if there is anything which Mrs. Jordan or I or the staff of New Zealand House can attend to for him, he will not hesitate to let us know.

With kindest good wishes,

I am,
Yours sincerely,

Mr. and Mrs. E. P. Brown,
7, Bourne Street,
Mount Eden,
Auckland,
New Zealand.

Tuesday, 29 September 1942

I had a four-day camera course. It was meant to be an assessment course and now the gear is fitted I'm meant to be able to tell how many strikes there are on the enemy aircraft. I can assure you I will need a hell of a lot of notes if I ever go into action! I saw most of the films of Dieppe showing action from both sides as part of the training.

We got short notice to shift south to Llandow, South Wales, via Churchstanton, Somerset. It was a lousy day and we did not have a very enjoyable trip down. The winter is starting and we have had quite a bit of rain, which is practically useless for flying. However, we got to our destination and were in the air some hours afterwards as withdrawal cover for US Fortresses. The weather was poor, and we lost 15 spitfires from the other squadrons. It was jolly cold up high and thanks to our CO's good leadership we got back without even calling for a homing, but very low on fuel.

Due to the weather we were stuck down there until yesterday. All we did was readiness but as the weather was duff it was impossible to take off. Yesterday we all got into our kites at about three, hoping to get off, but Group would not let us go. We pestered them so much during the afternoon that in a weak moment they said we could go. Believe me we wasted no time and as it was rather late we had to give the planes all we had. The blighters tried to recall us with no luck as we took no notice and we reached Kings Cliffe at dusk, thankfully without incident. We hope to go south permanently in a month or so as it will be jolly cold where we are.

I have not smoked the old pipe for months now so don't send 'baccy' for it please, Dad. I think quite a bit of mail must have gone down as few of the boys have had any for a long time.
I am sending you our Xmas card in this mail.

Love to all,

Doug

Carlisle
Sunday, 11 October 1942

Dear Mum, Dad and Girls,

I did not have my week's leave as anticipated as we were all held back in preparation for a trip down south and to do a show. As we were not due to go till after Saturday, Reg Grant asked me to come down with him for a couple of days. We flew down to Kenley on Thursday afternoon. We got into Smoke as soon as we could and once we had booked in at the pub we buzzed off and saw the flicks – 'My Gal Sal', which had some good tunes in it. After a feed of steak, onions and chips we hopped off to the Chez Moi where we had arranged to meet a couple of lassies. We had a few beers there until it closed at 11 p.m. Reg's girl insisted on going on to a nightclub which was not exactly in accordance with my wishes but off we went, and we took the Nut House by storm – the first time I've been there and the last if I have a say in the matter. Nevertheless it was 8.30 next morning before we got back to the hotel and for breakfast we popped up to the Sussex. After lunch we spent about three hours getting records for the squadron and then went our various ways, for myself I took a lass to dinner and then to the flicks and afterwards we had a couple of beers at the Chez Moi. I was in bed well before midnight, which was a good thing as we had to get up soon after six next morning so that we could get home early.

We took off from Kenley in pretty duff weather and it was really the only clear patch we saw. When we got near base Reg called up and asked how the weather was to which they answered it was on the deck for miles around. Just at that time we spotted a patch in the fog and as luck would have it there was a drome[52] so down we went none too soon for when we got there the fog came over and so we had to stay for four or five hours. It was a Yankee outfit and they looked after us pretty well.

We went south to Hornchurch about three days ago to do a job. We took part in a diversionary sweep while the Yanks did a raid over Lille with Fortresses and Liberators. They are beauts, the Yanks. They claimed some 45 destroyed, which is ridiculous. In a formation of such a size with about 20 guns brought to bear on any attacking planes they all seem to claim if the

52 Podington

plane goes down in flames. In their case they would claim 20 kites destroyed when they have actually only got one. The sooner they have cameras attached to their gun mountings the better.

Our hierarchy had clamped down on the practice of overclaiming by fitting cameras. If caught out by camera evidence the consequence was coming up before the AOC and inevitably a less-desirable posting. The chaps who inspect the films could tell you exactly how many strikes are registered on the enemy aircraft. Overclaiming also gave the squadron a bad name so the cameras stopped it quickly!

[Letter continues]

We have started rugby up here and have had a couple of games against Wittering and Black Friars Schools, both of which we won very easily. We have got quite a good team and with some practice we should have a good season.

Cheerio,

Doug

(Northern Ireland)
5 November 1942

Dear Mum Dad and Girls,

Three weeks ago we were detailed to action elsewhere. The 'big chiefs' seemed to think it was a big deal, but as far as we are concerned, it is of little significance. Unfortunately we will be here for another week or so and what is the bad part is that I can write nothing which has any bearing to our whereabouts and tell of nothing I've done since we left our home base, which makes news negligible!

Once again my leave got it in the neck, which makes it 12 weeks since I had any. I had planned two nights in London prior to a few days in Derby with Bruce and Mac Wallace. I have not seen Mac since Mick McNeil and I went up last February and now I have missed catching up with Bruce again!

I did not leave Kings Cliffe till a day after the others. Mick Shand came out of hospital that day so we went over to Wittering for the sergeants' mess dance and ran into Garry Barnett, who was shot down some four or five months ago and was lucky enough to escape. He was full of fettle and is pleased to be with the squadron again, as is Stan Browne. They certainly had some great experiences in France and got caught through bad luck. Garry was in such a hurry to go to the lavatory he did not take the usual precautions and got snapped up as a result. During my trip from Kings Cliffe I had to drop down at a drome[53] for the night, and who should I run into but a chap Burrett who was at King's School with me. So we had a bit of a session on the strength of it and yarned about odds and ends.

Tons of love to all. How is Mr Harvey? Hope old Agnes[54] is OK. She would like to be with me now.

Cheerio for now.

Love, Doug

When we were at Kings Cliffe in the last week of October the squadron was instructed to fly to RAF Kirkiston, Ballyhalbert in Northern Ireland. The day we were due to fly out I mentioned to Reg that I had a date that night. Reg said: 'That's all right, take off, but say you've got engine trouble.' The plan worked well. I had my date and took off for Ireland a day later.

It was a bit of a business getting there as the weather had started to close in. I was flying over England and saw a drome below so I landed [Mildenhall], asked where I was and took off again. I tried to get to Hawarden, a drome near Chester. Every time I tried to land they tried to push me to Welsh Hills. I remembered Colin Gray was down at a place called Rednal so I landed down there and had lunch with Col. The next day I took off again, flying close to the deck the whole way – so close I could have touched the southern end of the Isle of Man en route.

Initially in Ireland we partied and enjoyed ourselves but soon Reg Grant and the two Flight Commanders, Reg Baker and Mick Shand, decided to return

53 Hawarden
54 Agnes was Irish and staff at Bourne St and is code for now being in Ireland.

to Kings Cliffe and go down to London so we were left there. I was in charge by default. The parties in the mess and Bangor were well supplemented with scampi we got from the local fishermen. The locals were very anti-British.

On one occasion Tony Robson, Mick Maskill and I drank Irish stout all night, stopping only for breakfast the next morning. It took some sleeping off. Eventually the job came up and as I was in charge of the squadron at the time I took Slim Robson and two others up to RAF Eglington at north east Ireland where US Squadrons had taken over. We were there for the night and met Mrs Roosevelt and the next morning we took off at dawn.

Our job was to patrol the convoy deploying as Operation Torch for the invasion of North Africa. The weather was down on the deck and when we took off we were certain we would be shot out of the sky due to lack of identification. We circled the convoy a few times, not that we could do much anyway to verify there were no enemy aircraft. Coincidently, the *Awatea*, which had transported me from Auckland to Vancouver, was part of the fleet.

The Group Captain there, by the name of 'King' Cole, didn't want to release us. He was RAAF and a WWI ace. Reg Grant phoned us so I explained the situation. He said: 'Refuel all the aircraft, and at nine o'clock tomorrow morning take off without clearance for Valley at Anglesey, Wales. There's a Groupie there who'll look after you.' We left at nine and went down to see Ramsbottom-Isherwood at Valley, spent the night there, and then on to Kings Cliffe with the squadron intact.

Ramsbottom-Isherwood was an NZer and Battle of Britain veteran. He was Wing Commander of 151 Wing which had operated Hurricanes from Murmansk-Vaenga in the latter stages of 1941 alongside the Soviets and received the Order of Lenin for his efforts.

Kings Cliffe
Friday, 13 November 1942

Dear Mum Dad and Girls,

As you will have no doubt gathered from my last letter when I made reference to Agnes, we were in Northern Ireland. The first place we were stationed at as a squadron was well out in the wilds and the countryside reminded me of some of the country around Pukekohe and Huntly. Not far distant was a fishing village, which kept us well supplied. After a few days we split up: one flight at one drome and one at another. We remained in this state for about ten days and then we reformed the squadron again and worked as such. The country was a grand spot as far as flying went and I had one or two flips looking the place over and seeing the sights by air. In the hills there are brick places built few and far between and I very much doubt if the inhabitants ever see any town life in the whole of their existence.

We visited Belfast a couple of times, once to have a look around the place and we had a night out there – a 'buck' party which was jolly good and enjoyed by all. We had a night in Bangor at a seaside resort – a very fine place – at the invitation of half a dozen WAAFs and the night was really good. I met a chap there who said he knew Alex Kirker, I think that was the name – who if I remember correctly played golf at Middlemore. The chap's name was Henderson. As we were not stationed far away we had a gaze around Londonderry but I was not overly impressed. It is rather ironic that around that part of Londonderry it is blacked out but over the harbour there is a blaze of light showing Eire. Ireland is of course the dread of any squadron but they have entertainment for the troops very well organised.

We had the good word to 'up traps' three days ago but of course the weather was unserviceable as is always the case when you want to move camp. We got away yesterday morning as far as North Wales. I went into the Ops room and when I saw the controller, an S/L, I thought I knew him but gave up the idea when I saw 'VR' on his shoulder. We were having a few beers in the bar and he asked me if I came from Auckland. It turned out I was at King's Prep with him: Lusk was his name, a nephew of HB. You should tell the old boy, Dad, he would be tickled pink and *might* buy you a drink.

HB Lusk was on the staff at King's College from 1920 (and headmaster from 1940) until his retirement in 1947. Bordering the College is the Auckland Golf Club where HB Lusk was captain in 1930–31. My father, EB Brown, was on the committee and the incumbent for the captaincy. There had been some disagreement between the two, which was resolved by AM Howden filling in during 1932. My father was captain in 1933–34 but the relationship he had with HB Lusk was probably the reason I had my secondary education at Wanganui Collegiate an overnight train ride away as opposed to King's College which was close to home. The falling out is all the more intriguing when my father gave to the College the not-inconsiderable sum of £500 in 1931.

[Letter continues]

We managed to return to Kings Cliffe today, though the weather was still duff. We were none too sorry to be back and get a change of clothes and a good bath. I received a letter from you both, Mum and Dad, and also one from Ewie, which amazed me rather and I think he deserved a Purple Heart decoration for his grand effort of putting pen to paper!

Tons of love to you all. Cheerio for now,

Doug

Kings Cliffe
Sunday, 15 November 1942

Dear Mum, Dad and Girls,

They have introduced the good old airgraph for purposes of wishing you all a Merry Xmas and Happy New Year. To tell you the truth I have little news as I wrote to you the night before last. I have not had any leave for about three months. If all goes well I hope to spend New Year in Carlisle and if it turns out like last year I shall have a pretty good week. I hope you will all be able to get enough petrol to get down to Manly. I wish I was with you. Merry Xmas to you all and hope I will be home or near home next Xmas.

Tons of love,

Doug

Kings Cliffe
Friday, 27 November 1942

Dear Mum Dad and Girls,

Johnny Pattison, Bruce Gordon, and self did a rhubarb in Holland and Belgium in the vicinity of Knokke-Eeklo. It was a good day for the job but a few other pilots had the same idea before us and there was light flak as we went over the coast. We attacked a train but the Huns had quite a few guns handy and threw all they had at us. I was in among the poplars on the deck in no time and then we all made for cloud and came home over France. The weather closed right in and we had to spend the night at our hopping-off drome, Martlesham Heath, and that was quite a night as Johnnie Checketts was there.

Tony Robson and self went for a trip in a Master to pick up a Spit in South Wales. On the way down we stopped and had lunch with a couple of chaps, namely Les Scorer and Jim Gardner who used to be in 602 Squadron with us at Kenley. They were full of fettle but fed up with the job of instructing and wanting to get out of it one way or another. When we arrived there was no Spit, so we had to make the whole trip back.

On 17 November Tony Robson and I were flying a Miles Master from Llandow, Wales, following a trip to collect a Spitfire. No Spitfire was there so we returned again in the Master. Crossing the Bristol Channel the engine stopped. We managed to restart the engine by diving and landed at Aston Down to refuel. As there was a party at Wittering that night we decided to fly back in the dark. We were soon lost and I could not get a reply on the radio from the four contacts we had. The way we saw it there were two options: force land in the dark or bale out. I tried the radio once more and was relieved to get a reply so they could guide us in.

[Letter continues]

We have been playing a fair amount of rugby and have not lost a match. We played our two big games this week one against Oundle Public School who we beat 17–5. It was the first time they have been beaten for 16 games including other RAF teams so we did well. Group has always been of the opinion they have a great team so we went and beat the Group team 30–3, so that disproved their theory. On the way home we had a hectic night in Nottingham. It is a pretty good thing to have a team out of one squadron, all NZers, who can beat any station team.

There was an alabaster elephant in the pub that Tony Robson took a liking to. It wasn't until we were returning to base that the uplifted piece popped up amidst much cheering on the bus. A couple of days later Groupy was hounded by the publican and contacted Reg Grant so that a return of the trophy could be negotiated. We came up with the idea that the team would return to the pub and make a presentation. There would be an exchange on the basis of free drinks for the evening. This seemed to be an amicable solution for both sides.

Murray Metcalfe, Mick Maskill, Rev Steed, Reg Grant, Tony Robson, Doug, Lindsay Black, Buck Buchanan, Tommy Tucker

Parties seem to be the order on weekends with a sergeants' mess do here tonight, and tomorrow night a blow out at the officers' mess at Wittering, which should be pretty good with loads of good food and drink. Lobster is on the menu again – there must be a war on!

We have had a lot of mist and rain. It has been jolly cold, which is not too good for early rising. I hope we shift south before the snow decides to fall in great quantity.

A funny thing happened to Bruce Gibbs: he cracked his leg at footy and had to go to hospital down south. He was playing snooker one day and along came a couple of Jerries and dropped a 500-pound bomb apiece and hit the hospital. Poor old Gibby did not know what was going on so stood where he was and all he got out of it was an inch or so of powdered plaster all over him. He was certainly lucky and I think got quite a fright. Some 30-odd of the others were killed.

Cheerio for now. Tons of love to all,

Doug

LEFT Ian and Reg Grant   RIGHT Doug, WAAF, Tony Robson

With regard to dawn readiness, Mick Shand hated getting up early so he slept at dispersal when he was scheduled on. Mick and his No 2 took off one dawn. His No2 already dressed and Mick put a flying suit over his pyjamas. Unfortunately when they came to return to Kings Cliffe the weather had clamped up and Mick and his No 2 were diverted to an American drome. When they went to the mess it was suggested to Mick that it was not protocol to wear a flying suit to have breakfast in a US mess – much to his consternation he had to breakfast in his pyjamas!

Officers' Mess
Kings Cliffe
Monday, 30 November 1942

Dear Mum, Dad and Girls,

We had a very sad day on Saturday. Last week Johnny Pattison and I did a rhubarb. Four of the boys decided to follow us up and the CO did a recce

Hugh 'Tommy' Tucker

of his own. The Huns must have been waiting and we lost Mick Shand[55] and Bill Norris.[56] Hugh 'Tommy' Tucker who has only been with us since September was very lucky indeed to get home. He was on his first operation, a rhubarb with Mick, when they were set upon by FW190s. Tommy had a lucky escape. He came down low and almost crashed when he scraped a mound of earth. He struggled back to base at low level and was peppered by flak – an exciting start to his career!

The boys did a bit of damage and one redeeming feature is that Reg Grant cleaned up a Heinkel 115. Mick will be missed and I sincerely hope he is at present carrying out a tour of Belgium and Holland. If he gets back we will close shop for a few days for one big party. We had a big do at Wittering on Saturday night and drowned our sorrows having one for Mick every round. I did well in the eating line: I started with a lobster and then in sequence had half a fowl, half a duck and half a pheasant with splashings of ham and finished off with another lobster. I was in fine trim and very bright but was not so well next day! We had a few others join us like Dickie Barrett, an old cobber of the squadron, and G/C Isitt, and the next day we had a lunch in the mess for all the boys and girls who had come for the dance. The CO put Tony Robson up for Flight Lieutenant but those rotters in the RAF won't give it to him as we have too many Flight Lieutenants learning the trade.

A very Merry Xmas and New Year in spite of all.

Tons and tons of love,

Doug

55 Mick's stay as a POW in Stalag Luft III led to a few minutes of freedom in March 1944 as a participant in The Great Escape.
56 Bill Norris was killed on this operation.

The 'Black Velvet' show came up from London to the theatre in Peterborough. As I knew the leading lady 'Queenie',[57] Reg Grant asked me to organise the girls to come out to our mess after the show on Saturday. We took the CO's car and our own car, which we called the 'sexy six', and a couple of taxis and brought all the girls out to the mess. It was quite a party. They were still there in the morning and we all had breakfast together. On the Sunday Reg Grant had a call from Basil Embry, the Wittering Station Commander to say that the Group Chaplain wanted to come over and visit the squadron. Reg mentioned there were a few local girls here and perhaps the chaplain may prefer to visit another time. Basil said that was even more reason why they should come so they both arrived when the majority were still suffering from alcohol. The chaplain considered us all such a fine group of people and was most impressed in the manner we were putting ourselves out and looking after the local girls with such enthusiasm on a Sunday morning! The girls came out another five nights. As a result my mess bill for the month was more than my total pay.

Kings Cliffe
Thursday, 10 December 1942

Dear Mum Dad and Girls,

After turning down Tony Robson for a flight they tried to give us another F/Lt but we were not having any of it so we have now got Johnny Pattison back with us. He is a real good lad and though he has not had so much experience in sweeps he will be very good as he has his head screwed on the right way.

I had rather a hectic couple of days in London with Mick Maskill last week, which had disastrous results. It was a 'pea souper' in London again when we arrived. After booking in at the pub we went to our little café to have steak and mushrooms – very tasty too and then went to the Chez Moi where I met Queenie and at about nine we went around to the Panama Club where she was singing. We then danced till the place shut down – quite an enjoyable evening and quite expensive.

After some shopping we thought we would call in at the Forces Club and see if we knew anyone there. We visited the usual haunts and at the Sussex

57 Queenie was daughter of the proprietress at the Chez Moi, Denman St, Piccadilly Circus.

we ran into Digger Robertson and Jack Miller, as well as Doug Nilsson, Jock Dunlop and a few other scoundrels. As you can imagine, quite a session began which continued more or less all afternoon except for a lunch break and a trip back to the pub for a bath and shave. The night was spent in trips between the Sussex and Chez Moi with, for the most part, Digger, Jack, Doug Nilsson, Mick and self – quite a party! I had to leave early next morning to play rugby and was up at about eight. It was a horrible day and I could not get a taxi so I played around in the tubes for a while and then caught the 9.30 train, reaching camp not long after midday to find that the rugby was cancelled and there was a show in the offing.

On 6 December we left here early in the afternoon to refuel at a forward base, Coltishall in Norfolk. We acted as support for Venturas bombing the Phillips works in Holland, but we saw no Hun fighters.

It was to be a very sad day for 489 NZ Ventura Squadron. They were attacked while they had little cover during the raid and only one aircraft of the 12 returned to base. 489 was an NZ Squadron and S/L Len Trent, the CO who was shot down but survived and received a VC in this action.

[Letter continues]

I spotted one Ventura that had crossed the Dutch coast with smoke coming from an engine. I escorted the damaged plane on the homeward run but it crashed into the sea. One of the crew though he looked nearly done, was hanging on to his dinghy with odd bits of aircraft such as a wheel floating about. I flew around giving an R/T fix. My petrol gauge registered zero so I elected to land at a small drome Horsham St Faith as I had no show of reaching Coltishall. The engine stopped on my approach so I did a dead prop landing. Apart from hitting a tree as I passed over the fence I put down successfully. This aerodrome was so small there was no way I could refuel and take off so the Spit had to be dismantled and removed by truck to Coltishall where eight of us were stuck for the night.

Reg Grant and Reg Baker went down and saw the King the day before yesterday to get their 'gongs'. I wish I had been with them as I should think quite a time would be had.

A couple of boys who we trained with in Canada have been awarded DFCs, namely Bill Jameson and Harry Coldbeck – who is now missing, as is also poor old Toby Webster. Jack Rae also got a DFC, which he rightly deserves. We were over at Wittering the other night and ran into Dutch

Stenborg line shooting as usual. He is a good flier and deserved his 'gong' but he puts his foot in it at times.

I received a bundle of Xmas parcels from you all during the past few weeks. By the way, Dad, you mentioned in your last letter I should drop a note to the Auckland Golf Club, but I sent them a Xmas card a couple of months ago which should suffice. I hope they get it.

Tons of love to all. Cheers for now,

Doug

Kings Cliffe
Saturday, 26 December 1942

Dear Mum Dad and Girls,

We are in the middle of Xmas/New Year celebrations and I wish I was with you right now, sunbathing and preparing for a snappy New Year on the court.

Celebrations over here have been hectic. On Xmas Eve there was a Dinner-Dance at Wittering, after which a few of us went down to Bill Tomkins' till morning. Yesterday we started with a few beers in the sergeants' mess at 11, after which we served Xmas dinner to the airmen and did our stuff pretty well. The boys certainly appreciate occasions such as Xmas when they get waited upon and looked after by the officer types. Tomato soup was the starter, followed by a really large dose of goose, pork with all the trimmings, sprouts, peas, and spuds. Finishing off with Xmas pud, but not as good as Mum's. The American boys were well on their bikes at the dinner, drinking their 'double Scotch' all morning. Amazingly, a couple of them kept on the same drink all afternoon and were still on their feet.

The past two days have kept up the reputation of good cold England, the fog cutting down the visibility to about 30 yards, which means no flying. Tonight we are all due to go to a dance held by the girls at Operations. Tomorrow night there is a dance here, the next night the WAAF officers' mess, and then the following night, though I hope to be in Carlisle, there is a dance to be held by the 485 boys.

We have had grand news that Mick Shand is POW and was not wounded, so we were cheered up no end when it became official. We have done a couple of shows since I last wrote – the first was a withdrawal for Fortresses and Liberators bombing Rouen. It was the first time I've seen Huns for a very long while although they were too far away for us to do anything about it.

I expect we will shift south any time now, which would be a good thing and we might see what action there is going on in France in new model aircraft. The NZ Squadron Harvey Sweetman joined has been doing well and they have collected six or seven hit and run raiders in the last week which is jolly good going.

Tony Robson and self got offered jobs as Flight Lieutenants a couple of days after our F/Os came through, which naturally I did not take. Tony said the job was for three months to instruct S/L and Wincos who so far this war have not seen any operations. I know training command – very easy to get in and damn hard to get out of again. I don't think I'll leave the squadron till I have to unless I get a flight offered me down south.

We had Mr Jordan up here for the night last Sunday and we got all our toheroa soup and oysters out to give him a treat. With white wine and Drambuie and a cigar after the meal, he did well. He is a grand old fellow and the Government is lucky to have such a chap representing them, though I don't think they cut much cheese with him.

Tons of love to all and I wish I was at the beach now.

Cheerio all,

Doug

Westhampnett

*

*Westhampnett Command: W/C Peter Brothers, CO Reg Grant.
Flight Commanders Reg Baker and John Pattison.*

Westhampnett was a satellite of Tangmere built as an emergency airfield on land owned by the Goodwood Estate. After the war, Westhampnett became the Goodwood Racing Circuit.

610 Squadron joined a couple of weeks afterwards under Johnny Johnson. He became the highest scoring British fighter ace with 34 destroyed. After the war he had a career in the RAF and retired as an Air Vice Marshall.

Our accommodation was a house, Fishers Cottage, on the edge of the drome. Our mess was a Nissen Hut 100 yards off the road.

Life was very wild and parties were held in Fishers Cottage almost every night. It was a tiring business and fortunately did not seem to affect our flying ability. When we had leave, instead of going to London for more of the same, I usually went to Katie's, Fergie's or Cumberland for a rest.

In January we did a number of operations as the wing had a permanent patrol on anti-rhubarb operations run effectively by the Germans. They used mainly FW190s usually in a flight of four to fly in at low level and bomb the coastal towns. On another occasion, on 20 January, we were scrambled when about 30 Fighter Bombers tried to bomb London.

Westhampnett
Sussex
Tuesday, 5 January 1943

Dear Mum Dad and Girls,

Well here we are again into another year and I will start this scrawl by wishing you all over there 'Kia Ora' and all the best for the coming year – maybe I will be able to see the next in with you all? One thing I do miss over here – and memories are certainly sent forth in a mad upheaval around Xmas and New Year – Manly! When my time comes I'll have to be buried there to make the sand productive.

We have returned to the battle zone under 11 Group, the squadron shifting south a few days ago. All we need now are the new later-model aircraft. The trips into France will be far more extensive as we will be able to cut deeper into the land of the Frogs. I don't mind how far we go so long as we have aircraft, which are at least on a par with the Jerry jobs.

Before we came down here I spent New Year up north so I will recap. I was rather late getting to London but got a room OK. After a quick visit to the

Sussex I hurried up to the Chez Moi. I was not feeling in the best of spirits – quite a few of the boys had gone to bed back at camp so I thought I had a mild chill. I ran into Philip Pheloung and his wife, all the local roughs, and also Doug Nilsson and Bruce Tidy who will probably visit you as they are returning home anytime now. I had a couple of hot rums and went to bed. Next morning I was up early but I did not feel particularly fit and my head was properly blocked up. I went to the nearby chemist and had a bit of dope, which cleared me up. Luckily I was at the station an hour before the train was due to leave for Carlisle, as it was nearly full.

The Rickerbys were all pleased to see me and looked jolly well. As I had not eaten all day, I was pleased to be able to hog into a good amount of goose including the parson's nose! The next day I wasn't feeling any better and did not get up till late. After a spot of brunch I popped out to Harraby Grange where I saw Mr and Mrs Cavaghan and Harold. All transport for private means is of course outski, so I caught the bus back to Rickerby's. My temperature was now 102. I popped into bed and had a rotten night and so New Year's Eve was spent in bed till 9 p.m. when I got up. A New Year could not be seen in bed by any member of the Brown family, especially as there was a fair crowd congregating downstairs. I had a few beers and we saw in the New Year in the usual fashion.

Next morning I was greeted with a telegram: 'Return to base immediately!' I sent a telegram back: 'Can't make, it in bed with flu', and turned over. At about three in the afternoon a cop visited and on being shown in said the squadron had been in touch with him and wanted to know if I could get back by the following evening. This made me think that there must be something really in the wind. I got dressed on the spot and contacted Reg Grant. It was the return south again. This news bucked me up no end and I felt better on the spot and stayed up till after tea. Next day I got up at ten and had lunch with the Cavaghans.

I caught the train back to London just after midday on Sunday. I had some good standing hours coming down and only managed to get a seat at Rugby. The trains are generally fairly well packed, especially over the Xmas and New Year. I saw no one I liked better than myself in the Sussex except Jack Miller who gave me an update on how Digger Robertson was. Not long after I saw him last he crashed into a hill, killed his observer and knocked himself about a bit.

I had a fair trip back to our new abode right on the south coast. The billets are not particularly good. We've got a large house which has seen quite a number of squadrons and is beginning to show signs of wear. As the mess is not over-large we have converted a large room into a jolly nice sitting room where we run our own bar and have got the place looking fairly smart. The meals are very good and I've got no complaints in that direction. Two other squadrons in the wing are doing courses, which means we keep constant readiness and we have to do all of the work. I was on this afternoon and got a scramble to patrol from Shoreham to Selsey. We had a heavy fall of snow last night, which thawed during the day. Although I was a bit dicky about taking off and landing it was OK but with plenty of slush flying right and left.

The boys finished at Kings Cliffe in their usual style when I was away and had some really hectic nights especially New Year when few of them saw bed before six – thank goodness I was up north. I got a large batch of *Weeklies* in Carlisle, which were all appreciated when I brought them back.

Well I will buzz off and get some sleep.

Tons of love to all,

Doug

Westhampnett
Wednesday, 20 January 1943

Dear Mum Dad and Girls,

We are now well settled in and have things well organised and our sitting room-cum-bar is going well. Most of the boys seem to be out but Reg and Ian Grant, Reg Baker and Mac Sutherland are sinking the odd pint and yarning. As usual the wireless is going flat out. It is certainly a pity that we need a war to bring such a grand mob of chaps together. Ian Grant is a great organiser and we are never short of WAAF company each night.

We have been doing a lot of flying, mostly anti-rhubarb patrols along the coast. Although we have had quite a number of shows laid on for us bad weather has prevented some of them. We did a rather good circus to Abbeville. We went over as independent wings while two bombing raids were undertaken on two dromes to try and get the Huns up. The Fortresses went farther in. We got the Huns up OK but did not get a bounce. One of the other

Aerial view of Westhampnett airfield today with Goodwood Racing Circuit surrounding the drome. WWW.SEALANDAP.CO.UK

wings got a few. It was good to be at least close enough to mark the good old 'black crosses'. I was watching the Jerry come down, but I could not quite get into position to get a shot.

Today I should think was reminiscent of the Battle of Britain. About 30 fighter bombers tried to bomb London and got a tremendous shock as they lost 11 definitely and a further 12 probables or damaged. All our squadrons were scrambled but we were a bit late and only one section of our squadron got on the chase. I hope they come over a few more times so we can get among them. Down here we have quite a few air raid alarms, and the other NZ squadron[58] knocked over about eight 'tip and run' raiders. The other night we did a spot of night flying – a beautiful night – and as it happened the Jerries decided to do a reprisal raid on London with little success. We had to crack the deck with little light. Poor old Ops, what a 'flap'! The only trouble with this type of flying is that if we put up too many op hours, the hierarchy will want to park us up to an OTU.

58   486 Squadron based at Tangmere, at that time flying Hawker Typhoons.

I may take a flight out East if it offers. There is only one snag and that is we will in all probability get a new-type kite soon, which will be the goods. If I go out East I'll send a coded cable 'Many happy returns to Peg and Shirl', so you will get the gen.

We have played a couple of games of rugby down here, the first against the other NZ squadron and we managed to beat them 13–9. A couple of us played for the main station at the naval place where Bruce Wallace was commissioned and we beat them 11–6 after a jolly good game. Bruce has gone overseas and we have never managed to meet up, all through bad luck.

Any leave I have I try to fit in a few 'rest days' as every night at base there is a party at Fishers Cottage. Our operational flying ability doesn't seem impaired – we put it down to the oxygen on which we overdose when hungover.

Cheerio for now. Love to you all,

Doug

Yet another party! Back: Garry Barnett, Mac Sutherland, Murray Metcalfe, George Moorehead, Peter Gaskin / John Ainge, Bruce Gibbs, Doug, Lindsay Black, Reg Grant. For indoor photos Lindsay Black (front) would light an incendiary. He often missed getting into the shot!

ABOVE LEFT Fishers Cottage – one of few photos retrieved from a fire

ABOVE RIGHT Thea Hoddinott, Doug

LEFT S/L Reg Grant, F/Lt J Pattison (recounting combat action), F/Lt R Baker, 21 January 1943. IMPERIAL WAR MUSEUM IMAGE CH008385

Rosie Mackie was with the squadron until 1943 when he also left to fly in the Middle East and Italy. He had great success as Commander of 92 and 80 Squadrons, finishing the war as Wing Commander 122 Wing in Europe. He was a quiet gentleman who neither smoked nor drank alcohol – unlike the rest of the boys!

Having worked as an electrician in the Waihi gold mines prior to the war, following the war he worked with the Bay of Plenty Electric Power Board. He died aged 68. For further reading, see: *Spitfire Leader* by Avery and Shores.

Tadworth
Surrey
Thursday, 4 February 1943

Dear Mum Dad and Girls,

I'm spending a few days with Katie and Werner eating and sleeping well and in general having a jolly good rest.

We have not done much flying during the past few weeks. We've been very lucky so far this year as the snow has kept away. It has been very mild but I think the really cold weather will be this month and the beginning of the next. I've done a couple of trips over France since last writing. Both were in the Abbeville area and bombers played a part. First trip we got a good bounce on some 12 or so FW190s. Although they were numerically superior, they were over on their backs and left us smartly. A couple of them followed a section of ours out and two other sections of us had bad luck in not intercepting them. The closest I got to them was 800 yards. I opened fire but at that range there is little chance of a result. The next trip we got on to about a dozen on the water. Before they had time to scram our Winco Pete Brothers knocked one over and the chap baled out, the plane making a lovely splash. Another went into the water and the other squadron claimed it though it is still rather doubtful who got it. One attacked our section but I was in a rotten position and so did not even get a poop at him.

We went up north, to the last station we were at, to play the semi-final of the rugby for the Group, which we managed to win 12–3 after a good and hard game. I played with a few of our lads for the main station team against the Navy at Portsmouth and we managed to win OK. I still enjoy my footy and I think there is nothing better for keeping one fit.

Reg Grant and I set sail for London last Monday. Reg has a flat for the week. We saw the flicks in the afternoon, a musical show, and then after a meal we went around to the den of inequity, the Chez Moi, where we ran into Garry Barnett and also Jack Rae who was full of life as usual. Phil Pheloung and his wife came in later in the evening so we had a good pow-wow.

On Tuesday Reg had to see the Air Commodore for NZ so we were up reasonably early. On the way we ran into Rosie Mackie who is going away as a Flight Lieutenant. While we were there Noble Lowndes rang up and asked us to lunch. He is an NZer who has been over here for 20-odd years and is in the insurance game. He does not live far from Kenley. He is a grand fellow and looks after us well. We know what his lunches are like and as we did not feel in the mood for another big night – I intended coming to Katie's – we tried to get out of it but arguing with him is like arguing with a post so that was that. We met him at his favourite eating ground in the Haymarket. He started us on Gin and French. To tell you the truth I hate gin but I must admit these drinks were well mixed. We had three of these real whoppers, worth 7/6d a pop. The meal was really good and with it we had a bottle of Burgundy, very nice and we finished off with pancakes drowned in brandy which had to be lit first like the old Xmas pud and we finished the lot with a liqueur brandy – jolly nice! A typical London lunch, started at one and finished at four. After lunch we dropped off Noble and went to the NZ Club where we had a yarn with the odds and sods there and Mitchell the London reporter for most of the papers in NZ. He does all the write-ups for the squadron. We were just going out of the place when we ran into a couple of WAAFs we knew very well at Kenley and took them out for a meal and spent a pleasant evening. I stayed at the pub as Reg's flat was not made to accommodate two!

We were due to meet Miss Steffens of the Forces Club at 11 but we did not make it – instead we had lunch with Jock Dunlop at the Sussex. I've been trying to get you a book, *The Last Enemy*, written by a chap Hillary who, incidentally, was killed not so long ago. It is a grand book and gives you a great insight into the life of a Spitfire pilot with very little bull. Jock said he will get a copy and send it on to you. After a meal with Jock I caught the 2.20 p.m. train to Tadworth and arrived here at about 3.30. The Leuch family has had a bad few months. Werner has been ill for some time, Katie had flu and jaundice, and Paul has had about four operations on his foot during the past two months.

The news of late has been grand and if the Russians can only continue their advance when the winter is over we should be in the pound seats. I think the continual bombing we are keeping up day and night is bound to have some effect on the people as well as the superficial damage caused.

Love to all and tons for yourselves,

Doug

Combat report for 13 February 1943 at 12:15 in the Le Touquet area: National Archives of the UK

I was flying Red 3. In the general mêlée my No.2 was attacked and though I called on the R/T failed to break. An FW190 was climbing from the opposite direction to our section. I delivered an attack of about 1 ½ seconds with cannon and machine guns at an angle of 20-30 degrees at 200-250 yards and noticed one cannon strike between the pilot's cockpit and tail unit on top of the fuselage. As the aircraft shot from sight beneath me I was unable to see the effect of the attack. After this, having been split up I went for the deck and set course for home at sea level. My Cine camera gun was u/s. The FW190 was camouflaged dark green-gray. I claim one FW190 damaged.

Woodbridge
Suffolk
Monday, 15 February 1943

Dear Mum, Dad and Girls,

When I last wrote I was with Katie and had another day with them eating and sleeping well. The night before I was to report back I spent in the 'Big Smoke' and caught an early train back to camp, getting there at about lunchtime. Before I arrived George Moorhead and Bruce Gordon did a rhubarb but Bruce got smacked by flak and had to crash land over there but from what George saw he should be OK.

As regards flying, I have only done a couple of sweeps since I last wrote. The weather though without snow so far, has generally been full of rain and cloud. On 10 February we did close escort to 12 Venturas when they bombed Caen aerodrome and though fighter opposition was nil, 610 Squadron, which covered us, ran into a packet and lost three pilots. For their part I thought the bombers did well, and their bombing was very accurate. The results were grand to see.

The next show was a sad one for us. Reg Grant led the wing with us as bottom squadron and we started a climb from base, making the French coast not much under 20,000 feet. We played around inland a bit and for a while I thought we were in for a quiet show until we got a report of Huns below and south of us. One of the boys saw a few and down we went into a trap. We were about 1000 feet above these fellows going up-sun. I looked to port and could hardly believe my eyes when I saw about 20 or more FW190s above us and coming in to attack. Then it was as if hell had been let loose – Spits and Huns all over the sky, weaving and diving with an odd bit of flak from below thrown in for good measure. I had

Ian Grant, the CO's brother, as my No 2 and he got one right up his tail and though Reg and I yelled to him he made no attempt to break so all I could do was turn like blazes in the hope he would follow, but I'm afraid he went down. I managed to plant a high explosive just behind a Hun pilot's cockpit, and as I did not see where he buzzed off to I claimed a damaged. The CO got one about the same time. It climbed, stalled and belched out smoke and came down in flames. In the mêlée I only had one squirt. As there were 40 of them to our 12, I was not about to take undue risk. A couple got rather affectionate while I was closing my attack so I headed for earth and came out on the deck. We picked one another up during the home flight across the sea. When we got back I got a hell of a shock for though I was one of the last to leave France I was the first of our flight to land and all the other flights were on the ground. Besides losing Ian Grant, we lost Tony Robson of all people and Sgt Steed. I can't understand how Slim went. It must have been a damn good Hun and I guarantee Slim got two of them before they got him. All we can hope is that they baled out OK.[59] As Johnny Pattison was on leave I had some worries that afternoon. Besides the three kites we lost, Lindsay Black was shot up and I hit a bird or some such object, which made a lovely dent on my wing. However, we managed to see the day through with borrowed aircraft and pilots. What a day!

It was a tough fight and we had to carry out a few repairs when we got back. The only consolation was that Reg dispatched the FW190 that had shot down his brother.

We had one very dirty day with a visit from the Jerries who bombed, among other places, our nearby town, making a terrific mess. The ack-ack boys had a lot of fun. As the weather was really bad we left it all to them and they did well getting three out of the eight sent over. One crashed about five miles from us so we looked it over. With unexploded bombs in the vicinity it kept most people away. The Hun plane was strewn over a fair area and he certainly must have hit the ground with a bang as there were four crew scattered about in a different paddock to the crash. They were all dead but not badly bashed about. I had my eye on a watch one of them was wearing but the cops were too shrewd and kept their eyes open so I did not get a freebie out of it. The same afternoon we had a visit from the AOC of RNZAF personnel and he was in his usual good humour.

Cheerio for now. Hope you are all fit and well. Love to all.

Doug

---

59   Steed and Ian Grant were killed and Tony Robson ended up as a POW.

Martlesham Heath
Suffolk
Friday, 5 March 1943

Dear Mum, Dad and Girls,

The last two or three weeks have been spent doing a fair amount of air firing and very little else. The boys get quite good at it after a few goes and some good scores were put up, though I can only assess my efforts as average. All the censor will let me say is that we are here on a gunnery course and staying in a local castle.

Apart from flying, the order of the day was the odd game of rugby and a few parties. I played three games. In the first, four of us from the squadron played for the station against the Navy. The second game was between the squadron and the station team and we won easily. The last game was a Group match and the squadron supplied nine of the team and in a very good game we managed to make the grade 9–0, which thoroughly thrilled the station CO. He could not thank us enough and he had the band in the mess that night. We sank quite a number of beers and sang the usual RAF songs – no doubt as you did in the last war, Dad – pretty swingy and plenty of gusto but not for feminine ears. We went out on a squadron party in our dispersal and the station CO McGregor really enjoyed himself. He is a very likeable fellow with DSO and bar from the last war.

The war seems to go on well from our point of view and I would certainly hate to be in any of those towns the bomber boys are giving hell – good luck to them. The Huns dropped a few eggs not far distant from us and gave the ack-ack boys a bit of practice. Today a couple of recce machines came over at a great height making smoke and then buzzed smartly home.

Love to all,

Doug

Glebefield
Tadworth
Monday, 15 March 1943

Dear Mum, Dad and Girls,

I'm at Katie's again, having a damn easy time, which I appreciate to the full.

We have done a couple of shows since last writing and both times we did not even see a Hun in the distance. The second of the two trips was a beautiful day and you wouldn't have realised there was a war on, no flak, no other aircraft and you could see into France for miles. It would have been possible to follow the Seine as far as Paris. The weather over here has been mild this winter. This time last year it was a shocker. Now the sun has

Portraiture by Olive Snell

warmth in it and flowers like daffodils and primroses are in full bloom. I saw in the paper where we have had the most sun for some 41 years and I can fully believe it, it has been really grand and I hope the summer is equally as good.

Down near the drome is a very good artist, Olive Snell by name. Nine of us (the older members of the clan) have had our portraits done all on one sheet and what a marvellous job she has made of them. They are far better than photographs. The CO is having the original and we are all to have reproductions. I will also pay my friend Pearl Freeman a visit and get her to send you the odd photo to see how I look.

We had the Huns over the other night and they put on a bit of a show though it was quite a way off. We have been having the usual 'tip and run' raiders and I think on the Hun profit and loss account there is a hell of a debit.

Love to all the folks. Cheerio for now.

Tons of love to you,

Doug

From sketches by Olive Snell

ABOVE LEFT Tommy Tucker, Bluey Meagher, Tusker McNeil

ABOVE RIGHT George Moorhead, Murray Metcalfe

LEFT AND BELOW Peter Gaskin, Mac Sutherland, Chalky White, Johnnie Houlton

OPPOSITE Back: Lindsay Black, Mick Maskill, Reg Baker /
Middle: John Pattison, Reg Grant, Bruce Gibbs /
Front: Garry Barnett, Marty Hume, Doug

MICK

'UNKY

LIN

PAT.

DUMBO
C.O.

GIBBY.

MUGSIE.

MARTY

BRUNO

Olive Snell

485 NEW ZEALAND SQUADRON

Westhampnett
Saturday, 27 March 1943

Dear Mum, Dad and Girls,

I've bought a car – a black Super Deluxe model Standard 1931 with the registration of 'mileage stonkered' with so much use – price £16, rather amazing! One of the lads – a Free French boy – from a squadron that is moving wanted to sell, so I thought as it is a damn good little car I'd buy it. He wanted £20 so I offered him £15, and his answer was, 'One pound as a teep (tip!), which I agreed to. It is a nine horse job and does not cost much to register, just over £3 a quarter plus insurance. With the long days coming

Rev Steed, Bluey Meagher, Tommy Tucker, Murray Metcalfe, Johnny Pattison, Doug, Ian Grant, Mick Maskill, Lindsay Black. RNZAF MUSEUM

along we will have a lot of fun with it so long as the petrol is OK. There is enough for pilots at present but one never knows. There are some jolly good spots to visit around here.

We had a dance to celebrate two years since the squadron was formed and 40 Hun planes shot down.

After the last letter to you from Katie's, I paid a visit to Fergie and family and he was in good fettle but very hard hit by the loss of his son John in an aircraft accident. He was very proud to show me the grave at Limpsfield. He is a real lad and the night we were there he did a bit of home guard – Cpl Ferguson style. I had a game of golf in the afternoon. The course was in great nick and, as far as my long game was, I was good and on the green generally in two. I two-putted on two greens and got birdies on both. I really enjoyed the game and with the car I may be able to fit in a few more rounds.

On the Thursday I was in London and contacted Bruce Gibbs in the NZ Forces Club with Dutch Stenborg.[60] Incidentally, who should I meet but Ian McKenzie, son of Sir Clutha, who went to Sandhurst just before the outbreak of war and has spent most of his time at Gibraltar. We went and saw Noble Lowndes who took us to his club, Bon Viveur – where we had a drink with Prince Bernard of the Netherlands – nice chap – and met a Colonel Parks. Noble has just filed for divorce and was endeavouring to find out what I knew about any of the squadron being involved whom he was citing as co-respondents. It was an interesting situation as Noble seemed to trust me, and at the same time some of the lads were plying me for detail. Next call was the Sussex where I ran into Jack Rae and he came with us to the Tivoli. Another fellow I came across was Reg Crawford an All Black who is from Mt Eden and is an in-law of the Hughes – not a friend of them though. In his younger days he used to play in our drive and was always scared Dad would come out and tick him off. Small world! I went to the Chez Moi Club in Piccadilly when the Tivoli closed and caught the 5.30 back. I had dinner in town and took a taxi to the hall where we had the Squadron Anniversary dance. It was a jolly good 'do' and a fitting end to a quiet leave.

We decided to invite the owner of the Chez Moi, Harry the 'Frog' (Harry France) down to visit. He arrived with a wallet full of cash. We thought it good sport to gang up on him in a card game called 'shoot' and relieve him of some of the profit he made out of us when we visited his club.

---

60 We both trained at Moose Jaw. Stenborg was killed on operations with 91 Squadron in September 1943.

We have lost Reg Grant and Reg Baker has taken his place. Marty Hume got A Flight. Reg Grant was overdue for rest and I believe will be going to Canada to show the boys how it is done – and the girls too I expect!

Flying has not been what I would call excessive and we have only done a couple of sweeps since I last wrote – one small show to France in which we saw nothing and another over southern France where we encountered no fighter opposition. The ack-ack boys thought they would get in some practice and let go all they had but it was not over-accurate and did not worry us much. We have done plenty of readiness but we now have got a fair supply of pilots so that it is really not so bad. We had good news that Tony Robson is a POW. As yet there is still no word of Ian Grant but we live in hope.

Tons of love to all,

Doug

Westhampnett
Sunday, 11 April 1943

Dear Mum, Dad and Girls,

The weather has not been particularly good of late and we have done few shows. We have done a couple of bomber escorts to Caen and a small fighter sweep. On one show to Caen aerodrome we ran into a bit of trouble and lost one of ours, Sergeant Oxley who was killed, and the other squadron had one who failed to get back. The bombing was very good but there were two Venturas lost as well.

We had John Dasent and Ken Lee join us a little while ago. Ken was at school with me and an instructor at Whenuapai. We aren't in the same flight but will still see a bit of each other.

This morning we had some excitement. We were on dawn readiness and the bomber boys were late coming home so we were in the air early just in case of trouble. With my No 2, John Houlton, I was vectored on to one Stirling in trouble and not long after I got with it, it crash-landed on the sea three miles off Shoreham. It went under and I thought the crew had 'had it' but it bobbed to the surface again and the crew got into the dinghy, all except one who was

John Dasent, Adj. Boucher.

stranded. A Walrus flying boat was out in no time after I'd given a fix but when he had got the boys in the dinghy aboard, his engine petered out, and so the other lad would be in the water for a while before another Walrus could arrive. As no help seemed to be in sight I thought I would be smart and having heard of it being done before I planned to get my own dinghy from under my chute. My plan was to drop it near the poor unfortunate in the water and with flaps down reduced speed close to stalling at 120 mph.

There was little room to move in the cockpit but after a lot of contortions managed to get the dinghy out of its cover beneath my legs. I opened the canopy and pushed the dinghy out, hoping to land it somewhere near the chap in the sea. I had forgotten that the dinghy was attached to me via the parachute (in the event that if you did have to ditch you could pull the dinghy towards you). The lanyard holding the dinghy got caught in the tailplane. The situation was becoming desperate and it was more by good luck than good management that I did not 'buy it'. I opened the throttle, the lanyard broke loose and the dinghy fell to the sea and landed just 30 yards away from the bomber boy. While he was heading towards it another Walrus came into sight and so all my efforts were in vain!

You would not believe that when I got back the Equipment Officer wanted me to pay for the dinghy. Needless to say, the CO Reg Grant took him to task.

We have been doing a lot of readiness, which is rather annoying and now that summer time is in force it means we do not finish our day till well after nine.

I have been coughing a lot in the past few months and I had an X-ray and overhaul on the chest thinking I may have a bit of TB. I have not got a trace, thank God, but I've got Chronic Catarrh Bronchitis. I may have to go on a bit of a rest for a month or so, though with the summer coming on health may improve.

Well I will buzz now,

Love Doug

Westhampnett
Tuesday, 27 April 1943

Dear Mum, Dad and Girls,

I have had five days leave since I last wrote but as the weather was excellent I spent most of it about the camp sunbathing. I spent one night with Mac Sutherland at the King's Beach Hotel at Pagham where we ate and slept well. We went up to London for one night and saw 'Commandos Raid at Dawn' which was quite good and very exciting. We went to the Sussex[61] and I ran into the Canadian crew of the bomber I had helped to get out of the drink a few days previously. They were damn glad to see me and I did not have to pay for a beer all night. They certainly appreciated what we did for them. Later in the evening we met Hori Hansen who gave me my first flip in a Tiger Moth at Whenuapai. He had just arrived back here and gave an update of what's been happening on your side of the world. The next day we met Digger Robertson, who was just going to have a medical, though I doubt if he passed it as he had a pretty bad limp.

We have done some bomber escort, which has proved uneventful except for one show when the Hun got amongst us. One of the boys managed to get a Hun. They are hard to get on these sorts of shows, even if you run into them,

61 This was my last visit to the Sussex as the proprietor AV Cakebread had a fatal heart attack.

Office of the Minister of Defence.

WELLINGTON C. 1.

20th August, 1943.

Dear Sir,

When I was in England I met many New Zealanders serving in the R.A.F., and I thought you might be interested to know that I had the pleasure of meeting your son during my visit to No. 485 (N.Z.) Squadron.

He was then quite fit and well and I hope you will continue to hear good news of him. The lads in this particular Squadron seemed very cheery and happy, and their superior Officers spoke to me in very high praise of them.

Yours faithfully,

Mr. E.B.Brown,
7 Bourne Street,
Mount Eden,
AUCKLAND.

Letter from Jones

as you are escort you must remain with the bomber boys. On 18 April we lost Sgt Denholm, killed doing close escort to Venturas at Dieppe. The new boys we refer to as sergeants because they have often been with us for only a few days.[62] At least with bomber escort you can see some result of your trip. The bomber boys are quite good shots with their eggs – a real pleasure to watch. The bombers at night have been doing well and have been dropping plenty of stuff.

Hawk Wells paid us a visit as well as Jones, Minister of Defence – great guy! Hawk stayed the night, a night that happened to coincide with a sergeants' mess dance so, as you can imagine, we had a right royal time. He is jolly glad to be back here. He said he was sorry he was not able to get to see you but he

---

62 Often these pilots were shot down early in their first couple of operations due to lack of experience. From statistics, over 29% of bomber and fighter aircrew were lost either in training or in their first three operations.

did not spend much time in the big city of Auckland. From what Hawk told us the Yanks are spreading a bit of culture such as is not laid down in the true Ethics of Mankind. It is a damn pity. Jones gave us a talk, which was up to the usual bull. Halfway through his speech Reg Grant decided we'd had enough and we all walked off.

I had an airgraph from Ewan Johnston who seems well settled down among sand and flies. I have not heard from Gus Taylor or Colin McGruther of late but Ewie is apparently not far from Gus as he popped over to see him in order to get my address – so he says. The Tunisian news is good and I should think if the good weather holds the Air Force will have the Hun out before this letter reaches you!

The bedside clock you gave me and the cigarette lighter Mrs Gyllies gave me prior to my departure were stolen some weeks ago when we were on the gunnery course. We are lucky we lose little but it is still a nuisance and a pity people have not got better things to do.

Tons of love to all,

Doug

Westhampnett
Sunday, 16 May 1943

Dear Mum, Dad and Girls,

The weather has been very good during the past four or five days and we've done a show or two each day though we've had no success in knocking over the Hun as we've been close escort each time. The American bomber boys have been having their fun in daylight and have been putting the odd dent in the German occupied towns and fields of France. Our work generally with the medium bombers is jolly interesting and though we seldom get a shot it is quite enlivening especially when the flak gets a bit too close.

I have had five days leave at Oxted with Fergie. The weather was lousy except for one day when I made good use of the golf course and played quite well managing to beat both my opponents by a fair margin. The first night I had with Johnnie Checketts and his cobbers at a dance in the local pub.

As soon as I arrived at Fergie's, the first thing he said to me was that he wanted a fighter pilot to speak at a Wings for Victory at East Grinstead. I smartly put the job on to Johnnie Checketts as he was an F/O. We motored down to East Grinstead and it transpired it was more than saying a few words. It took the form of a pageant with a BBC announcer more or less outlining the whole affair. RAF 'erks' and WAAFs attended, McIndoe's boys who had been burnt and repaired were there, and the ATC trooped in carrying the flags of all the fighting nations, followed by a crew of bomber boys.

Johnnie had to march up the aisle, followed by another mob of flag bearers and sit down in the middle of the stage all on his lonesome and spout forth at the appropriate moment with a few words, starting with 'I am a fighter pilot . . .' Poor old John just managed to stagger through but he did earn us beers afterwards at the expense of all the officials.

The next two days and nights were spent in a quiet fashion. Monday we went to the flicks – 'Casablanca', which I'd seen before but enjoyed far more the second time. At the end of my leave I went up to Johnnie Checkett's drome and he flew me home – an excellent leave and the second time running I've kept out of London. London is nice but I've had the place for many reasons and I think that is becoming a general outlook by the squadron.

Before I went on leave I did some test flying in a Spit XII. I got to 10,000 feet in 1 minute, 40 seconds and attained airspeed of 340 mph.

Rosie Mackie who used to be with us has got a gong in North Africa. He has done damn well and since he has been over there has destroyed six so far. He was also put up for a gong for his work over here and if they keep going in Africa the way they are he will likely get a bar to it.

I posted you a *Tattler* today which contains in it some sketches of the boys as seen by Olive Snell. There is also the etching of yours truly, which you probably won't be able to recognize, but the lads say it is a bit like me. Olive Snell said I had a good 'fighter pilot's nose', a standing joke in the squadron for a while.

A couple of the honourable Government officials, namely WP Endean and a Labour job, visited us this week. I meant to have a yarn to Endean about Manly but I was flying at the time so missed out.

Cheerio for now. Love to all,

Doug

Wine, Women and Song
ground crew – Vic Strange
(centre), Ron in cockpit

Westhampnett
Sunday, 30 May 1943

Dear Mum, Dad and Girls,

I had a glorious five days at a 'rest home' at East Grinstead where there was a recuperation area for fighter boys. Mick Maskill and I had suggested to Reg Grant that we needed some rejuvenation and an 'operational rest cure' was required. The weather was beautiful and I got quite a tan on. At the railway station we were picked up by transport and taken out to our temporary residence in the wonderful old home of Haig the 'whiskey man'. The place is a grand spot with very large rooms panelled for the most part with oak and with massive oak doors.

The first thing I did when I got settled in was get into a pair of shorts, which brought back memories. I had my first game of tennis, except for a game in Canada, since I left NZ. By Jove I was good! The ball came off the

Vic Strange, Doug. Vic arranged the *Wine, Women and Song* artwork on my plane

bat at some amazing angles. As the weather was perfect my usual day's work consisted of arising at about nine, having breakfast of a couple of eggs and bacon – browsing over the *Daily Mirror* – 'Jane' and her pals! After breakers I went down to the swimming pool, got into a bathing suit and lay in the sun in comfort till about midday. Then I popped into the pool, after which I again lay in the sun till lunchtime. After lunch the same thing till about four – teatime – when I popped up to the mansion to have a shave and a bath, got dressed, had some tea and met up with Nadia Thomas in East Grinstead. We had some jolly good evenings as round about that district there are some Road Houses where they serve a good meal and a few beers. As you can see, business is very stressful at present. What it is to be in the Air Force!

I don't know whether you know or ever knew a Dr McIndoe who is in charge of the hospital that does all the resetting of broken jaws and skin grafting for badly burnt RAF boys? I seem to remember you mentioning a Dr Gillies, Dad, who was his partner.[63] It is marvellous what a great job can be made of these bad cases. One fellow there has had a new nose and chin added.

---

63 McIndoe and Gillies were New Zealanders and both later received knighthoods for their work.

485 Squadron formation

At night Nadia, Mick and I would mix with McIndoe's team at the pub. Dr McIndoe's wife was there also, an American, and their two daughters with whom we played tennis.

Imagine it – five days sitting in the sun, swimming and an occasional game of tennis. There were only nine of us on the course, quite a mixture: three Poles, an American, an Aussie, an Indian, two Englishmen and myself.

I resumed normal activity the day before yesterday on a run with Venturas to Zeebrugge. Though we ran into no fighters one of the bombers lost a wing through flak and went straight into the drink. Yesterday was a grand day and a couple of Huns came over just after lunch, giving off a vapour trail, which spread across the sky for miles. They were being chased by Spits, which were also making trails and though they failed to intercept it was quite a sight. Later the Fortress boys went out and we watched them give off 'smoke'. Quite a cloud was created by them. We had bad luck this morning when George Moorehead went into the drink when on a shipping recce. Flying too low he hit the water with his prop.

Cheerio for now.

Love, Doug

Landing mishap

11 Group decided our squadron would carry out some landings on a carrier. This was while we were at Westhampnett prior to going to Biggin Hill. Churchill had devised some scheme that when we invaded the continent and could not get back due to lack of fuel that we would land on a large strip in the water like an aircraft carrier. Then, if necessary, refuel and then come home. We spent 10 days from early June doing deck landing practice.

On 6 June I landed and my oleo leg for the left wheel collapsed. I managed to hold it on one wheel until the speed dropped off and the plane slewed on the wing tip. All hell broke loose, the propeller fractured and OUQ was a write off.

Merston
Tuesday, 15 June 1943

Dear Mum, Dad and Girls,

At the end of May we had quite a trip into Holland with bombers and gave the Hun ack-ack boys a bit of practice. One of the bomber boys did very well and flew his kite back on one engine within about five miles of the coast and did some good ditching and they were pulled out of the water within about

20 minutes. On 10 June we did a deep penetration with Mitchell bombers to Ghent. About 25–30 Huns got amongst us and though we made no claim we had the odd poop and the Hun did not stay long. One bomber was hit and I hope the crew got out. Another did jolly well and plugged away on one engine getting attacked by the Huns and we brought it back to England OK where it force landed. We did a trip down to Caen and ran into the heaviest ack-ack I've ever seen. Unfortunately it collected one of the bombers.

The radio boys caught up with me and I had to shoot a line over the air. It should come over 1YA. After dropping Checks in it up at East Grinstead there was no getting out of it. There were three of us put on the spot. A naval lad, a fellow just back form the Middle East and I did my story about the dinghy 'rescue' which seemed dull in comparison.

I've been doing some high-class exercise – squash. I'm not very good but it's a good game and it takes off a bit of the very extensive superfluous flesh I carry around with me.

I had a letter from Reg Grant a day or so ago. He has a bar to his DFC and is leading a life of luxury in North America.

Cheerio for now,

Love, Doug

On 16 June, 12 of us went to RAF Ayr for additional 'carrier landing practice' following on from the practice landings at Merston. With carrier landings it was necessary to come in right on the stall with full flap down and then drop on the deck. To be authentic we even had a real naval bats instructor.

On the 18th we went out on the carrier HMS *Argus* on the Firth of Forth. We were issued a daily ticket for 2/6p to cover food, cigarettes and alcohol. With 1/- for food we thought that 1/6p would not be enough to keep us going. A glass of beer was 7p and a large whiskey and a large gin was only 2p and cigarettes were 2p for 20. It was therefore much cheaper than we thought and though we weren't used to drinking spirits, we of course did. As a result we got very drunk on the ship. The skipper seemed to like us and let us stay an extra night. We had three nights on board and the food was great. In England at the time there was only one loaf available, a Bevin loaf. It was a sort of mixture between a white and brown loaf. The Navy had access to flour from their overseas ports of call and we were plied with large quantities of fresh white bread.

Woolton

ABOVE LEFT Seafires putting down on *HMS Argus*. IMPERIAL WAR MUSEUM IMAGE A018883

ABOVE RIGHT John Pattison on *Argus*

After the first night of drinking we did four deck landings in Seafires[64]. Despite the many hours flying Spitfires a high level of concentration was required; as with the Spit you couldn't see over the nose. There were 2 Fleet Air Arm, both lieutenants who went over the side due to their inexperience in these planes.

When taking off it was with full throttle and flaps partially down with a frightening drop off the end of the deck towards the sea – almost hitting the water before heading off on our trajectory. Not recommended after a big breakfast! Landing was also quite uncomfortable. In a Spitfire we normally would approach at 120 mph and come over the fence at 90 mph with flaps down. For carrier landings in Seafires we were trained to come in at 80 mph, full throttle, flaps down and almost on the stall.

When coming in for the first time I misjudged and by the time I came down the boat had moved and I had to follow it up. When doing this at 80 mph at a very slow speed and the sloppy way the 'Spit' reacted combined with the design where you cant see right in front under normal circumstances, it wasn't easy. I eventually caught up with the carrier and the Fleet Air Arm Batman's guidance and I just followed his directions in. The next three landings from there were a piece of cake.

The follow-up was at Ford Aerodrome, and Churchill came down. It was a

64 Seafires, or sea Spitfires were Spitfires adapted for use on aircraft carriers.

relatively big drome and they decided to use it as a dummy for the landing in the channel. The idea was to bring a large number of aircraft in. By the time they had landed and started taxiing the problems began: aircraft running in to each other resulting in a terrible mess. Churchill got into his car in disgust and departed and that was the end of that scheme.

Westhampnett
Monday, 28 June 1943

Dear Mum, Dad and Girls,

I think I remember that when you were last over here you spent some of your golfing hours round about Prestwick and Ayr in Scotland. I spent a few days in the vicinity although I did not manage to get any golf, the courses looked in good nick. As to be expected the weather was very poor and about all you could do on afternoons off was to go to the flicks or a dance. Gibby, Jack Rae, Marty Hume, Reg Baker and yours truly were going in for a meal and someone came out of the dining hall nearly knocking Gibby over. He got up looking very annoyed and hoping that whoever had knocked him over was much smaller. It was Dickie Barrett, as large as life, so we all adjourned to the bar.

There was one thing I did not like and that was the long trip back here by train. I am yet to find anything more uncomfortable than a train trip and I must admit that is why I do not get to Carlisle as much as I would like. I had a lengthy letter from Gus Taylor who seems to be doing OK. He is still mad on flying and manages to arrange the odd fly for himself. I think it is probably a good thing he is in the dental corps.

Cheerio,

Doug

ABOVE NAAFI van providing food and beverage services

LEFT Doug sunbathing

Biggin Hill

*

Biggin Hill Command: Station Commander Sailor Malan and W/C Al Deere. For 485 Squadron, CO Johnnie Checketts, Flight Commanders Marty Hume and Bruce Gibbs and 341 Free French Squadron CO René Mouchotte with Flight Commanders Chris Martell and Bobo Boudier.

On 1 July 1943 we moved to Biggin Hill in Kent, a relatively small pre-war RAF establishment. We replaced 611 West Lancashire Squadron and joined 341 Free French Squadron which had been at Biggin Hill since March.

This was our first experience in Spitfire IXBs. We took three days to adjust to the new Mark which had a Rolls-Royce 66 engine with a blower or supercharge system that cut in at 13,000 feet. It also carried a supplementary fuel tank under the fuselage for more range. This Mark of Spitfire was the first fighter aircraft to have overall superiority over the Me109G and the Fokker Wolf 190, naturally a great confidence booster to all Allied pilots. The extra power enabled a top speed of 400 mph. We became over-confident. Whenever we ran into Huns we attacked no matter how many there were. We flew in an open or 'finger non-defensive' formation rather than 'line astern' which was our previous formation. As production increased most Spitfire squadrons were equipped with this type of aircraft. Armaments in our IXBs were four 0.5 calibre machine guns and retained the two 20mm cannon but we had the ability to fit a 500lb bomb.

G/C Sailor Malan (Station Commander Biggin Hill), S/L Charles (611 Squadron), Winco Al Deere, May 1943. IMPERIAL WAR MUSEUM IMAGE CH009994

Prior to the introduction of auxiliary drop petrol tanks slung under the fuselage just forward of the cockpit, the Spitfire had limited range as the main tank only held 94 gallons. Initially at Biggin Hill the IXB were equipped with 30-gallon drop tanks and by D-day this had increased to 45 gallons. Later on, the Spitfire XIV had 90-gallon drop tanks. Normal procedure was to take off on the main tank and transfer to the auxiliary tank at 5000 feet. We would have an adrenalin boost if during the changeover the motor missed a beat. We then had to manually operate the toggle pump to recover the flow of the petrol.

It was always a thrill to take off for operations as each squadron was in a formation of 12 – a wonderful sight. On one such occasion, a dawn operation, Bruce Gibbs became airborne but due to engine failure did not gain height. He had sufficient speed up to carry him to the valley below where despite the concentration of houses he force landed in a paddock with little damage.

Leading up to our arrival at Biggin there was much speculation as to who would claim the thousandth Hun for the station. The tally was 997 and a sweep was running for who would shoot down number 1000, 999 and 998. There was a lot at stake, as the ticket holder, the ground crew and pilot of the plane would get a cut. So keen was the competition that G/C Malan, Winco Al Deere, a Canadian S/L Jack Charles, S/L Checketts (who flew as No 3 to Charles) and

Marty Hume, Garry Barnett, Bill Jordan, CO Johnnie Checketts, W/C Al Deere

S/L René Mouchotte were all on the show. Over Abbeville Al Deere came on the R/T and nonchalantly suggested the group investigate some action in the distance. Within a minute John Clouston was on the loudspeaker at the station announcing Charles had two and one of the Frenchies had another. Johnnie Checketts confirmed the kill. He was about to pounce on the FW190s when Charles snuck through. The first broke into pieces and the pilot got out, the second burst into flames and went straight down.

Glebefield
Tadworth
Monday, 12 July 1943

Dear Mum, Dad and Girls,

Our new station is near Kenley where I first joined the squadron – it is the envy of fighter pilots. It was an RFC base during the First World War and played a key defence role during the Battle of Britain.

Baldy Baker has left us and we have got Johnnie Checketts as CO. He has got plenty of what it needs and will bring the squadron back to the Reg Grant standard. As usual, Dad, you were right when you said I should have accepted the job as a Flight Lieutenant when it was offered to me. Johnnie and Al Deere were annoyed the other day when Johnny Pattison left and were concerned I did not get the job as Flight Commander. They are convinced that Baldy organised it that Garry Barnett, who has been a substantive F/Lt for a good year and a jolly good chap, got it.

You mentioned in your last letter that I must have finished my op tour. To tell you the truth, I have, but I think I will be able to work my hours for some time yet. I have not got far to go now to complete my hundred sweeps over enemy territory. I reckon on doing about 400 operational hours before I go on rest – assuming I don't get caught for excessive hours before that. You may say I need a rest but you know yourself, and I bet you did it in the last war, that there is no sense in pulling out if you are still OK and I am the same as the day I started, with more experience.

We have new aircraft, and are they good! Unfortunately in the five shows I did last week we never saw a Hun till one the day before yesterday on Fortress escort to Paris when they would not come near us at all. In my opinion the Huns may as well be doing a sector recce for the amount of work they do when in the air. On these trips apart from the Fortress do, we never saw a thing although we were over there for a fair time on each occasion. It is rather annoying when we are up before six each morning for no result.

The Middle East boys are away again and seem to have air superiority although they have only been going a day or so[65]. I think they will break all resistance that is put up against them. The Hun must regret what he called his 'blitzes' on English towns. He did say that every raid the RAF made would be repaid five times over – I'm afraid we've repaid his debt that he owed us. The night bomber boys are dropping a few on German cities, but it is nothing to the destruction and dislocation that is taking place on Hun works and their war machine generally. It annoys us to hear the likes of Jones, Nash and co. tell us about the war and how *they* are winning it. Perhaps they should join up and show us how it's done!

I've just completed my first leave for some time. I started on Saturday and Johnny Dasent and I set out in the high-powered 8.9 Standard. We steered a course south and headed for Oxted. John went to London for the night and I stayed with Fergie who is as fit as ever and, as usual, glad to see me. Yesterday

---

65 The Axis Forces capitulated in North Africa in May 1943 and the invasion of Italy began soon after.

morning though it was wet and windy I played a round of golf with Fergie. The golf was rotten but I enjoyed it thoroughly. I left Oxted after a hearty lunch yesterday and arrived at Katie's not long after five which was good going considering it was Sunday travel. After a jolly good supper and listening to the nine o'clock news, I went to bed and practically slept around the clock. I had a good rest, building up both the sleeping and eating hours.

A couple of afternoons we had a few Huns over in very bad weather, so bad in fact that we could not get off the ground. One of the Jerries popped out of the cloud just above the drome and let a few eggs go but they were badly aimed and missed by miles. There was no damage at all with the bombs falling in some nearby fields. Just as well. They apparently had some good luck in that they hit a cinema a few miles away and quite a number of people were killed or badly injured.

Tons of love to all the family,

Doug

Combat Reports of 15 July on a rodeo to the Dieppe/Abbeville area.

Combat Reports were completed by pilots returning from an operation where there was contact with enemy aircraft (E/A) that resulted in a damaged or a destroyed. Details would include where the enemy aircraft was hit, how many rounds were fired, and whether other aircraft in the squadron were involved in combat. The reports provided first hand commentary of the war and were used to verify any claims made by pilots.

S/Ldr JM Checketts of 485 (NZ) Squadron recorded in his Combat Report for 15 July 1943: National Archives of the UK
When we were over the Forêt de Crécy on our way back to England at 20,000 feet, I saw five FW190s at about 15,000 feet flying straight and level in the direction of Fécamp. They saw us and turned towards Gris Nez, and I ordered the section I was leading, Green Section, and White Section to go down on to them. We went down on to them and I fired at one of them from line astern without seeing any results. Immediately after this, we were jumped by 15–20 190s and I asked my Black Section and 341 Squadron for assistance. We avoided the initial attack and I managed to get a shot at one of them from 300 yards astern. I closed to 100 yards and saw strikes on the port mainplane close to the fuselage. I continued firing and suddenly he rolled

slowly onto his back and went straight down with flames streaming from all round his belly. By this time we were down to 5,000 feet and were attacked again by four 190s and climbed rapidly up to 23,000 feet. My No 2, F/Sgt Kearins, did not climb hard enough and was hit and started to stream glycol. I called to him to climb and bale out but apparently he did not hear me for the FW190 closed to very close range and shot him down in flames, blowing his tail off. I also saw a FW190 hit the beach just north of the Somme Estuary. The pilot had baled out and was being guarded during his parachute descent by another FW190, which I attacked but was attacked myself and forced to break. I turned for home and lost height reaching Dungeness at 2000 feet. I claim one FW190 destroyed.

F/O JD Rae of 485 (NZ) Squadron recorded in his Combat Report for 15 July 1943: National Archives of the UK
I was flying Black 3, and after we had come down from 20,000 to 15,000 ft to attack five FW190s, two more 190s tried to get behind Black 1 and 2, so I and Black 4 made a head-on attack at them. As they passed by after our attack, Black 4 swung round on to the leading aircraft but was himself attacked by 4 FW190s. I dived in to attack and, after several turns and dogfights, I made a 30-degree attack from 450–500 yards, closing to about 400 yards. The E/A went over on its back and then went straight down streaming thick smoke. This was witnessed by Black 4. After several more inconclusive dogfights with about 12 FW190s, I became separated from the rest of the squadron, and managed to get on to one of the 190s. I attacked from 30 to 10 degrees closing from 400 to 100 yards at ground level. I saw strikes on his port wing root and on the port of his fuselage and on the engine. The E/A's engine appeared to stop entirely and I nearly rammed him as I overshot and turning, I saw him crash in flames from 500 ft as considerable height had been lost in this combat. During these actions I made a few wild short bursts. I claim 1 FW190 probably destroyed and 1 FW190 destroyed.

Biggin Hill
Saturday, 24 July 1943

Dear Mum, Dad and Girls,

The weather the past week has been typically English – rotten! It has been on the deck with no rain to clear it.

I wrote my previous letter from Katie's when on leave. The last two days I went back to Fergie's. The first afternoon I spent playing around with the car,

Old Jail Hotel

mending a puncture and changing wheels around. I think I'll try and get a couple of retreads as she is going so well. The trip from Fergie's means coping with a rather steep and long hill, which is a bit of a strain on the old blitzer – her maximum speed in such conditions is very little over 5 mph. The second day John Dasent came down from London and a fellow by the name of Bing. Old Bing is a typical Oxted resident and took us home for a drink after a game of golf. He had no beer at all but we were not too proud to clean up his pre-war sherry. He was very lucky and bought up a cellar full of grog and has got piles of Champagne ready for the Day of Peace – what a day that will be.

While I was away – just my luck – the boys twice ran into Huns and we got two destroyed, three probables and a few damaged. The first few days after leave we did the odd show but it was generally uneventful. One day we got among them and chased them upstairs where another of our mob was waiting for them and they got the pickings and we got nothing.

The weather being duff has produced 'release' and numerous parties. We have only been to London once and that was about a week ago. Marty Hume, Mick Maskill, Gibby and Garry Barnett and self intended to go to a picture and then return, but we could not get into the flicks so we went round the hotels had a meal at the Boulogne Restaurant in Gerrard Street, where you can get a feed of ravioli, half a lobster and raspberries with lager or wine very reasonably.

Gun Harmonisation, Biggin Hill. Armourers adjust gun on Spitfire IXB of 341 Free French Squadron. IMPERIAL WAR MUSEUM IMAGE CH018603

After a feed we caught the train back as far as Hayes and first went to the Country Club and then a place called the Crooked Billet – a spot of ill repute. Sunday and Monday were nights of rest and nothing much happened. Tuesday we all went down to the local – The Jail, of all names – and had the odd noggin. Wednesday night was one of the best parties I've been to for many a day. The whole squadron was there in their true colours. The party started when the Navy brought down a supply of Wrens to do a bit of liaison with the boys. At 11 the WAAFs from Operations arrived and I spent most of the evening dancing with one we knew as Jean. She is a great girl and it was not until the next morning I found out that her name is The Lady Jean.[66]

The night before last we had a party at Oxted at Soutrow's, a great affair held in his barn. We were released early in the afternoon so John Dasent and I went down in the 8.9 and played another round of golf before the fun commenced. It was a grand show especially as the release did not run out till nearly midday.

Tons of love to all the mob,

Doug.

66 Lady Jean Bruce. Her father, Edward Bruce, was the 10th Earl of Elgin.

27 July 1943 was a successful day for the wing. The operation was high cover for 12 Marauder medium bombers attacking Triqueville Aerodrome. The Germans were active with about 30 FW190 entering the fray. 341 Free French Squadron destroyed five FW190 and 485 was accredited with four, with no loss to us. Bruce Gibbs was attacked and put the nose down with two 190s on his tail. His speed was such that the effect of him aggressively pulling back on the stick increased the incident angle of each wing and permanently bent them both – the port by 10 degrees and the starboard by 13 degrees. Under these circumstances one 'blacks out'. Gibby recovered flying upside down and fortunately his two adversaries had disappeared.

The following Combat Reports give a perspective of the same joint operation involving five pilots from two squadrons: Combat Reports, 27 July, During High Cover for Marauders to Triqueville

Sgt/Chef P H Closterman of 341 (Free French) Squadron recorded in his Combat Report for 27 July 1943: National Archives of the UK AIR50/132

I was flying as Yellow 2. Going north-west out of the sun at 21,000 feet, I saw two FW190s followed by four more. My No 1 engaged the first whilst I fired a short burst at the second from 600 yards with no observed results. By now, the first FW came into my sights, my No 1 having gone over to attack the second. Giving him three short bursts using from 30–10 degrees deflection from 300–200 yards, I saw strikes all round the cockpit with volumes of black smoke issuing from him. As the Boche went down in a dive upside down completely out of control, I broke away and fired a quick burst at another FW190, and came up above another on which I dived firing a series of short bursts using 1½ ring deflection and closing to within 10 yards when I passed behind him. By now, thick black smoke was coming from him. Pulling out of the dive, I flew parallel with him and saw the pilot jettison the cockpit cover and bale out.

Capitaine C Martell of 341 (FF) Squadron recorded in his Combat Report for 27 July 1943: National Archives of the UK AIR50/132

I was flying as Yellow 1 leading my Section to the assistance of 485 Squadron who were engaged by approximately 14–20 FW190s. Seeing two FW 190s with others behind coming head on, I gave the leader a short burst and immediately climbed to starboard opening fire at the second after manoeuvring behind him from 250 yards closing to 150 yards seeing strikes on the cockpit and wing with black smoke coming from it. The plane burst into flames and went down. Breaking away in a turn, I easily got up with one of the other Boche opening fire at 300 yards with a short burst and closed in a dive to 200 yards firing again till I was within 100 yards. Cannon shells were hitting the Hun all over the fuselage; a large piece of the E/A came away and a sheet of flame issued from the cockpit. Further pieces flew off and I disengaged as, in my opinion, the Boche was finished. Two FW190s destroyed.

F/Sgt W Strahan of 485 (NZ) Squadron recorded in his Combat Report for 27 July 1943: National Archives of the UK AIR50/159
I was flying White 4 when, near Triqueville at 8000 feet, I saw a FW190 turning towards me on my port side from slightly above. I turned into him and opened fire at approximately 300 yards and 20 degrees. I saw a strike just below the windshield and then a large orange flame burst from around the cockpit. The aircraft went into a spin with black smoke pouring from the engine and I saw it hit the ground south-west of Triqueville. I claim one FW190 destroyed.

F/O JD Rae of 485 (NZ) Squadron recorded in his Combat Report for 27 July 1943: National Archives of the UK AIR50/159
Ramrod south east of Triqueville and further inland 18:40 hours.
When flying as Black 3 in the above area at approximately 20000 feet several E/A approached from 6 o'clock slightly above. As a squadron we climbed into them. After manoeuvring for position I picked out 4 menacing FW190s above and climbed after them. One after another flicked away downwards attempting to lure us obviously under instruction from their leader. I continued to climb up however and the FW190 leading found himself alone and then realising his predicament nosed over and dived vertically down. I gave chase with Black 4 still right with me. A long chase resulted with extensive low flying. The FW190 tried every trick he knew from flying under high tension cables to going round church steeples, but could not shake us off. My cannons both had stoppages although I observed strikes with the machine gun and slight smoking. I decided that Black 4 who had stayed with me magnificently could finish him off. So I flew formation with the FW190 and had the pleasure of watching Black 4 blast him into the ground with a short burst. In the first engagements I fired on other E/As one of which I observed to smoke profusely but this may have been caused by boost.

P/O HS Tucker report of the same action:
I was flying Black 4 throughout the above engagement observing all that took place. On request from Black 3 I continued the attack from 10 degrees. Only a short burst was necessary. Cannon strikes were seen along the fuselage especially in the cockpit and engine. He then exploded into the ground.

Gun Harmonisation. Small outer disk for machine guns, large inner for cannon, upper disk represents pilot's reflector sight. IMPERIAL WAR MUSEUM IMAGE CH018605

On 28 July 1943 we were to act as high cover to Bostons bombing Schiphol, Amsterdam. This trip was on the limit of our range so we flew to Coltishall in Norfolk to refuel. As the trips extended further inland it became easier for the Germans to attack the bombers and the intensity of flak increased. On this occasion, despite the German aggression, all the bombers returned home. We made no claims.

Combat Report: 31 July, during high cover for Marauders to Triqueville

**S/Ldr JM Checketts of 485 (NZ) Squadron recorded in his Combat Report for
31 July 1943: National Archives of the UK**
I was leading Green Section of 485 (NZ) Squadron near Triqueville. At approximately 16.45 hours I sighted 14 E/A comprising FW190s and Me109Gs coming from inland at 19,000 feet to attack the Marauders. I ordered my squadron to attack in sections and Black and White Sections went in to attack. I stayed above and after a few minutes, saw two FW190Gs orbiting. I made an attack on the No 2 and the No 1 promptly made off. I fired at the Me109 and he evaded, losing height. I made several attacks but he broke each time and I blacked out. I finally damaged him at 5000 feet and he dived down to the ground. I broke away and saw no other E/A so I went down after him again. I got on his tail and opened fire from 200 yards. I saw my cannon strikes hit the field ahead and below and lifted my nose and hit him full in the cockpit. The E/A hit the tops of some apple trees and caught fire and fell in

the orchard and finally skidded into a barn. I took a cine film of the fire. My No 2 F/O Gaskin confirms seeing this E/A destroyed as does Comm Mouchotte, of 341 Squadron also. I claim 1 Me109G destroyed.

Biggin Hill
Monday, 2 August 1943

Dear Mum, Dad and Girls,

The past ten days over here have been really grand with cloudless skies and very hot days, which meant plenty of work for us. We have, generally speaking, not found the Hun at all, but on a show about a week ago the Hun fighters turned up and as you have no doubt heard, as the R/T conversation was broadcasted in the 'news', the wing – two squadrons of us – destroyed, nine for no loss, which is pretty fair going. It was a good scrap[67] and though I made no claim I had a few odd shots. The poor old Hun must have wondered what in the hell he had struck as we were sailing along straight and level when we saw them in the distance and Johnnie called out to us 'Throttle back and let them catch up' which we did, and, when they were nearly in range, we opened out and climbed like blazes leaving poor old Jerry nicely below. Then the fun started. Jack Rae and Tommy Tucker chased one to the ground and Jack's guns stopped on him so he formatted on the Hun and left Tuck to the rest, which he did very well and the Hun found himself sitting in a large-sized fire in the middle of a French town. Johnnie got two and one of the sergeants the other.

Next morning we got among the Huns again but we frightened them and only got a destroyed and a damaged. My No 2 and I had bad luck as I stalked five of them and just as I was delivering the attack four of our boys came in and the Huns disappeared smartly.

The other show[68] we ran into them was the day before yesterday also to Triqueville and again I had quite a fair crack at a Hun but could not quite get on to him so all he got was a good fright and maybe a bullet or two in his wings. Johnnie got another and Gibby a damaged. Johnnie's was spectacular. He chased Jerry to the ground and when he finally got him the Hun went smack into the middle of an orchard, cutting down some poor French farmer's

67 Combat Reports 27 July 1943.
68 Combat Report 31 July 1943.

apple trees and collected a barn at the end of the field which carried on with him and made a good bonfire. The squadron has had a good week – six destroyed and the odd damaged for no loss. I've had bad luck so far but my turn will come. Johnnie Checketts got his DFC yesterday which he more than deserves as he has now got seven destroyed.

As far as social activity is, it has been more or less off the cards as we have been going from dawn to dusk. We did let ourselves go last Thursday when the Ops girls put on a party. I took the night off as I had done nine shows running – Garry being on leave. I'll always remember that do and I took Her Ladyship Jean Bruce out or rather she took me, seeing it was their party. I hit bed at about 4.30 a.m. as did five or six others and just as they were getting into their pyjamas the phone went telling them to get up for breakfast and briefing – did I have a laugh as I gently got out of bed at midday.

Cheerio for now,

Doug

The four Combat Reports below track the progress of the same action through the eyes of one section of the squadron. Of the eight Messerschmitts, six were destroyed. Four burning on the ground and two disappeared in black smoke with fragments of plane scattering. This took place at 400 mph over Lille-Merville. With cannon fire lasting only a few seconds the battle was over in a minute.

Combat Reports for 9 August

S/Ldr JM Checketts of 485 (NZ) Squadron recorded in his Combat Report for 9 August 1943: National Archives of the UK
While leading Green Section 485 (NZ) Squadron, I sighted four E/A 5,000 feet below approximately, in the Lille–Merville area, and I led my section down to attack. When I got there, there were eight Me109s and I attacked the port one of the line abreast formation. This E/A was fired at from 200/250 yards at 10,000 feet and blew up. I shifted over to the starboard one, because the Hun formation turned 45 degrees port without seeing us. I opened fire at 200 yards and he blew to pieces, and I had trouble avoiding the debris. I then closed on the next E/A and I fired from about 250–300 yards and observed only machine gun strikes so I gave him another burst and he also

shed pieces and burst into flames. I called frantically to my No 2, 3 and 4 to help me and I closed on the extreme starboard one, the others selecting their targets. Just then, one Hun saw us and dived away; I closed on my target and was almost line abreast of F/O Rae's target when I fired. I observed heavy strikes and pieces flew off, and just then, F/O Rae's Hun blew up beside me. F/O Gibb's one, which was about 20 yards from the port side of F/O Rae's, shed cowlings and turned over on his back with his flaps down and started to burn. I looked round for F/O Tucker, and saw a Hun going down in flames. I presume he shot it down. I called my Section together and we returned to base. Green Section reported fires on the ground. I claim three Me109s destroyed and one probably destroyed.

F/O JD Rae of 485 (NZ) Squadron recorded in his Combat Report for 9 August 1943: National Archives of the UK

While as Green 2, I followed Green 1 (S/Ldr Checketts) into the attack of 8 Me109s which were about 10,000 feet, i.e. 9000 feet below us and to the port side heading inland. They were flying a close line abreast formation with one E/A slightly behind and to the port of the formation. Green 1 dived slightly below and behind this formation and then climbed up behind the trailing E/A and opened fire; the E/A commenced burning and then came to pieces as it fell away. Green Leader then swung across to the starboard E/A and again opened fire. This E/A disintegrated and Green 1 appeared enveloped in debris. He then closed into the next E/A on the starboard side and after a short burst, this third E/A fell away enveloped in flames. Up to this juncture in the proceedings, I had remained behind my Leader as I felt that this party was just too good to be true, but after having a final look behind, decided that I might as well pick one off too. The next E/A in line on the Starboard side apparently saw Green Leader as he broke away and so, at the same time as Green 1 was closing on his next victim, I was attacking the Leader who was slightly ahead of the others and Green 3 was attacking the E/A on my port side also. I opened fire at about 250 yards dead astern, gave about 2 second burst, and this E/A exploded. I had another half second burst from about 200 yards, more with the intention of obtaining a picture, and he disintegrated even more and pieces flew past my cockpit. In breaking from the engagement and rejoining Green 1, I observed his last victim falling in an inverted spin; this one I understood Green Leader claims as probable. I also observed the result of Green 3's attack; his E/A had large pieces falling from it and flaps and wheels appeared to be down and it was burning.

F/O BE Gibbs of 485 (NZ) Squadron recorded in his Combat Report for 9 August 1943: National Archives of the UK

I was flying Green 3 to Squadron Leader Checketts in Lille area at 19,000 feet, when he reported four E/A at nine o'clock below. He led Green Section down below and astern of the E/A, which were identified as eight Me109s. He then fired at the port A/C, which blew up. Crossing over to the starboard A/C, he again fired and this A/C was also seen to shed pieces and explode. Selecting his third E/A on the starboard side, he gave it a burst, which set it on fire. F/O Rae, Green 2, F/O Tucker, Green 4, and myself, each selected one of three E/A, which were flying in line abreast. I fired at the port A/C observing strikes by cannon fire all over fuselage and wing roots followed by large explosion. This A/C rolled over on its back with flaps down and caught fire. My attack was from dead astern, 250 yards range and about 2½ seconds burst.

P/O HS Tucker of 485 (NZ) Squadron recorded in his Combat Report for 9 August 1943: National Archives of the UK

I was flying Green 4 to S/Ldr Checketts when, at 19,000 feet in Lille area, he reported 4 E/A at nine o'clock below. He then led Green Section down to below and astern of the E/A which were identified as eight Me109s. After S/Ldr Checketts had shot three of the E/A down and was selecting a fourth, F/O Rae, F/O Gibbs and myself attacked the remaining three. I attacked from about 30 degrees, range about 350 yards, and gave a short burst. I observed strikes on the engine and cockpit, and cowlings flew off the E/A and after streaming black smoke, the E/A burst into flames. I also saw F/O Rae's and F/O Gibbs' E/A blow to pieces and after turning back for the coast, saw four fires on the ground.

Biggin Hill
Tuesday, 17 August 1943

Dear Mum, Dad and Girls,

Since last writing I've had five days leave. John Dasent and I spent it together, most of the time in Oxted with Fergie. The first night we went to the local cinema taking Mrs Fergie and Fergie with us, after which we had a few beers followed by supper. We were up fairly early next morning and had a round of golf before lunch after which we came back to the drome to have a bit of a party, as the boys ran into some mugs the night before and got six Huns for none. We went back to Oxted that afternoon. Next day, John and I went to London with Norman Roberts who has just arrived over here and is a great pal of Fergie's. We had a spot of lunch when we got there and a few beers going to the Matinée show of Lupino Lane's, which was very amusing. After the show we had a few beers and went to the Boulogne for supper, and then did a bit of a pub crawl, getting a train from Victoria shortly after nine. We spent the next day on the golf course and in the evening went to the pictures again – a very quiet leave.

On Saturday night the Frenchmen threw a party at the Hyde Park Hotel and a very well-organised do it was. As my car is getting new tyres on it, Mick Maskill and I borrowed Marty Hume's Morris Ten and set course for London following the Winco. All went well till we got a bit north of Bramley and we had to apply the brakes in a hurry. After that everything seemed to go wrong and we could get no power out of the car at all and we thought she must be pretty bad when the tram cars started to pass us. Nevertheless, we kept plugging along and eventually reached our destination. When we got out we thought we were on fire as there was smoke issuing out from both the rear wheel hubs. All we could do was park the thing and go off and have a meal. Some two hours later we came back, gave the car a test and it was perfectly OK though I expect the strippers are pretty well worn out. Anyway she took us home OK which was all we wanted.

We have done two shows a day the past few days without any excitement and this morning I was not on the show but they met a few Huns and Jack Rae got a destroyed and a probable.

We had Bill Jordan and a few of the big wigs here while I was on leave and they took a row of pictures though my pretty face will not appear – probably a good thing. I expect you heard yours truly as a radio man again. We had quite a mob here and I had to say the odd word or two. We put all the names in a hat and I was one of the mugs drawn out. I made sure I had a script this time so that all I had to do was sit and read.

Cheerio for now,

Love, Doug

With the recent successes the wing was becoming over confident and as a result had a number of close calls. Whenever we ran into Huns we broke into pairs and although we didn't know it at the time, it made us vulnerable on defence.

An example of this occurred on 22 August. The squadron acted as withdrawal cover to 36 Marauders bombing Beaumont Aerodrome. Johnnie Checketts led the squadron and Bruce Gibbs and I were flight leaders. As we crossed the coast north of Le Havre at 20,000 feet, Ops advised us there were '40 plus bandits ahead and

Bill Jordan (NZ High Comm), John Checketts, Bruce Gibbs, Jack Rae, Tommy Tucker – a few days before Jack Rae was shot down

below.' There were indeed 40 FW190s, however, the squadron was attacked from above despite previous advice that they were below us. We broke and attacked but in the battle we lost four: Jack Rae, Mac Sutherland, Chalky White and Snow Clark, who was killed. Most of us fired our guns but there was no chance of a result. Fortunately the Huns did not hang around even though they had superior numbers. The eight of us remaining pressed on as cover for the Marauders.

Jack Rae had engine failure. He and Chalky White both made a wheels-up landing in France.

Bert Wipiti, a young Maori lad who had been flying in Singapore joined us in August. He was up with Sailor Malan our G/C as No 2 one day and Sailor had been hit and was making a forced wheels-up landing. Wipiti called out on the R/T and said, 'Excuse me, Sir, you haven't got your wheels down.' This caused a lot of amusement and Sailor dined out on this one for a long time.

L eslie Samuel McQueen 'Chalky' White, had a 350 acre farm at the Waikaka Valley, Gore. Before the war he had the world sheep-shearing record of 432 sheep in eight and a half hours. Chalky had been with us a year when he was shot down.

Chalky briefly evaded capture but was then caught and held under guard by a German Corporal from whom he was able to overpower and escape. He spent the next few days hiding by day and in the evening knocking on doors. With the exception of one household he was given food and drink but not encouraged to stay.

In Errol Brathwaite's book *Pilot on the Run*, Chalky mentioned there were three German FW190s on the ground. He put this down to contributing to his evading capture as the Germans focused on looking after their own casualties. Following the mêlée we had made no claims despite the Hun planes downed in the skirmish. I had fired at a couple but didn't see any strikes so I didn't claim. Fighter Command had been accused in the past of making too many claims so we had become wary of this and probably were more conscious of under claiming. It is possible some of the German planes had been shot down by the four pilots we lost. In *Pilot on the Run* Chalky describes shooting down one FW190 before he in turn was attacked. His engine was overheating so he decided to force land when another four came at him. Film of Chalky's plane on the ground indicated the guns were still capped. It remains unclear who got the kills as the film was not perfect.

In our briefings on escape we were advised to approach humble dwellings but Chalky soon became frustrated with rejection and hunger so he approached a large château. The lady owner not only spoke English but fed him and hosted him for the night despite the rest of the château being occupied by Germans. She put him in touch with a guide to initiate his escape through Spain. At the border there was a scuffle and Chalky had no option but to shoot a German guard. His troubles were still not over as he made his way through Franco-controlled Spain to Gibraltar. Just before take off from Gibraltar he was offloaded in preference for some more important-looking officials. Unfortunately for them the plane plunged into the sea. Chalky took the next flight and after formalities in the UK made his way back to 485 Squadron.

After the war, Chalky married Lorna and farmed a large holding in Ruatoria, near Gisborne. He was one of the great characters in 485 Squadron. The farmhouse was at the end of a meandering rutted track a fair distance from the main road. At the main gate hung a large sign 'close the fucking gate' and 'salesmen by appointment only'. Those that did dare penetrate the defences and made it to the cattle-stop at the house with their vehicle still in working order were greeted by a pile of old bones resembling a skeleton and another sign 'last salesman lies here'.

Biggin Hill
Monday, 30 August 1943

Dear Mum, Dad and Girls,

We have done quite a bit of flying, but whenever I've been up we have never run into anything, except one day when we ran into the Hun and we were rather outnumbered and did not come off well. We lost Chalky White, Mac Sutherland, Snowy Clark and Jack Rae. Jack had called up for a fix and said he had engine trouble and was coming home. A minute or so later he called up as casual as the day and said he was landing over there. On the way down he said, 'Say goodbye to the chaps for me.' I retorted that we would send his dirty washing on to him. I don't think I've seen so many Huns in my life, and thank God I had such a good aircraft to keep me out of trouble. I only got in a small squirt but saw no results. Jack ranks as one of the best fighter pilots over here at present. It was bad luck as he was due for promotion to Flight Lieutenant the next day.

The day operations nowadays are extensive. We have mainly been doing cover for bombers. This month I've been on ten trips doing high cover to Marauders into France bombing areas like St Omer, Beaumont and Triqueville. Also high cover and escort to Fortresses. The bombers are a great sight. We ran into Huns a few times but I did not get among them and the only ones I got really close to were head-on jobs.

The bomber boys are also going well at night. Bomber trips are expected to intensify over the coming months – weather permitting! I'm glad they went to Berlin the other night. Give them no mercy! The Russians seem to be plodding forwards and any idea of an offensive on the part of the Germans seems to have petered out – in other words, they have had it.

Funny that Peg should mention a fellow Ainge whom she 'maltreated' while executing her physio duties, as his brother is in the squadron and a real lad he is.

Ken Lee's wife has just arrived over here. She was Marjorie Hughen before they married and lived just next to the Mt Eden Fire Station.

I've not been off the station for the past few weeks except for one day when I was not feeling the best, so I went down to Oxted and had a round of golf with Fergie and followed it with a steak. The car is now serviceable once again with a couple of new tyres – now all it needs is a new body and a new engine!

Well, folks, there seems to be no more news so I will buzz off,

Doug

Marty and I were at the local pub one day when a lass came up and said 'Hello Brownie.' I looked at Marty and he in turn at me. I could not recall immediately who she was or where we had met, but she was somewhat larger than life – some months pregnant! We hadn't recognised her as the last time we had met she was in WAAF uniform. It transpired the prospective father was one of our boys. We had a chat for a while and put two and two together but I did not have the heart to tell her he had been killed on operations.

Some of the boys got themselves into terrible trouble with the ladies. However, it has to be said, 'it takes two to tango'.

One of the lads was engaged to three girls at the same time and one of them was apparently about to produce a child. 'Brownie, what will I do?' he confided in me. Of course, I could offer no suggestions. However, for better or worse, he was shot down and disappeared from the scene for a while. On his return he decided to do the decent thing and knocked on the door of his 'fiancée' but the greeting he received was the door slammed in his face. It transpired she had not been pregnant and the passage of time had got him out of his predicament. Unfortunately in the interim he had sent a letter to his family in NZ advising of his imminent marriage and fatherhood!

It was not uncommon for forces men to be caught out. There was another who had supposedly caused some 'embarrassment' to one lass to the extent that it was going to cost £68 to terminate the pregnancy. The fellow was in a terrible state and sold his car, watch and camera to produce the necessary funds to resolve the issue. We never saw her again – I am convinced it was a ruse to extract some funds from the Kiwi pilot.

Biggin Hill
Sunday, 12 September 1943

Dear Mum, Dad and Girls,

Today is a typically English day, plenty of fog or rather mist which tried to clear up at about midday with no luck, and it looks as though there will be nothing cooking. If I know it, this weather will hang about for a day or so yet, which will be very annoying – I don't mind one day of it but after that I'm bored stiff with lack of flying.

I attained one of the ambitions of my life this week and am now a Flight Commander with the squadron – Acting Flight Lieutenant Brown. To tell

ABOVE Doug with his high-powered 8.9

BELOW Gary Barnett, Mick Maskill, Murray Metcalfe, Peter Gaskin in front of the 8.9

you the truth I thought I would never get it as there are so many substantive Flight Lieutenants in the RAF nowadays. My substantive F/Lt is not due for about a year, which is a long way off. It was mainly due to Al Deere, Hawk Wells, Jamie Jameson and Bill Compton that I got it – they all know me well as I've flown with them. I've found it rather expensive and have had 'shouts' demanded of me left, right and centre. As it is an acting rank, when I go on 'rest' at the end of my tour I am liable to lose the rank. It was probably the same way in the last war with you, Dad. We had bad luck in losing Johnnie

Checketts last week. We were on high cover to Marauders near Rouen. He got a Hun and went after another and one of the boys saw him get it from a 109 but he baled out.

We have heard Jack Rae was caught and is a guest of Stalag Luft III. Apparently he is very much disliked by the Huns for the continual mischief he gets into in the POW camp. The bar to his DFC, which he well deserves, came through yesterday. Marty Hume is now CO.

We have been fairly lucky with the weather and have done quite a few shows and now I'll be on practically every one. The Huns have been scarce, and if we do get a bounce, they do not stay long and go smartly towards ground to get home quickly. Gone are the days when they outnumber us.

The news from Italy was grand.[69] Hitler and his Hun compatriots must be having an odd amount of worry on all fronts. The Russians seem to be plodding along as well, and my one wish is that they get amongst the Hun population before we do – as you have always said, Dad, 'There is only one good Hun and that is a dead 'un!'

Our social activities have been curbed due to the need to be near the drome and I've been restricted mostly to the Country Club up the road at Hayes. I went up to London the day before yesterday when we got a release, and I was so depressed with the place when I got there I bought a pair of shoes and came home again. I paid 4/6d for a seat at the flicks but the seats were so rotten we came out again smartly and went to the News Cinema. The day Johnnie was shot down I went down and saw Fergie. I had a steak and a few beers, and watched him at work with the Home Guard. Quite a few of the boys went down to Oxted to a party last night, but I did not go as I had a date in the local village.

I saw Noble Lowndes the other day when he came up to the mess to see us, and I asked him if he had gone to Samoa with your lot last time and it is the fellow who was with you right enough, Dad. He asked me to give you his very best regards. We have not been up to his place for a meal of late as they are having alterations done to the house. Last time I was there we had, after a terrific meal, melons which he grows himself – very tasty, very sweet!

The car is going like a bomb and has given no trouble at all. Mick Maskill has joined the club and bought an MG.

Cheerio,

Doug

69 Armistice between Allies and Italy declared on 8 September 1943.

Mick Maskill was quite a lad particularly when it came to pyrotechnics. One of Mick's great bar tricks was to fill his mouth with lighter fluid and then blast out a flame of a few feet. While we were at Biggin Hill we had an adjutant who was renowned for dozing off while he was reading the newspaper. Mick would creep up with his cigarette lighter and 'put it to the flame'. Adj would wake up rather startled.

He finished the war as CO of Number 1 Squadron, replacing Johnnie Checketts.

Mick had various interests after the war, ending up as a 'maltster' at the Castlemaine Brewery in Brisbane. Eve and I had a wild day and night with Mick, Flower his wife, and family, starting at the brewery and then at his home. He died of throat cancer around 1970.

Biggin Hill
Sunday, 26 September, 1943

Dear Mum, Dad and Girls,

I'm afraid I have not much news for you this fortnight, mainly because I've spent the last nine days in sick quarters. If the hospital was not full up, I'd be there, so I'm thankful for that. As far as the sickness goes, it is not very serious but can be readily passed on. I've got a mild attack of dysentery and I've got myself to blame for it. Early last week the boys started to 'spend pennies' regularly and at short intervals. It must have been something we had eaten in the mess or something we caught from one of the boys back from the ME.

Most of them went smartly to the MO and had a good dose of castor oil and were off for a day or so. As we were short-handed I did not take the dose but flew for the next four days until a few of them were OK. When I was tested the result was that I had dysentery – what a thought, and bad luck just when I had got the flight. Three of us are in 'Clink' – Al Deere, Red Roberts and yours truly. I've built up the reading hours and think when I get out I'll be able to write quite a successful murder. I should be pretty fit too as I've not had beer for two weeks now. Before I came in here I had no inclination to drink beer at all. I went to a party one night and did not have a single drink. Our other main occupation is crossword puzzles – the *Telegraph* and the *Times* and with all day to think we get quite a bit done. From last Saturday when I came in till a couple of days ago we had no cure except a light diet, mainly because the dope which is the cure – sulphur something or other – is sent to other theatres of war where the disease is more prevalent. We have now got the pills and with any luck I should be on my feet again in a day or so. Food, not that I'm very hungry, consists of buttered toast and tea for breakfast, lunch, tea and supper, so there is no fear of putting on too much weight. I expect I will need an overhaul when I get out of here! One really annoying part of being stuck in here is that during the past five or six days the weather has been perfect, not a cloud in the sky – I think this will be the last good spell we will have till next year – what luck! The squadron has been doing well and the last two days the wing accounted for three each day without loss.

I led the squadron for the first time on just a couple of days before I came into this place. The next day we did quite a good show as high cover to Marauder bombers to Beaumont Le Roger. My tummy was giving me hell so I nearly turned back but as Huns were plotted I persevered. Our squadron ran into about 20 Jerries above so we opened up and climbed up behind them. You would hardly believe it unless you saw it, but when they spotted us they stuck their noses down and headed for Paris – too far inland for us to follow. 20 against 12 with height and they go home – I don't know! Later on Gibby and his section which was a bit behind us got amongst some and the four of them accounted for three but unfortunately lost Murray Metcalfe – a great pity as apart from being a grand chap he was a good pilot. He was shot down while attacking a Hun, which was eventually destroyed. Prior to this we had not seen Jerry for a week or so.

I've got a damn good mob of chaps in the flight and for the most part very experienced which is an asset. I only hope I don't have to lose them for being in sick quarters.

Love to all,

Doug

Towards the end of my time at Biggin Hill it got to the stage that every time we flew we made a mess in our pants. Even worse, we couldn't hold a beer down! Al Deere and I were in the bar and Doc Thomson came along to Al and said, 'Excuse me, Sir, I want you to go to hospital.' Al replied in the normal manner and said, 'I'm not going to any bloody hospital.' To which Doc added, 'Well, Sir, if you don't go to hospital you could well be dead in three days – and that goes for you too, Brownie.'

That was the end of the tour for me. I went to hospital with amoebic dysentery. Most of us who got it went on a course of sulphur tablets which seemed to cure it.

On the day we were certified 'unfit' John Ainge and Bert Wipiti were shot down while the squadron engaged enemy aircraft over Cayeux-sur-Mer, on the coast near Abbeville. F/O Mortimer was shot down and escaped through France and Sergeant Frehner baled out, was picked up and returned to the squadron.

*

A Fighter Command First Tour was supposed to be a 350-hour operation. Like many others, I was well over that and was close to 500 hours. We used to rig our returns. Every month we put in a return that was generally not looked at. When at about 280, we would put in lesser returns, for example 250, 230, and so on. Once in hospital the log books were checked, the figures reconciled, and that's when we got caught out. My second tour, however, was only about 150 hours.

Although I did around 280 trips altogether, some were only about 30 minutes. We might be on readiness, receive a scramble, see nothing and come back. In a normal trip in a Spit we carried 94 gallons of fuel, which gave a range of 90 minutes. There were some close calls with the fuel gauge on empty and the occasional dead prop landing.

For D-Day we got 45-gallon supplementary tanks which extended our range to over two and a half hours, and with the Spitfire XIVs we had 90-gallon supplementary tanks which took us out to over three hours. During the build up to D-Day we were sometimes doing three trips a day which increased our hours rapidly.

485 Squadron, October 1943, Hornchurch. Bill Crawford-Compton (cap under arm) was Winco Hornchurch at that time

485 Squadron

*

AFTER MY DEPARTURE

M Y FLIGHT WAS TAKEN OVER BY LINDSAY BLACK. He was a top-notch chap and we spent many a 'happy and hectic time' together. He was killed near the end of the war.

485 Squadron moved on to Hornchurch where it was for about a month. Bill Crawford-Compton was Wing Commander. Marty Hume took what was left up to Drem near Edinburgh to regroup until the end of February 1944 when the unit returned to Hornchurch.

Johnny Niven, a Scot, became CO when 485 moved back down to 11 Group based at a number of dromes in the south near Beachy Head. He took them on to France then Johnny Pattison took over as CO in September 1944.

Lindsay Black

Of the 'new recruits' who joined 485 in 1944, Max Collett and Owen Hardy are the two I see most. Max plays an indispensable role organising our reunions. Owen had an interesting career with the RAF and has just published his book, *Though My Eyes*. Owen joined 485 following a successful tour in North Africa.

While on the Continent, Des Scott, then the Groupy, Chalky White and one other had somewhat of a scheme going. They would fly to England and purchase goods that were in short supply, such as coffee and tea, and sell them on the black market in France and Germany. On the return journey they loaded up with items of value readily saleable in England either obtained in exchange for the coffee and tea or other means! They must have made a bundle out of this business enterprise.

ABOVE LEFT Group playing cards, seated: Al Stead, Bill Strahan, Doug Clarke, Des Roberts while Chalky White and Tommy Tucker look on

ABOVE RIGHT Back: Lyn Griffith, Chalky White, Tommy Tucker, Bill Compton, _, Bill Strahan, Jack Yeatman, Lindsay Black, Herb Patterson / Front right: JJ Robinson. CO with pipe and five others with cigarettes

ABOVE Flying Officers Mayston and De Touret walk away from their planes with Ground Crew Bongard and Parker looking on.
RNZAF MUSEUM

Bruce Gibbs was a good friend and a great lad. He returned to NZ early in 1944 and flew with the RNZAF in the Pacific. He was based for a while at Seagrove Airfield near Pukekohe and visited us regularly. Gibby and Pat produced four boys and farmed at Utiku near Taihape. He died in the early 1960s. When 'Gibby' left, Ken Lee became A Flight Commander.

Ken Lee and I were good friends before and after the war. I went to King's School and Wanganui Collegiate with Ken. He qualified for a pilot's licence before the war and was accepted in one of the first flying courses. He was retained as an instructor in NZ and was instructing at Whenuapai when I was doing my training there.

It was only through his own determination that he was able to get to UK for operational service with 485 Squadron.

Ken stayed in the RNZAF after the war on the promise of a W/C post on ballistics. This was not forthcoming and he continued his professional career as a lecturer at Auckland School of Engineering where he taught my son Hamish.

Bruce Gibbs (top) and Ken Lee

Doug, Johnny Pattison

John Pattison, a Battle of Britain veteran, was shot down on his second operation and also hospitalised for over a year. He was hit in the arse and couldn't move or bale out so he did a forced landing. He reckoned if he had baled he would have died due to loss of blood. By the end of the war he had completed over 250 sorties during his three tours and been shot down twice with two E/A destroyed to his name.

John and Pauline (ex WAAF) married before returning to NZ and ran a sheep farm in Waipawa.

On 6 June 2004, John received the Légion d'Honneur from Jacques Chirac. This took place at the 60th anniversary commemoration of the Invasion of Normandy in the presence of a number of world leaders gathered at Caen. When President Chirac kissed him on both cheeks, Johnny said to him, 'I'd rather be kissed by one of the girls, Sir!' Vladimir Putin was standing alongside Chirac and by the look on his face certainly appreciated the levity of the comment.

485 Squadron circa August 1944. Left: Lindsay Black, Frank Transom / Mac McInnes, Athol Downer, John Houlton. Right: Johnny Niven, Maurice Mayston, Bill Newenham, Joe Eyre / Herb Patterson, Bill Strahan, Russ Clarke

Aston Down

*

FIGHTER LEADER SCHOOL

Aston Down Command: CO W/C EH Thomas, S/L 'Wag' Haw, S/L Bobbie Hall, F/Lt Michel 'Mike' Donnet, F/Lt Doug Brown – instructors

On 7 October when I recovered from hospital I was posted as an instructor to Fighter Leader School at Aston Down (near Minchinhampton) in Gloucester. It was part of Fighter Command as was Central Gunnery School. Our Wing Commander Tommy Thomas was great company. He had a fox terrier, which he took on operations in his Spitfire.

'Wag' Haw had been posted to Russia in the latter half of 1941 with 81 Hurricane Squadron which was transported on HMS *Argus*. Ramsbottom-Isherwood who helped us when we were stuck in Ireland was Wag Haw's Winco. They were based in Murmansk and trained Soviet pilots to counter the German invasion. Wag, in shooting down the most German planes, was also awarded the Order of Lenin. This entitled him to the extraordinary perk of first-class travel for life – in Russia.

A Belgian, Michel 'Mike' Donnet was born in England in 1917. While serving in the Belgian Air Force he was captured and became a POW. Early in January 1941 he was released and returned to Belgium where a group of friends secretly

CLOCKWISE FROM TOP LET
Michel Donnet in a re-enactment of his historic escape from Belgium in an SV-4B
Michel Donnet (left) and Léon Divoy (right) with colleague at the time of the re-enactment of their historic flight
Instruments made for flight from Belgium to England
Compass used on SV4B

restored a Stampe-Vertongen 4B. On 4 July 1941 Michel Donnet and Sgt Léon Divoy flew from German-occupied Belgium to Britain and joined the RAF. We became good friends, both at FLS, Aston Down and when posted in 1944 to Milfield Pre-Invasion School. In March Mike was posted as Commander of RAF 350 Belgian Squadron. After the war he assumed a number of senior positions including head of the Belgian Air Force as Baron Donnet. He came to NZ in the early 1990s and spent one night with us. For further reading, see *Flight to Freedom*.

Our function was to train future Squadron Commanders and Flight Commanders in operational procedure. We did practical work in the air and theoretical on the ground over a two-week period. After each course we had frequent allocations of leave through to the end of December. We had a Spitfire to fly wherever we wanted to all over England. I went to places like Biggin Hill and visited my old squadron up in Edinburgh; I went to see the Fergusons in Oxted and I would go to Longtown, the aerodrome in Carlisle and stay with the Rickerbys there. This was a well worthwhile bonus to the job.

A Pam Barton came out to New Zealand about 1935 as a member of the ladies golf team and when they were at Wanganui a few of us were invited to play with them at the Belmont Course. I was at Wanganui Collegiate and she would have been a couple of years my senior. In 1936 she held the British and USGA Championship titles. When I was at Kenley Pam Barton was a WAAF officer and I used to play tennis with her as she was a good tennis player as well as golfer.

Shortly after I had arrived at Aston Down I heard she had been killed in an accident. At the time she was based at Manston and had flown with a pilot friend to a dance at Detling some 40 miles distant. Afterwards Pam was due back in Manston where she was on duty. However, in the morning of 13 November, the weather was bad. There was a slight improvement in the conditions so they attempted to take off across an adjacent rugby field. Unfortunately, the Tiger Moth struggled to get off the boggy ground and hit a petrol bowser. She was killed and buried at Margate, Kent. The pilot F/Lt Ruffhead from 184 Squadron survived but was killed on operations over France in January 1944.

Aston Down
Gloucester
Monday, 11 October 1943

Dear Mum, Dad and Girls,

The powers that be have at last caught me out. My first tour is officially over and I'm now on rest so to speak. The hardest part of this outfit will be finding enough news to give you each fortnight as for the next six months day after day, week after week, I will be doing the same thing.

Given that I have to go on rest, this is as good as it gets. I've got 'Hawkeye' Wells to thank for that. I still retain my F/Lt rank and my work is for the most part just flying. I'm an instructor for a school they have had in operation for some time now, which gives 'Advanced Operational Experience' to eligible fighter pilots. There are five instructors flying: a Winco, two S/Leaders and two F/Lieuts as well as a P/O and Naval Officer, a good homely crowd. A number of the boys on the first course I've met previously and they are all on 'op' squadrons. Each course usually lasts about three weeks and when that time is up the instructors get leave from 48 hours to five days to go to a forward drome and get the latest gen or do what we want.

My actual time when they caught up with me was about 480 'ops' hours and I'd done about 180 sweeps. A rest will do me a bit of good and another point is that winter is nearly upon us.

When I last wrote I was safely tucked in between the sheets with dysentery and not exceptionally happy with life. I spent altogether 12 days in the hospital and when I came out they wanted me to take a week's leave. I knocked it down to four days, which I spent with Fergie in a very quiet manner. I intended to go to Katie's but I did not feel 100% so I stayed put and tried to regain the stone and a bit I had lost in weight. One day Fergie took me to Bernard Thorpe's estate near East Grinstead. I had been there before so I gave him an update on how the war was going.

I played golf on three days. The second day up I just managed to play nine holes after which I was absolutely stonkered. I played with our doctor, a Scotsman, who also had a day off and had not played for a couple of years. The first night I was in bed early but I had to go and shoot a line to the local ATC boys who were all ears and eyes as I would have been in their shoes.

When I got back to base at Biggin I was greeted by Mick Maskill, who said, 'Heard the news?', and when I said, 'No', he said, 'You've had it and are going on rest.' He kidded me for a while that I was the only one but later admitted he was also on rest. As the weather was bad during my last couple of days with the boys I did not fly with them again but we had a party or two to see me on my way.

The journey up here was not as bad as I expected. I had a lot of gear to cart along with me and from past experience had some rather dark visions of the journey. However, I only had to change at London and unbelievably porters came to my aid. I got a taxi from Victoria to Paddington, which left me an hour before the train was to go so I got a bit of lunch before my trip west on to my new camp.

This first course should have packed up this week but the weather has been against us.

Well I'll buzz. Give my love to all.

Cheerio,

Doug

Aston Down
Sunday, 24 October 1943

Dear Mum, Dad and Girls,

The weather has had it for the year. If we are lucky the fog clears enough from about one o'clock to get some flying in – even then it is not ideal and many of the valleys around remain full of fog.

At the end of the last course I went to Hornchurch where 485 Squadron is now based. Two of us took the Maggie but, as the weather was no good, I had to go most of the way by tube, which involved a trip of some two hours. All the lads were fit but fed up, having done no shows at all since I left them. They are under Bill Crawford-Compton's command. Lindsay Black jumped at the chance to get my flight. He will be good as he knows the score and had a flight for five months in another squadron. I could not have a better man to replace me. The night I got there the boys were pretty tired after a rather large party the previous night. On Saturday the boys were to go on a show but it was cancelled. I borrowed a Spit to go over to Biggin Hill and find out how the flying was going. They were not particularly enlightening. I wandered into the watch office after I had landed and noticed an NZ boy in there with battle dress and thought I knew him as a fellow who was at Whenuapai with me and got turfed off flying. As I wandered out he came up and introduced himself as Jim Sanders and I knew him to be the chap I trained with. He is over here as an Aerodrome Control Officer.

On Saturday night they had a big party, partly as a welcome, and they imported a few girls from a show in town. The party was a great success with chickens, lobsters and oysters to the fore, though I'm afraid I don't like raw oysters, but I did justice to the other stuff. Al Deere was there with Joan, his fiancée. From what Al said, he is off ops for good and I expect he will join Johnny Pattison and get married. Colin Gray, just back from North Africa, was there and had had a few and was keen to take me on at billiards. It was the first time I've seen Paul Hayward for about eight months and he slung off at me having been taken off ops. I got my own back as the squadron he is in does not do much work except continual readiness so he does not build the hours up. The party was a real success however and next morning I felt very fit!

In the course of the party the previous evening we had a ring from Reg Grant who had just arrived at Noble Lowndes'. I rang Reg up in the morning and asked him if it would be OK if I went over, which Noble affirmed for me in a loud voice. I went up to London with Ken Lee's wife Marge and Chalky White who has just escaped from France. His effort was all the more amazing given the only French word he knew was *anglais*!

I got to Noble's at about one in the afternoon and there was Reg, typical of him, in the kitchen hacking the skin off a pumpkin, as happy as a lark. All he wants to do now is get back to flying. He will be back on a squadron when he gets settled down and will be given a wing. Noble is well and sends his regards to you, Dad. Noble is like you, Dad, and likes his meals to be well cooked. That evening we had a great feed: oxtail soup, corn on the cob with plenty of butter, pepper and salt, cold lamb and salads with a bottle of Burgundy. Reg brought back a bottle of American 'Bourbon' whiskey and he mixed up a drink popular in the Southern States called Mint Julep. I stayed the night at Noble's and after scrambled eggs we went to London. I left Reg at about ten then went back to Hornchurch for lunch with the boys and to collect the Maggie.

The group in the new course is not bad, though a few of them have not got any idea. Hopefully they will when they leave us!

I heard rather a good story the other day: Two Americans went and saw 'Desert Victory' – a film that should be out your way by now. One of them died of shellshock halfway through, the other saw the picture to the bitter end and was awarded the North African Star for his efforts!

Cheerio,

Doug

Aston Down
Saturday, 6 November 1943

Dear Mum, Dad and Girls,

This course finishes tomorrow and we will have a break of about three days. I will probably take a spot of leave while the next course is here and spend a few days with Katie, as I have not seen her for ages. I've written piles of boloney today, writing out repetitive reports for each pilot on the course, whether he is good, bad or indifferent – good for this and that etc. For the most part this course was more or less average, with one or two really good and one or two not so.

Wag Haw, Mike Donnet and I have taken up some serious squash, playing most evenings. I'm not so hot but we get some really good rallies going, after which we sit down and gasp for breath for a minute or so. During these duff days we have had the course playing hockey and basketball and they have been very amusing and tough games. For the hockey, the main thing is to hit the ball either side of the stick – just like the old Manly games. The basketball, so called, seemed to be a cross between rugby, soccer and basketball, the former two being most prevalent. I can see myself losing weight in the near future with all this activity.

Tons of love to all and a Happy Xmas from me. And a Happy New Year!

Doug

Aston Down
Monday, 22 November 1943

Dear Mum, Dad and Girls,

We had a good farewell party for the course and got them off on the Monday. Boozy Sims, Wag and I intended to go to Bath as everyone was away, but Wag was made Station Commander and so that was the end of that jaunt. Next day I took the train to London and had a couple of days with Fergie in the hope of seeing Johnnie Checketts. Unfortunately Johnnie left the day before I arrived and he got back in time for me to say 'how are you' and 'goodbye.' He has been awarded the DSO, which he has certainly earned. He was burned and wounded in one leg when he baled out but was lucky to get among the right people practically as soon as he hit the ground. He had lost his pants on the way down due to fire.

I got back on Thursday afternoon in time to meet the new course, which seem a pretty good crowd and all out for a bit of fun. They got quite a bit of flying in during the first few days, which is a bonus.

I just returned from a week's leave this afternoon, which is the first leave I've had for a few months, and I had quite a good time. Last Tuesday Boozy flew me down to Gatwick. I took the train to Tadworth and got to Katie's just after six. After a couple of days at Leuchs I spent some time in London with Norm Roberts and then went back to Fergie's and finished a pleasant leave at the Thomases with Nadia.

I caught a rotten cold yesterday and I finished off the day with a hot bath, a shot of whiskey, and two more pills. The cold was nearly gone today and I felt much better, though I had a hell of a night and lost buckets of sweat!

I had a letter from Reg Baker just before I went on leave and he is now apparently in Italy. Good luck to him!

Tons of love,

Doug

Aston Down
Monday, 6 December 1943

Dear Mum, Dad and Girls,

A few days ago I came in to the drome at Aston Down and there was snow on both sides of the runway. One tyre burst on landing so I was on one wheel. On losing speed the plane came down on the left wing and the prop broke resulting in a spectacular snow cloud.

The only other excitement I have had while flying was when doing a simulated attack on the squadron of FLS trainees. My wing tip came so close to one of the aircraft that a static electricity flash was created. It could have been a disaster but the only damage was to some paint at the static contact.

The last course finished well, a day before scheduled which was very good indeed for this time of the year. They were a good mob of chaps and did quite well. We had a very good dance that Saturday night before they left. It was not large by any means but everyone was full of beans and let themselves go properly. The bar closed at about 3 a.m. and I made bed at about 4.30. I'm afraid that I did not get up in the morning till about ten but it was duff yet again so it did not matter. The course put a party on for the ground crews on Monday night at the local, which they certainly appreciated. When they broke up last Wednesday, Boozy and I went up with them in the train and met them at Shepherds – the gathering place of the boys nowadays, and had the odd ale to see the evening through. Boozy and I did ourselves proud and stayed at the Park Lane that night, which cost us a packet.

On Thursday I went down to stay with Reg Grant who has now got a mixed squadron at Hornchurch – they are a grand mob of boys and worship Reg. Reg picked me up in his Jeep and we went up to the mess for tea which consisted of pheasant, shot by the boys. After a feed we went back to Smoke and first went to the Kimul club,[70] another RAF rendezvous, where we met Al Deere, Marty Hume, Jack Charles and a few of the fellows from the NZ Headquarters and after the odd ale we went over to Shepherds where there was a terrific mob and as a result quite a party developed.

That evening I went back to Reg's camp for a good night's sleep. The weather was still no good so we went to the pictures in the morning and after lunch we went shooting. We had no dog and nevertheless four of us got five pheasants in just under an hour. As the country was full of bracken you had to practically tread on the birds to put them up. After some tea I went back to London and met Boozy. The next day we went round to Shepherds where we ran into Bill Compton and his mob who had got the day off and spent most of it in Watneys' Brewery – sightseeing they called it! Dickie Barrett, Bobbie Oxspring and a host of others were there. Later in the evening, who should walk in but good old Digger Robertson and he looks very fit with his scruffy beard. From what I could gather he has been to Canada. Lindsay Black came in, having arrived from Scotland on leave.

70 Kimul Club, Burleigh St, formed by Bobbie Page before the war.

The 485 boys are having a good rest up at Drem but have had a plague of the flu. There is a lot of it about and a few have been snuffed out as a result. I got it about two weeks ago and when I felt it coming took quinine by the ounce and in the evening had a hot bath and a hot whiskey – a kill or cure method!

Cheerio for now. Many thanks for the Xmas presents,

Doug

Aston Down
Monday, 20 December 1943

Dear Mum, Dad and Girls,

I hope you are able to get enough petrol to go down to Manly for a week or so. Give it the once over for me – maybe I'll be there for next year. I hope you are able to get the odd dash of whiskey to see in a successful 1944.

We've had no snow or very little – it fell for about five or ten minutes one lunchtime. Other parts of England have seen quite a bit and they had about a foot around London, Kent and Surrey. It has been very cold here and the frost and freezing atmosphere is such that you can barely see 20 yards ahead. The course has been so badly affected by the weather that we have had to extend it a week so we can now allow all the boys to go back to their stations or go home for a couple of days over Christmas. I feel it is my duty to stay on the drome here and we will be able to get plenty of fun out of life. The bar seems well stocked so we won't go dry.

I had a letter from Lewis Eady a day or so ago and he has finished his first part of the training, which amounted to the same sort of thing we did at Levin. He is now off for three months at sea and I hope he has a better experience than Bruce Wallace and Harold Mace. He seems very keen and I'm sorry I have not been able to see him.

Most of the boys over here are now wearing the ribbon of the 1939–1943 Star including yours truly, rather a gaudy arrangement comprising about 1½" of dark blue, red and pale blue. It could be a damn good decoration, only it is so easily earned. To attain it all a chap has to do is two months in a squadron or one operational trip.

As the weather has been so rough lately we have been having quite a number of lectures to keep the boys amused and we have played rugby, soccer, hockey and indoor basketball. Practically no rules and very little whistle.

Tons of love to all and all the best for 1944,

Doug

Oxted
Tuesday, 4 January 1944

Dear Mum, Dad and Girls,

I'm now at Fergie's having a spell in between courses.

Since I last wrote Xmas and New Year have been and gone. Both involved a certain amount of elbow bending. I did not have any after-effects, which seemed to be worrying a majority of the mess when it was all over. On Xmas Eve day we sent all the boys off and I flew down and had a few beers with the boys of 486 NZ Typhoon Squadron at Tangmere. The bombers and fighters have been flying over in streams and a grand sight they are. They seemed to be busy so I left them to it and got back to Aston about four. The bar opened at six and we stood around and yarned, knocking back the odd noggin till about ten when we proceeded to an all-ranks dance which finished at one in the morning. After the dance I was back in the mess at about two and there were only two people there. The place looked like a morgue until a mob of the sergeants arrived with a home-composed band consisting of a big drum, two small ones, a bugle, an accordion, and a majority of the cooking utensils. By this time there were one or two more of the officers assembled so we proceeded to pull the barman out of bed and got the bar open long enough to give out a round or two. After a beer and with the band leading the way we trooped in a mighty procession all through the camp and went through all the billets, including the WAAF officers', who took a rather dim view of proceedings.

Next day we started by dishing out drink for the mess staff at about 10 a.m. and then had the sergeants in till about midday when we all went over to the airmen's mess and dished out the Xmas dinner, which is customary in the RAF and is much appreciated by the troops. After the troops had their midday meal we went over to the sergeants' mess and ate large sandwiches and drank pints of beer till four when we adjourned in preparation for Xmas dinner, which was to be held in both messes at about 6.30. The bar opened at five and we duly had our meal. I felt a bit clapped out so I went to a pantomime, which was put on by members of the station. After the panto a dance developed in the mess, which went on till about three in the morning. On Sunday I did not get up till about midday. I was relieved to see the boys arrive back that night and know that we would do the odd spot of flying again instead of partying. The weather was grand and we finished the course by the 31st and the farewell coincided with New Year's Eve.

New Year developed in customary fashion and we all started in our little bar and knocked back the odd ales which cost me little as I was in fine form on the dartboard. After a meal we had cigars and liqueurs but it was not long before we were back in the bar and then off to the local all-ranks dance till after twelve. We returned to the mess where we had another party organised. 1944 was well and truly in at about four o'clock.

I got up at eight in the morning and went up with the chaps to London. There were about a dozen of us and the majority was somewhat the worst for wear so we had a couple of lagers, followed by steak and onions, and then we went our devious ways. I went down to Fergie's and have been living a rather quiet life.

Tons of love to all,

Doug

Aston Down
Tuesday, 18 January 1944

Dear Mum, Dad and Girls,

Once again I am 'on the air' to give you what little news I have. There is a new job coming up which is supposedly 'Top Secret' so I'll be restricted in what can be related in letters. We shall see what happens. These invaluable men, you know!

At the end of my stay in Oxted, Fergie, Norman Roberts and yours truly went up to London and saw Max Miller's show at the Palladium. After the show, I took Fergie down to meet Harry at the Chez Moi for a few beers. We then had a ginormous feed at Genardi's and headed home. Next day I met Boozy at Chalford Station on the way to the next course.

The weather has hampered flying a bit – fog for the most part, and during the past seven days, we have been in the air one day only.

When I first got back on this course I flew to Scotland and saw Mick Maskill who is a Flight Lieutenant instructor. Al Deere and Johnnie Checketts were away whooping it up in town. Mick gave me all the gen and Marty Hume was also there so we had a good catch up. You'll be sorry to hear Johnny Dasent – The Champ – has had it. Soon after I had left the squadron in November he was killed in a flying accident near Edinburgh. He apparently was doing some practice interceptions and went too low to the sea, which he hit. He was seen to climb up to about 1000 feet and called on the R/T that he was baling out, but his chute did not open properly and he was forked out of the Firth of Forth dead with the cord around his neck. Very bad luck to befall such a good pilot and likeable character.

We did a lot together and became good friends at a time when a few of my pilot colleagues had moved on to other squadrons, been killed or despatched to POW camps.

We have a fellow Strachan on the course who was in my flight at Biggin. He was in the RAF pre-war and is only a Flight Lieutenant now. He takes a very poor view of us 'new' boys and tells us so as he sees fit.

We had a rather large-scale party in the mess last Saturday night. It was well organised with two large bars and very good running buffet. The mess had managed to get half a dozen turkeys, and at about three all that were left of the party went into the kitchen and cleaned up the remains. It looked damn funny all the boys and girls with carcasses and drumsticks in their hands. One of the boys had a ham bone of terrific size. Bill Statham, another NZ boy, and self were not satisfied with that and at about 4.30 when the party finally came to rest we had a tin of oysters – very tasty.

The war news continues to be good and I think the Ruskies are giving the old Hun more than he bargained for. As regards the Japs we don't hear much from that sphere and we little realise what conditions the boys over there are fighting in.

Cheerio for now. Tons and tons of love to you all,

Doug

Doug carrying out test flights in Spitfire XIV

Milfield

*

PRE-INVASION SCHOOL

RAF HEADQUARTERS DECIDED TO ESTABLISH A PRE-INVASION SCHOOL IN Northumberland. Fighter Leader School at Aston Down had come under the jurisdiction of Fighter Command. The majority of the instructors of FLS were then directed to form a pre-invasion school at Milfield, Northumberland in late January, 1944. We were part of 2nd Tactical Air Force (TAF) which was charged with supporting the Allied Invasion and subsequent Land Force progress through France, Belgium and Holland.

Air Marshall Sir Arthur Coningham was the Air Commander of 2nd TAF. Group Captain Adams and I did not get on. I believe he hindered my progress and, at the end of the school, tried to hold me back when I wanted to get involved in D-Day. Fighter Command Headquarters appreciated that the role of Fighter Squadrons after D-Day would be significantly different from the period during the Battle of Britain where it was purely a defensive role. The advantage, then, if you could call it that was that it took place over England, over familiar soil, with a full fuel tank, and with back-up from ground ammunition.

During the three years or so following the Battle of Britain we had adopted an offensive role and operations such as bomber escorts, ramrods and circuses were flown over France, usually at 10,000 feet plus. These operations were carried out to encourage German fighters to engage in battle. If combat did occur it was

One of the courses at Milfield pre-invasion school. We trained experienced fighter pilots in the art of dive bombing and rocket firing for air-to-ground attack following the D-Day invasion

all over very quickly. There was a frenzy of aircraft going in seemingly random directions and no time to think about being shot at. You had to remember to turn everything on, turn on the gun sight and make the trigger live, otherwise you push the button and nothing happens, you just take a photograph. And then, in the next moment, there is nothing to be seen and it is an almost eerie quiet. With limited range we regroup and head for home.

With D-Day looming and with the experience of the Italian campaign it was realised that the Spitfires would basically be involved in air-to-ground operations and were fitted with cannon and 500lb bombs. Typhoons were converted to rocket-firing operations. Tempests initially involved in destroying V1 bombs would then also adopt an air-to-ground role.

The beach from Berwick-upon-Tweed to Holy Island was littered with transport and tanks for target practice. The school comprised two squadrons of Spitfires fitted with bomb racks and one squadron of Typhoons fitted with rocket racks. The RAF squadron was joined by one squadron of Mustangs and one squadron of Thunderbolts controlled by the US Air Force (this gave me an opportunity to fly in both these planes). Wing Commander Tommy Thomas allocated responsibilities and I found myself instructing Spitfire pilots in the art of dive bombing. I knew little about 500lb bombs and had to learn very rapidly. I was, however, able to obtain a copy of the recommended procedure for Stuka Ju87 dive bombing and used this as a guide.

Those instructed were wing commanders, squadron leaders, and future squadron commanders. When the first course started in early March 1944, although I knew little of the bombing procedure to adopt, I had to instil confidence as the pilots were not too keen to use Spitfires for bombing purposes. The method established was to roll over onto your side at 10,000 feet and with the target in the gun sight at 3000 feet ease out of the dive, count 1, 2, 3, and release the bombs. It sounds Heath-Robinson but it was very successful.

We carried out a number of exercises specifically with the invasion in mind. These included straffing, beach cover, low-level attacks on gun emplacements, dive bombing and cab rank. Cab rank was devised in the Italian campaign and Billy Drake and Arthur 'Mary' Coningham[71] came over from Italy and taught us the procedure.

The system developed from Coningham's time in North Africa where he saw the need for coordinated Close Air Support (CAS) for ground forces operating in proximity of the enemy. Cab rank was the term assigned to a reserve of fighter-bombers in the air. They were called up sequentially at a particular map reference to attack identified ground targets efficiently and accurately.

This system proved to be very successful against the German tanks and was one of the turning points in the war. For example, the Typhoons fitted with rockets knocked out the Tiger tanks, which had a range of 4000 yards, while the US and British tanks only had 2000-yard range.

Exercises were carried out with live 500lb bombs and rockets. On 9 March, one member of the first course, Captain Bouguen, thought that more accuracy would be achieved if the bomb was released before easing out of the dive – he blew up in mid-air. The bombs had their own drive propeller and, when released, slipped forward along the trajectory of the plane. If released before pulling out of the dive, the bomb would catch up and hit the prop of the Spit with disastrous results.

There were discussion groups set up to decide co-operation with Army, Navy and bomber command, how airfields would be established following the invasion,

71 Coningham called himself a New Zealander but was born in Brisbane. His father played one cricket test for Australia in 1894 and had a colourful life. In 1900 he accused Dr Francis O'Haran, the secretary and administrator to Cardinal Moran, the Head of the Australian Catholic Church, of committing adultery with his wife. Coningham lost the case despite his wife admitting in court her third child was O'Haran's. The family moved to New Zealand where he was convicted of fraud involving £6 and spent six months in prison. Young Arthur entered the Great War in the NZ Expeditionary Force at Gallipoli before joining the Royal Flying Corps. He was a highly decorated RAF officer during World War II and also received a knighthood. In 1948, after retirement he disappeared in the Bermuda Triangle on a flight from the Azores to Bermuda. There were 31 passengers and crew on board.

38, *Lowndes Street,*
London, S.W.1.

31st January, 1944.

Dear Brownie,

      I must apologise for the delay in answering your welcome letter of the 5th instant but, as you will in due course learn, there have been very special reasons.

      If you are coming on leave shortly, even though you be in London for no longer than a day or so, please give me a ring at the Office so that we can meet and discuss a programme.

      With kindest regards,

              Yours sincerely,

                Noble

Ft. Lt. Douglas Brown,
   (R.N.Z.A.F),
      R.A.F.Station,
         Aston Down,
            Gloucester.

Letter from Noble Lowndes

utilisation of cab rank, methods of identifying allied aircraft to minimise friendly flak fire,[72] and the many problems that were likely to be met. Although we were not told of the landing area for the invasion, the inference was that it would be in the vicinity of 100 miles from the English coast. The beaches of Normandy were the natural landing area. The Germans had convinced themselves that the main landing force would be in the Calais area.

Rocket-firing Typhoons and dive-bombing Spitfires were used from D-Day extensively up to the end of hostilities.

While at Milfield I did a few test flights on a Spitfire XIV, which had not yet entered service. It was more powerful than the IXB with specifications of 12-boost and 100-octane fuel. The engine was a Rolls-Royce Griffin 65 with five-bladed

---

72 One such method was painting black and white stripes on the underside of Allied aircraft.

prop which developed tremendous torque during take off. The test exercise was to trial 18-boost and 150-octane fuel. The first trip was rather nerve-racking with a full boost climb to 20,000 feet. The heat generated, the noise and vibration was unlike anything I had experienced before and I wondered if I would survive this test flight. The tests did prove successful and the aircraft reached 418 mph in low-level flying.

Milfield
Northumberland
Tuesday, 1 February 1944

Dear Mum, Dad and Girls,

We are now in north-east England. There is no fog but the wind has not been below about 50 mph since I got here. The ground crew has to hold the tail down pre-take off. OK for flying but not so good for taxiing. It can also be quite dangerous. Wag Haw told me they lost a couple when he was flying Hurricanes in Murmansk. Ground crew had to hold the tail down due to the often icy and slippery runway. If the tail was held too long the plane flipped on take off.

After I last wrote we eventually got rid of the course after having about nine days continual fog, so it mainly consisted of coffee drinking. I got a 48, which I spent with Katie, where I ate well and built up sleeping hours. The wily Hun was rather bumptious and decided to put on some fireworks, which kept us occupied for an hour or so watching the searchlights and ack-ack in action and the results of the bombing. Though several kites flew right over Katie's, there were no bombs dropped in our vicinity and I judged from what appeared as a good fire that the odd bomb had fallen some 20 miles to the north. The lights got a big fat Dornier just over Katie's and after a rather frightening experience in the flak he got fixed by a nightfighter. They came over first after supper and not satisfied with that they had another go at about four or five in the morning which did not interest me but Katie and Werner were up and about for about an hour. I left for Aston on Saturday. Passing through London I first paid a visit to Kitty Steffens at the NZ Forces Club to catch up with what the boys were up to. I had such a good breakfast of eggs that I did not bother to have any lunch at all.

The next few days were spent cleaning up prior to moving and also being social with the local WAAFs, whom we had befriended at Aston. When we finally got organised we did a bit of ferrying, moving our kites. We got quite a number of imported chaps who did the bulk of the job. Flying the Spits to Milfield was not so bad but the journey back to Aston Down in an Oxford was tedious. They are an eight-seater and quite tricky to land. Boozy tried to kill us one afternoon when he overshot on landing and more by luck (or as we say in the Air Force let everything go and 'Take over, Jesus') we ended in a pile of rocks and rubble. It could quite easily have been worse if we had hit the cars and the offices of the local ATA. Quite fun!

There was a Captain Bogle in charge of the ATA who used to always come and have the odd ale with us in the evening. At a party night about two or three Saturdays ago after a small session in our own bar we went into the larger bar where the dance was in full swing and one of the Polish boys managed to swing one of their patent drinks onto the Captain. It consists of double whiskey, double gin and double rum. Cap knocked back the half pint, turned round to get off his chair and spun nicely – out for keeps! We never sighted him in the bar again till our prang in the Oxford when he reckoned he could now show his face in public without shame.

My old squadron is at Drem near Milfield. There are only a few of the boys left who were in 485 with me. Gibby has now gone on rest and I expect Marty will soon follow. I had a meal with them and had a yarn to all the chaps. They should be flying as much as possible but they are doing as little flying as they can. They have got a lot of new boys willing to learn the form but at the current rate they are going they will go south again with little knowledge or experience.

I had a flip in a Hurricane yesterday. I've never flown one before and it was quite different from the Spit. One thing I will say for it is the vision from it is grand, and for low flying, good fun and safe, and you can see in every direction. Unlike the Spit where visibility is poor – during taxi and take off you need to weave about and raise the seat.

The mess where we are is not bad for an after-the-start-of-the-war-built camp and the food is very good. The trouble is that the billets are some half-mile from the mess and bathrooms, and a mile and a half to two miles from dispersal. However, we shouldn't grumble when we think of the type of living the boys are going through in the Middle East.

Love to all,

Doug

Milfield
Sunday, 13 February 1944

Dear Mum, Dad and Girls,

We have started off with a bang in the shape of a high-powered party. The mess has a large bar, which has just been constructed, and it adjoins the dining room. We opened the bar at six to the accompaniment of a very high-class band we have got on the station. We had a feed, which included the largest and best steak I've ever had in an RAF mess so far. After the supper had more or less finished the party began in earnest. A grand 'buck' do with piles of typical RAF songs and turns, which were helped along by the band. Bobby Oxspring and I left the mess at 4.45 a.m. and were not the last by a long way but before we went to bed we had a much treasured tin of oysters between us. At the moment Boozy and I have a tin of soup on the stove – looks good and will be enjoyed before we hit the hay tonight.

The flying has gone as well as we hoped and we have got a lot out of it. I generally manage to get a couple of trips in each day. Reg Grant is on the first course and is just the same as ever. I hadn't seen his ugly dial for a couple of months! Reg is now Wing Commander with 122 Wing flying Mustangs and should prove to be an excellent Winco.

I received all your welcome cables from NZ for my 25th birthday. February 6th was last Sunday: we flew in the morning and had a bit of a discussion in the afternoon. On Monday after a flip I was signing up the authorisation book and noticed the date, 6 February 1944. Reg was there at the time and I told him today was my birthday, but no sooner had I said it than the Flight Sergeant came in and altered the date to the seventh. Rather amusing but rather silly having a birthday and not realising it till the day after you have had it.

The weather here has continued to be fine and clear with windy days. I much prefer this type of weather to the damp fog we had at Aston. I've been very lucky this year and so far – touch wood – have had very little trouble with this bronchial catarrh of mine. The day before yesterday was not as windy as usual and out in the sun it was quite warm. Yet, the night of last Thursday week it snowed for about an hour. Snow fell generally throughout England that night.

We had a big night in Edinburgh and did not get back to Milfield until about one the next day. The band was in the mess and the big bar was open, so we had a couple more ales and a good lunch. We do not starve up here. For instance, today we had soup, lamb chops and boiled spuds, leeks and peas and mixed fruit – just a normal meal. This afternoon we had a combat film show so most of the boys built up their sleeping hours.

Cheerio for now.

Love to you all,

Doug

Milfield
Tuesday, 29 February 1944

Dear Mum, Dad and Girls,

Yesterday I heard the worst news I've heard for a long time when Jamie Rankin came in to tea and said that Reg Grant had been killed that lunchtime. As far as we can ascertain – the line not being very clear – he was killed just after take off from his base at Gravesend due to engine failure. It was too low for his chute to open. Such an end for so distinguished a fighter pilot and a year after Ian was shot down. When I get the details and Reg's sister's address, I'll drop a line and tell her all I know for I'm sure she would like to know how the whole thing happened. He was a damn good friend to all who came in contact with him and will be missed by many chaps who have served with him as well as known him. He was fixing me up for my return to ops but that is of little importance. He was here only a week to ten days ago as bright as a light, drinking his 'Bulls Blood' stout, great pity.

We had a rather large party when the last course went out. We imported a few nurses from the local hospital and we had some beautiful salmon as the buffet which we caught ourselves. We have great fishing around Milfield as there are a number of streams and pools in which fish thrive. Our method is fruitful, if not in accordance with the laws of the land. We select a pool likely to contain a good catch and then drop in a thunderflash obtained from Army 'Surplus'. One of the boys hops into a rubber dinghy and gets to work retrieving the stunned fish.

As the last course broke up early I got a Spit and flew up to Drem, which is not so far from here, and spent Saturday and Sunday night with the 485 boys. The Saturday I got there was of course a dance in the mess, which was a damn good do and it was just like old times again. The hierarchy has at last caught

R eg Grant and I had an arrangement that I would take over one of his Mustang Squadrons where he was Wing Commander. Reg 'Dumbo' Grant and I became good friends. As CO his philosophy was to develop a close bond among the pilots and he became a great leader. 485 had developed into a squadron of real character. A strong bond of camaraderie grew built from the individual personality and spirit of each member.

Reg Grant

Reg did not think twice about posting on any that did not meet his criteria of strengthening the unit. In March 1943 he went on rest, having completed 150 sorties. He spent a few months in Canada lecturing NZ trainees. In November 1943 he returned to become CO of 65 Squadron and then he became the Winco of the RAF 122 Mustang Wing. I was looking forward to getting back on operations but sadly Reg was killed so I had to search for a job elsewhere.

We also heard Reg 'Baldy' Baker had been killed on 12 February 1944. Following a rest period after his first tour he flew Mosquitos on Intrusion Operations. He was a gentleman and good friend.

up with Marty for rest and his place has been taken over by Johnny Niven, a Scotsman. He was with another squadron at Kenley when we were there[73]. He is on the course at present and is still the same Johnny Niven despite missing a finger when shot down on the Dieppe show.

The car I had at Biggin is still going like a bomb. Terry Kearins who was a French 'visitor' and now back with 485 has got it at present and he reckons it's pretty good. He got married not so long ago and as they live near the drome he takes the car home each night.

This course has gone along as well as can be expected and I think the boys are getting a bit of gen from it, I know I am anyway.

Had a letter from Chalky White yesterday to say Mac Sutherland is a POW, which is the first news we have had since he was shot down some seven or eight months ago.

Love to all,

Doug

73 During the course of the war there were over 200 members of 485 Squadron. Johnny Niven was one of the very few non-NZers in 485 Squadron.

We had a few fishing trips when at Milfield with mixed success.

In a pub on the south side of the airfield the locals told me there was a large pike in the pool under the bridge east of the drome. No one had been able to catch it so I assured them we would do the deed and deliver the fish. The pool was 30 ft deep so I threw in three thunderflashes. About 300 small fish floated to the surface followed by a few trout, five salmon and a 15½lb pike which I delivered to the locals. Grand sport but rather costly if caught. Unfortunately the small fish drifted down the Tweed to Berwick whereupon the local fishery inspector was alerted. He traced the source to the bridge and had been referred to me. The excuse I used was one of the 500 lb bombs had fallen from a Spit on take off and landed under the bridge and exploded.

As well as 'fishing' around the streams and pools of Berwick using Army thunderflashes, we had the opportunity to grow the business with the Berwick Air-Sea rescue boys. I was approached by one of the chaps to see if we would be interested in getting fish from outside Berwick in the sea when the salmon were running. We of course agreed so long as we got some of the loot. The day came and they called me up. I took along five other planes with 500lb bombs. They marked the area with two orange buoys and we went up to 10,000 feet and dropped six 500lb bombs and expected to get quite a haul of salmon – all in the name of bomb training!

A couple of days later I called them up and asked: 'Where are those bloody salmon?'

'Oh', they said, 'we didn't get any, all we got was one cod.' I was not convinced. One cod was not a good return for six 500lb bombs!

Monday, 13 March 1944

Dear Mum, Dad and Girls,

I'm at Fergie's having a spot of leave but before I go into that I'll tell you a tale of woe.

Last Wednesday week at 11 p.m. the billet I'm in at camp caught alight and burnt to the ground. I lost all I have except for two uniforms and greatcoat. As I had battledress on at the time and a polo neck pullover, I do not even

TOP Fire in Milfield barracks

ABOVE Gold Sovereigns retrieved from fire

have a shirt – damn bad luck! What annoyed me most was the loss of my three volumes of photos I've collected since I've been over here. The camera 'had it' and all the films and negatives also went on their way. The Rolex watch you gave me when I left, Dad, will, I'm afraid, be only useful for salvage, if that. The cigarette case you brought back from Aussie for me is pretty badly knocked about but I may be able to get it put into some shape. The Parker Vacuumatic fountain pen as well as the Swan has gone the way of the weary. I did salvage the five sovereigns that you gave me, should I be posted to the Middle East. They are OK except for a slight tarnish.

They tell me the RAF will not pay back a sou. I think the fire was caused through faulty wiring. I wrote to Bill Jordan and got a personal letter back from him, which encourages me somewhat. It is not the actual loss of the cash involved so much as I hate to be diddled by the Government. I'm reasonably lucky as I pay no income tax and even though I spend a fair quota and enjoy myself, I've got over £100 in the bank. Some of the others are pretty broke – I don't know how they will fare. The little cash I have combined with a fairly liberal supply of coupons, I've been able to re-kit to a fair extent. I've bought five shirts, three pyjamas, seven pairs of underpants, eight pairs of socks, shoes, towels, handkerchiefs, gloves, vests, hat, scarves and ties. So far

Inventory of items lost in fire

this month I have cashed about £36 and I've spent about £25 on clothes and other gear. Suitcases are practically unprocurable over here but as luck would have it I rang Katie today and she has got a spare. I look like a tramp at present, wandering around with a kitbag of gear.

I started leave last Saturday. My week was due to start tomorrow but as the course finished on Friday I decided to come down early. G/C Adams would not sign my leave pass to start with, and I was rather angry and flew around to his office and demanded a mighty conference. When I told him I wanted my leave he said he had not had any for six months and wanted to know why I should have it. So I told him: firstly I wanted to get gear which I could not procure up north, secondly I had booked and paid for a room in London for the 16th and 17th, and lastly I was meant to be on a rest and was due to go back to ops next month. He then started to make odd excuses but I twisted him a bit and smartly got my pass signed and got out of his way!

Geoff Page and I flew Spitfires down to Detling where Geoff has got his squadron. I had lunch with Geoff and caught up with Vic Hall. As I was heading for Oxted I thought I'd try a new system and cover the journey by bus, which was not bad. It involved three changes from Maidstone to Oxted. I went to Sevenoaks, then to Westerham and on to Oxted, the whole journey took about two and a half hours.

I got here at about five o'clock in the evening and, as Fergie and Mrs Fergie were in London, I went down to my chemist pal and bought a razor, shaving brush and all and sundry. I'm sure he sold me the lot at a loss to himself. That night there was a dance at the Hoskins Arms. Colin Gray was also in attendance and quite a party developed. Colin was a short-service commission type and did well in the Battle of Britain as well as North Africa and heads the NZ boys with 27 destroyed and has got DSO, DFC and two bars – damn good going and well deserved. He is stuck at an OTU now and very fed up. On Sunday morning Fergie, Norm Roberts, a chap called Bing, the local pro, and Colin and I played a round of golf. In the afternoon we went and visited a few of Fergie's pals and did not get back to Oxted till after eight. Colin went off this morning in his car, an MG for which he paid £160 – a very good buy.

We had a good farewell party for the course at Milfield and Marty Hume came down from Drem for it. Marty suffers from hangovers to a certain extent, for he went to bed at about two or three while I hit the hay at about five. I was up at 8.30 and ate a hearty breakfast of sausages and egg. Marty got up in time for breakfast and he sat down for about two minutes, but left rapidly and we did not see him for an hour.

Cheerio for now,

Doug

Milfield
Monday, 27 March 1944

Dear Mum, Dad and Girls,

On Thursday I had lunch with Noble Lowndes and got all the chat from him, after which I met Gibby at the Kimul Club. It was a late night session and, consequently, the next day I did not arise till nearly midday and the first thing I did was have a mighty feed at Genardi's of spaghetti and hot lobster – very tasty! In the afternoon I met a lady friend and went to see 'Gone with the Wind', which I thoroughly enjoyed. After the flicks we went down to the Chez Moi but as Harry was not there I only had a couple of beers and we buzzed off to the pub and quietly sipped ale and feasted on buffet food. There was a bit of an air raid and as soon as Wailing Willie finished, the pub filled up, leaving no room to move as the shrapnel from the ack-ack continued to fall furiously outside.

Returning from leave, I caught a train from Oxted at about 11 o'clock on the Monday morning and caught a taxi to King's Cross with half an hour to spare, which I thought would enable me to get a good seat, but I was diddled and had to stand as far as Darlington – a matter of just over six hours. We were like sardines with the lavatories in the same state – too bad for anyone who wanted to pay a visit! I reached Berwick at 9.30 and met one of the Engineering Officers when I got off the train so we nipped up and had an ale before we caught a 10.30 bus back to camp.

Last Saturday the course went to Edinburgh for the weekend so I flew to Catfoss and spent the night with Johnnie Checketts, Mick Maskill and Gibby. I played rugby in the afternoon, which blew out my lungs a bit. In the evening eight of us got a taxi and went about nine miles to the nearby town of Beverley where we paid a social call to the local. Quite a night as you will guess!

Sunday, yesterday, was the start of spring and it was such a grand day. I was up at 7.30 and, after a breaker of a couple of eggs at Mick's expense, we sat in the sun and yarned till I left at about 11 o'clock. This morning was misty and we did not fly. As it was still down after lunch we cancelled flying for the day so Lindsay Black, Mick and three others including myself thought we would climb a local hill. The mist cleared and the sun came through as warm as yesterday. Lin and I did not get to the top as we ran into some local farmers administering first aid to some ewes in a paddock so we watched proceedings and shot a bit of a line.

Tons of love to you all,

Doug

Milfield
Monday, 10 April 1944

Dear Mum, Dad and Girls,

It seems incredible that it is nearly three years since I left fair Auckland. Just think of it, if there had been no war I would probably now be a farmer and married. I often wonder how it will be to settle down after this life and what I'll end up doing.

We have another course in – the last I'm told and this time we have got Garry Barnett and Ken Lee. The previous course finished with the usual gusto and I did not hit the hay till five. It was a perfect day and I was up at eight ready to fly south. Unfortunately there was the usual fog in the London area so the Winco Tommy Thomas and yours truly did not set course till about 11.30. We had a few beers and a meal at Biggin Hill and a pow-wow with those I knew there.

Sunday, Checks left to take over No 1 squadron and Mick Maskill managed to get one of the flights – lucky people as they fell right on their feet and should do well. That evening I met my ATS job and had a few ales with the locals. On Monday morning I went up to London in the ambulance with

Norm Roberts as he had to pick up some patient there and I had a few jobs to do. The ambulance job is Norman's war work and I believe he did a grand job in the blitz and should have got recognition for it.

When I hit town my first job was to get a new hat as I lost mine at the party the previous Friday night. I managed to get one off Kitty Steffans at the Forces Club, but had to buy a badge, which cost me 21/- which seemed rather steep. After that I went and saw Alan Mitchell, the war correspondent, and was directed by him to the Sport and General where I attempted to replace all the press photographs I lost in the 'Great Fire'. I did fairly well on that line and got several other interesting non-squadron photos for nix. When the girl who did all the organisation said she would sort out some other photos for me I took her to lunch but as yet have not received the photos and so do not know how successful my lunch was from a business point of view. After this mighty luncheon I caught a tube to Victoria, and went to the Army and Navy stores in Victoria Street to buy a photograph album.

On Tuesday I hoped to get back to Milfield. I went up to the aerodrome and met Winco Thomas there but as the weather report was no good we decided to take another day off, so back I went to Oxted. I rang up the Winco next morning and he said he had decided to stay as his leave commenced in a couple of days. I had lunch and took off to see how far I could get before the weather closed in. I got as far as Hull OK, though it was rough in parts. I had a pop at going up the coast but the weather beat me so I hit back to Catfoss where Gibby is and had quite a night with him and his rough friends. We finished the night in the kitchen frying and eating eggs as fast as we could go. Next day I could not get away as the fog was down. I got off after lunch and sallied north without trouble.

At present I'm doing a liaison job to some Yanks and as they are damn good fellows the job is easy and I'm having quite a bit of fun.

I had airgraphs from Gus and Ewen. Ewie told me Jock McG is back in the ME – he's a glutton for punishment. Lewis Eady has finished his three months at sea and is now training to be an officer. He enjoyed his time and was on one of the newest warships, which brought Churchill back.

Tons of love to you all and all the best,

Chin Chin,

Doug

Oxted
Tuesday, 25 April 1944

Dear Mum, Dad and Girls,

I flew down to Biggin Hill on Saturday after the usual hectic party. Garry Barnett arrived later so we headed for a quiet night at the Hoskins Arms with Fergie and the locals. On Sunday we did not arise till midday. Garry and I met our girlfriends and walked about three miles to a local tea house called the Old Wheel, went up to a local common and Garry and I went to sleep in the sun for about three hours.

Yesterday afternoon, Norm Roberts, Garry and I went out to the golf links and played nine holes and had tea. Fergie and Mr Bing joined us to complete the round. I won the money but after golf the trouble started. Mr Bing has rather a lot of money and a pretty good cellar, which he is always insisting we have the odd drop from. He started us off with a triple gin and lime followed by a fairly good helping of pre-war kummel and then a triple whiskey. Bing is a pretty good yarn spinner, as is Fergie. They were telling yarns, trying to keep them decent as Mrs Bing was there, not that she minds a good yarn. Norman Roberts rather carried away by the chat and the booze told a real shocker. A deathly hush reigned over the party – poor old Norm does not even now know that he spoke out of turn. It was a good night in spite of the blacks put up.

Garry and I had a date at the Hoskins' for eight o'clock and were not surprised when we arrived at five past nine to find our respective escorts absent. There was a message for us to ring a number and we got told off in no mean manner and were rather unpopular for the rest of the evening.

Garry caught the 9.30 bus this morning and if the aircraft is there to meet him should be on his way back to his base. I go on the bus this afternoon. As soon as I leave Biggin Hill I'll head flat out for Northumberland. If all goes well I should be back with a squadron in a couple of days which will certainly suit me as I've had enough of sitting around doing nothing.

Fergie has just had about half a bunch of bananas sent to him, the first I have seen for a long time and I've got one off the bunch which I will attempt to ripen and eat in due course. Marty Hume's cousin Bill Robjohn has sent them. He has been in the Med patrolling in submarines and gets a few perks. I'm not convinced a bunch of bananas would be enough to get me down in a sub.

Love to all the mob,

Doug

Milfield
Monday, 8 May 1944

Dear Mum, Dad and Girls,

In this good weather I've done the odd sightseeing tour of the country, which is at its best. A couple of days ago I went across to the Lake District by Spitfire XIV, shooting up Keswick on the way. Damn good fun whistling along the lakes at zero feet and giving the locals in their rowing boats a wave as I rip by. Keswick itself looked really grand with all the flowers adding the odd dash of bright colour to the green. I had a look at the Silloth golf links from a low altitude but they did not look so very interesting, and the course itself seemed to have a good share of bunkers. As yet I've not been able to find Aspatria from the air. It's a great pity I lost the camera in the fire as I might have got some damn good aerial shots.

I received the photos taken of you all on the verandah at Manly. I'm sending you a photo showing what was left of my hut after the fire.

Last Saturday I paid a nocturnal visit to Gibby and his rough crew at Catfoss and, as luck would have it, struck a night when they were having a large-sized dance, which was the dreaded end. It was a party too – free beer and plenty to eat, which suited me. I did not hit the hay till rather late and while I intended to be out of bed for breaker and back here for lunch, I did not wake up till midday. Gibby fared worse than me for later in the evening he decided to do some acrobatics, which got the better of him, and the last I saw of him was just before I left with a sprained ankle well-bandaged by the Doc and confined to bed as he could not walk.

Well, I seem to have come to the end of my news bulletin. I hope to go south again for a few days again this weekend.

Love, Doug

Milfield
Tuesday, 23 May 1944

Dear Mum, Dad and Girls,

When I last wrote we were in the last week of yet another course on the instruction of Spitfire bombing. It finished off with the usual farewell party, everyone saying what a hell of a good chap the next bloke was, though possibly thinking him a real stinker – such is life!

I was up bright and early on Saturday morning as I had a small job to do. I saw Bill Compton and Al Deere in the morning at Merston and had a few beers and lunch with them. After lunch I went and plonked down at our old station, Biggin Hill, and caught the bus to Oxted. I stayed with Fergie till Tuesday morning and managed to fit in a round of golf each day. On Saturday night Johnnie Checketts came up with Jamie Jameson. Beer was hard to get so we went to the Returned Soldiers joint and had a few pints and billiards prior to going to the local dance. Johnnie is now a Winco and doing well though they've not run into anything as yet. He had a grand cocker spaniel puppy which died after a bout of flu' or some such disease. Checks was very upset about it.

The trip to Milfield on Tuesday was foul as the weather was right down on the deck with plenty of rain and I got caught in the hills for a while which rather annoyed me as I had to refuel on the way. I got home and had tea and as the next course was not due to start for another five or six days I hopped in a Spit and went off to Carlisle. I landed at Crosby and took the bus to town and as I wanted some cigarettes I popped into the Silver Grill, had a couple of beers and wandered down to Rickerbys' where they were very surprised to see me. We had a fairly quiet night and had a few by the fire and yarned. On Wednesday I went to the bank and checked out Wilkinson the new manager. I went to Thursby to lunch with the Cavaghans, after which I went out with Mr Cav to one of his farms and looked the joint over, then we went back to the factory and after some tea in the canteen we caught the bus to the Grill where we met Mr Ken Harrison who sent his best regards to you. On Thursday he had a job in Penrith so I went with him and had lunch at the George with Jim Dias, and also bought a car – a Ford 8 – 1937 model. Jim bought it for £50 and, after fitting two new headlights, a tail light, a battery, two decent tyres and giving it a good clean up as well as a full tank of gas, I paid him £55, which really amounted to a net loss on his part but he would take no more. On Friday I did my usual morning rounds – bank, Dias Bros and the coffee shop

P re-invasion school closed down about mid-May and I then had the problem of getting back on operations. After Reg Grant was killed the only other alternative I had was Johnnie Checketts who ran 142 Wing at RAF Horne after only a month as CO of Number 1 Squadron at North Weald. Checks was instrumental in me joining 130 Squadron at Horne prior to D-Day. He moved on after about three weeks.

Marty Hume became CO of 485 when Johnnie Checketts was shot down and I was appointed B Flight Commander. Marty was a big man and spoke with a slow drawl. I spent more active service with Marty than any of the other pilots. He was with 485 for most of the time I was there. When I ended my tour and went to FLS, Marty led 485.

Marty and I were also both in 130 Squadron. Marty served under me. He was a good pilot but after the war he seemed to lose all interest in work and his future and virtually went back to 'the mat'. Marty had a stroke and died late in the 1980s.

Johnnie Checketts

to hear all the gossip and scandal. I had lunch at the Grill with the Ricks, Cavs and Creightons – quite a social gathering and very chatty. I caught a train to Penrith to collect the car and headed back to Carlisle – she ran damn well.

I flew back to Milfield, taking note of a good route to bring the car later.

Back at Milfield I found I was to be one of the Squadron Commanders although I would remain a Flight Lieutenant in rank. After a yarn with the Winco I managed to borrow a two-seater Miles Master and a pilot and I left here at about 9.45 and I was in the coffee shop at Carlisle by 10.30. The Dias Bros were fixing the lights. Mrs Rick gave me a salmon and some Cumberland ham and I set off and only got off course once during the journey, which only took about two and a half hours from Carlisle to base. The salmon I had done up and divided into seven good portions. The ham I had with a couple of eggs this morning and good it was too.

The next course has started and I find myself CO of one of the outfits. Mick Maskill and Howard Crafts are here. Last night I took Howard and Mick to a party we had for the ground crew and we sank a fair quota of beer and sang the usual songs. I got talked into giving the boys a solo, which amused them, and was the idea of the party anyway.

I've got a good cold on the way, which I imagine will keep me off flying for a day or so.

Love, Doug

Rendition by Mary Denton / RAF Heraldry Trust

130 (Punjab) Squadron

*

O N 5 APRIL 1944, 186 SQUADRON AT LYMPNE WAS RENUMBERED 130 Squadron. The 'Punjab' refers to the Punjab states, which had presented Spitfires to the original 130 Squadron in 1942. The planes were marked AP. I joined a few days before D-Day as a supernumerary F/Lt but obtained a Flight Commander's job and led the squadron on D-Day itself.

Initially we were equipped with old Spitfire VBs. We also had slipper tanks which gave us the extra range.

130 Squadron

In August the squadron converted to Spitfire XIVs to counter the VI flying-bomb attacks on southern England. At the end of September 1944 we moved to the Low Countries for armed reconnaissance sweeps over Germany. Attacks on enemy transport and airfields continued in the main until the end of the war.

130 was a squadron of mixed nationalities, mainly Brits, Canadians and a few Kiwis under S/L Bill Ireson. We all got on well together but it was quite a different feeling to the camaraderie that developed in 485. Conditions on the continent were well below par and the situation did not lend itself to much of a social life – this no doubt contributed to the lack of close friendships. I still correspond with Bambi Lawrence who was with 402 Squadron.

Horne, Surrey, 31 May 1944

Horne, in Surrey, was about 15 miles north of East Grinstead and the airfield had steel mesh runways. It was constructed rather rapidly and was used for only six weeks from mid-May until 27 June 1944.

At Horne we had three squadrons: 130, a mixed Squadron; 402, a Canadian Squadron; and 303, a Polish Squadron. That formed the whole 142 Wing and Johnnie Checketts was the Wing Commander Flying.

Doug, Bill Ireson, Russ Mathieson, Scotty Scott at Horne

Horne
Friday, 2 June 1944

Dear Mum, Dad and Girls,

I am back on ops again and very pleased about the whole outfit. I'm not with the old squadron but a mixed outfit, which is good for a change. I hope to get a flight in the near future but as I'm not a substantive Flight Lieutenant I can take it easy for a while with little to worry about.

The course at Milfield was going OK and the car was doing good work with Maskill and Crafts Ltd. We went to a country dance about 12 miles away one night at a place called Kirk Yetholm. We started off in the Border Hotel and left there for the dance before midnight where we stayed till the bitter end trying to keep up with all the local and old-time dances, of which I did not have a clue. The following day I got my posting as F/O to 130, the F/O being smartly changed to F/Lt again thanks to G/C Adams. I told Johnnie Checketts I did not care in what manner I got south so long as it could be done and he worked it so that I'm now in his wing.

The night of my posting a whole mob of us went out to the Black Bull at Etal. Next day I spent all day clearing up and packing. That night we started in the officers' mess at about seven and proceeded to the sergeants' mess

Bill Ireson,
Johnnie
Checketts,
Doug, Russ
Mathieson

Facilities at Horne were somewhat Spartan

where we stayed till about three in the morning – quite a session and after that we went along to my room and had a good feed of sardines and tongues – a damn good farewell party.

Next morning I packed up the car and set course south in the Ford 8. I came through Wooller on to Morpeth where I met the Great North Road on through Newcastle, Darlington, Doncaster, Grantham, Stamford, Huntington, on to London and towards Oxted, which I reached at about 8.30, very tired and thirsty. I had lunch between Darlington and Doncaster at a little place called the Orchard Café. It cost two bob for two poached eggs, cold ham, gooseberry pie and cream and homemade mince pies and tea. The average for the trip was 34 mph and the petrol consumption over 40 miles to the gallon.

I intended staying with Bill Tomkins at Kings Cliffe but as I got there just after five, I thought I may as well plod on and have a good sleep at Fergie's. I missed a few streets when I started through North London and when I got to the river I initially could not find a bridge to get across. On the way to Purley I had a great race with a chap in a Triumph – what a do and we did not even get a 'pinkie'. When I got to Oxted I was tired and thirsty so I went to the pub and got a pint shandy, which I downed all in one go. I felt 100% after a 24-hour sleep.

I had lunch with Fergie and then drove down to Horne. I've been down here now about five days and I'm feeling very fit. We've had some grand weather and we are living in the open air. I had a rotten cold when I got here which has more or less cleared now. I was up at Fergie's a couple of nights ago and Bill Robjohn was there and as Mrs Fergie was in London we were chief cooks and bottle washers. We had steak, whitebait fritters à la Brown, cabbage and fried potatoes à la Fergie. It was a grand feed.

I'm doing some night flying which keeps me out of trouble.

Tons of love to all,

Doug

D-Day Invasion

From my involvement as an instructor at pre-invasion school we had an idea when the whole thing was going to take place. The build-up to D-Day had been kept fairly secret. The first we knew about it at Horne we received a 'Form D'. The invasion was to take place on 5 June as we were advised at seven o'clock on 4 June.

The inevitable happened and it was called off so we had no leave and had to keep it quiet. We flew in the Dieppe area that day anyway, just to make the Germans think everything was normal.

I led the squadron on the pre-dawn show on 6 June and we arrived over the beachhead about 30 minutes before dawn. Our patrol was the east end of the Normandy beach. At that stage the emplacements, which were pretty well impregnable, were being bombed by RAF Mosquito bombers and also being shelled by the Navy which had arrived before the main force. As dawn arose the actual armada was about six miles offshore. There seemed to be nothing but ships as far as the eye could see. It was an incredible sight.

My next patrol was just before midday when I led the squadron again. We were again patrolling the east end of the beach. At that stage there were a tremendous number of tanks on the beach but it was difficult to see if they were making any progress because of the gun flashes, smoke and general mayhem.

From 6–27 June I had completed 24 operations, each of which was about two and a half hours. It was an intense three weeks. We lost a number of pilots, including P/O Meadows and Flight Sergeant Brown who were shot down, hit by our own ack-ack. F/Sgt Ferguson spun into the drink and our CO was hit by ack-ack but baled out.

130 Squadron en route to beachhead, Doug leading

Horne
Thursday, 15 June 1944

Dear Mum, Dad and Girls,

The big do is on. We were pretty pleased with the fact that we were the first day squadron over there. At that early hour there were no sea landings but night bombers were at work and the whole show was rather impressive. Once I crossed the coast at a low altitude they opened up on me. Just after I turned away, the Pathfinders lit up that particular spot and down came the bombs.

I was out again later in the day and it was a really impressive sight. There were hundreds of boats, all shapes and sizes, including the Navy, some were disembarking troops, others returning for more – the channel was literally chock-a-block. The air was full of aircraft all our own, bombers, large and small and fighters: the Hun was having a day off. The area was covered in gliders and parachutes of all colours. The Navy was periodically shelling combined with the RAF, and American bombing had more or less reduced the well-defended coast, about which the Huns boasted so much, to a ploughed field.

Generally speaking we have tried to work it so that no pilot does more than two shows a day. For the most part they are long trips lasting over two and a

D-Day, 11:30, 6 June 1944 Take off in pairs, Doug leading nearest camera

half hours, which builds rather large-sized corns on one's bottom – or so it feels. With dawn so early and dusk late we have been getting up before 3 a.m. and landing after midnight, so you can imagine what a grand job of work the ground crews are doing.

I've only seen one lot of Huns, last night – big juicy Ju88s and I should have got two if our ack-ack had not been keen, for I was right up the seat of one and at about 300 yards, closing in and just pressed the button when the Army sent up everything but the kitchen sink, so I lost two certs. I had to nip smartly off – bad luck and I was damn annoyed. I've had the odd shot at Hun transport which is rather good fun but generally we do patrol work, up and down, up and down again ad infinitum. We have a fair amount of rather accurate and frightening ack-ack to contend with. All our casualties, six in all, have been through it, and to come home with the odd hole or two is not uncommon.

I'm at Fergie's for the night as the Doc reckoned I had been doing too much and sent me off – sheets once again!

I'm very fit – don't worry.

Love, Doug

Westhampnett
Wednesday, 21 June 1944

Dear Mum, Dad and Girls,

We had a move in the weekend and having to keep up op requirements at the same time didn't give us much peace. We are now temporarily at Westhampnett where we were for the first few months of last year. We have a proper mess once again which is comfortable and will make us rather lazy after the open-air life we got accustomed to.

The latest thing in the air war is of course the V1. When we were at Horne they came over regularly day and night. In the day they make a rather terrifying noise and go like the clappers. At night they look like a small fire nipping through the air and seem to make more noise than usual. All this combined with the ack-ack boys creates rather a disturbance. The CO of the airfield offered £5 to the first chap to bring one down, so all the boys had machine guns at the ready – we actually got a couple from the ground. One morning I had a squirt at one from about 500 yards but I did not get it. A Typhoon blew it up in mid-air.

The £24 you kindly sent me, Dad, has arrived OK – many thanks. The RAF would not give me a sou to replace the gear lost in the fire so I complained to Bill Jordan. I received a letter from him yesterday to say all he could do was to give me £10 from the NZ Patriotic Funds, which is better than a kick in the pants.

Since I've been back here I've not had much time to visit any old haunts but we had a party with Bill Compton, Al Deere and a few of the French boys we knew at Biggin Hill.

I was up at 3.30 this morning and as it is now 10 a.m. I'll go and get some sleep.

Tons of love to all. I'm still damn fit so never worry.

Love, Doug

As well as patrols over the British and Canadian east end of the Normandy beach, we also did patrols at 10,000 feet protecting the ships and if we had time we would go inland and fire at any transport we might see. Eventually the beaches cleared

ABOVE Balloons to combat V1 Doodlebugs

BELOW Horse killed and cart demolished due V1 raid Aldwych

and the Mulberries – temporary wharves – were set up. The beach quietened down as the Army moved in and US Forces cut off Cherbourg Peninsula. One time we came across a couple of Ju88s which we claimed as shot down, but also the Navy claimed them and the search light claimed them!

I do remember that night quite clearly. We didn't get back until after dark from that operation. By the time we had something to eat and went on to intelligence for a briefing, it was 1 a.m. before I got to bed. I was up before 3 a.m. again to do another pre-dawn patrol. It was 22 June. The day wasn't the best with low cloud from 900 feet to 3000 feet. Usually I check courses but didn't this time as I had only slept two hours. I was tired as we had been at it for over a week and I followed the intelligence course. When I came through the cloud we were 30 miles south of the bridgehead over St Lo, which was held by the Germans, and all hell was let loose. All I could do was order the squadron to hit the deck and head north into our own ack-ack. Unfortunately, during that run up, four Spits were shot down with three killed. My No 2, an Australian F/O Shields, was on fire. When in cloud the fire looks much bigger. I thought, we wouldn't be seeing him again, but he managed to force land inside British lines. It seems he had opened the cockpit which is a mistake when you are on fire but had somehow managed to get his flaps down. To release the straps in the cockpit you pull out a key but it is likely he pressed his parachute release instead. On impact the straps restrained him just enough. The fire had partially burnt through and he was thrown out of the cockpit and landed in a haystack. Very lucky. He ended up in a hospital in south London where I went to see him three days later. He was slightly burnt on his hands where the leather gloves were and where the helmet had been. He was one of the survivors!

We lost another four about two days later in a daylight patrol through 'finger trouble'. When we flew through cloud we adopted a plan for the squadron of 12 to form three boxes of four. We came through cloud and on my left the box of four was intact, but on the right only one aircraft appeared. There had been a collision in the cloud. Two of them went into the sea and one fortunately got back to Ford aerodrome. The leader stupidly and against all orders flew on and was shot down by our own flak. He was picked up from the sea in his dinghy by air-sea rescue.

At the end of the month we lost Sgt Hircock and all up during that period we lost 11 of our pilots (many shot down by our own flak), some of whom were recovered. Once I was patrolling over the east end of Normandy and our own people started firing at us. We were at 8000 feet and I called on the R/T: 'If you bastards don't stop firing we're going home and we'll leave you to it!' I don't know if they had radio contact or if it was just coincidence, but the guns stopped immediately.

The whole period of that month was hard work. We were all tired and could well understand how the Army would feel – they would have been absolutely done. Air Command was starting to establish Spitfire squadrons into Europe and we were waiting in anticipation of our call up.

YEAR: 1944		AIRCRAFT.		PILOT, OR 1ST PILOT.	2ND PILOT, PUPIL, OR PASSENGER.	DUTY (INCLUDING RESULTS AND REMARKS).
MONTH.	DATE.	Type.	No.			
—	—	—	—	—	—	— Totals Brought Forward
		130 (Punjab) Sqdn. R.AF Airfield Horne Surrey				
MAY	31	Spitfire VB	AP- L	Self		Sector Recco
JUNE	2	"	AP. J	"		Line Gun
"	2	"	AP. G	"		A/c Test
"	3	"	AP. G	"		Dawn Patrol – Solent
"	3	"	AP. G	"		Dusk Patrol - Foreland
"	6	"	AP. G	"		Dawn Beachhead Cover
"	6	"	AP. G	"		Beachhead Support
"	7	"	AP. A	"		Dawn Beachhead Support
"	7	"	AP. D	"		Cover 'Utah'
"	8	"	AP. C	"		Cover 'Utah'
"	8	"	AP. G	"		Cover Utah
"	10	"	AP. G	"		Cover Utah
"	10	"	AP. G	"		Dusk Cover Utah
"	11	"	AP. G	"		Dawn Cover Eastern Area
"	12	"	AP. B	"		Cover Utah
"	13	"	AP. D	"		Dawn Cover Eastern Area
"	14	"	AP. G	"		Patrol Western Area
"	15	"	AP. G	"		Patrol Eastern Area
"	16	"	AP. G	"		Patrol Western Flank
"	17	"	AP. G	"		Dawn Patrol
"	17	"	AP. G	"		Omaha Patrol
"	18	"	AP. A	"		Chasing Hun Robot Planes - Beachy. Dungeness

GRAND TOTAL [Cols. (1) to (10)].

TOTALS CARRIED FORWARD

Extract from log book, June 1944, during D-Day

Oxted
Sunday, 2 July 1944

Dear Mum, Dad and Girls,

The war seems to be proceeding very well and I reckon once the big push starts over here, poor old Jerry won't have a clue as to which way to turn – a damn good thing. I've seen no Hun aircraft for ages in fact I've almost forgotten what they look like. A few of our boys who were shot down turned up again a day or so later rearing to go. Many of the Fighter Squadrons are now operating and based in France but we have been held back for a later push.

Down at the new abode [Shopwhyke House – officers' mess for Westhampnett and Merston] we now live like kings after the tent life we had before. The meals are grand and sheets again – what more could a man wish for. A couple of days ago I had quite a chat with Hawk, as I had not seen him for some time. With him are also Howard Crafts and Jack Barrett, both of whom I saw at Selsey. Johnny Pattison came over for the evening the night before I came on leave and he is hoping to go over to the 'other side' shortly. He reckons on finishing this tour and then going back to NZ, which I'll probably do myself depending on the state of affairs at the time.

Arthur King at the Mermaid was jolly glad to see me. Owing to the shortage of beer Arthur has to close down for three days a week but he always has a bar, which he keeps open for us boys. Now his pub is not unlike a club in London as a meeting place with some boys on their way to the 'other side' and others on a quick visit back. Jamie Rankin was here on my first day and he had brought back a whole lot of Camembert cheeses, which together with butter and cream are bountiful in France. Arthur on the other hand sends the boys lobsters, ducks, eggs and strawberries when he can get hold of them, and so he is rather popular. It has become a thriving business. The ten days I've spent so far I've had quite a few lobsters from him and the odd duck – all for nothing mind you – and I've also got the chap I used to get eggs from organised so we do pretty well one way and another.

Mick Maskill was down one day so I had a beer with him. He is the same old Mick and always in trouble. Garry Barnett came down to see Johnnie Checks and me one day. He has now got a pet tortoise with his squadron crest painted on its back and a hole drilled through the shell to which is attached about ten yards of string. Another visitor was Blackie Travis, an American who was with us at Biggin Hill last year. He has just finished a tour and is on his way back to the States on leave. They treat their boys pretty well and at the end of each tour they get a clear 30 days at home.

I came on leave on Friday and the Ford 8 got me to Oxted in two hours despite the traffic. It was rather a grand drive as the country now is really beautiful. After a cup of tea with Fergie I nipped out and played nine holes of golf. I must have worked rather too hard this month for I was rather tired. In the two nights I've been here I've crammed in 14 and 12 hours' sleep respectively. On Friday night I had a couple of beers and then had my fortune told by a certain Gypsy Smith. It cost me five bob and did not give me much gen I do not already know except that I am apparently going to have three children. She is quite a girl and gave me all the gen on the gypsies over here.

Best of luck to you all,

Love, Doug

On 27 June we were posted to Merston from where we operated until the end of July. We did about a dozen operations, mainly bomber escort. There was little of consequence as the bombing was taking place just beyond the lines of the Army south of Caen and there were no German aircraft seen in that vicinity.

Merston
Sunday, 16 July 1944

Dear Mum, Dad and Girls,

After I last wrote, Johnnie Checks phoned and came up that Sunday. We had a massive feed of toheroa soup, whitebait fritters, and pork chops with all the trimmings after which we went down to the Hoskins Arms. The beer ran out fairly early, so John and I decided we would visit the Jail Hotel, a rendezvous of ours when at Biggin Hill. They were very glad to see us as we arrived just on ten when everyone else had just been kicked out. We then got all our old local pals – those who weren't there were rung up – and ordered them to put in an appearance pronto. When all this was organised we opened up – yours truly barman – and drank beer which we blotted up with egg and tomato sandwiches. We continued the do till about three and then went to one of the local's houses and had some more beer to the tune of steak, eggs, tomatoes and chips – what a feed! We were disturbed by a V1 bomb which decided to drop rather close and broke up the party.

The trip back to camp was very enjoyable as the car buzzed along in great gusto. All I had to do was sit back and take in the scenery. I arrived back at about six and after supper I popped along to my local egg supplier and collected my 'ration' of five dozen a week, which I divide up among the boys.

As the weather has been poor we've done practically no flying to speak of and I'm rather annoyed about the whole thing. I've got a flight in the squadron again as Russ Mathieson had to go on rest, but I managed to get him the same job as I had while on rest. We had quite a do the other night in the local with Bill Compton, Colin Gray and Johnnie Johnson. I've known him for quite a while now and although he has done so well and the papers have got hold of him good and proper, you can notice no change in manner or general outlook on life at all.

Frank Transom, Chalky White and Red Roberts were over last night for tea and a bath, which cost me a few eggs.

Tons of love to all,

Doug

Merston
Sunday, 30 July 1944

Dear Mum, Dad and Girls

It is no wonder there hasn't been much progress from the Army as the weather has been rotten during the past couple of weeks. We have not been able to aid them or bust up the Hun surrounding them. The Yanks, however, have pushed ahead the last few days, which makes the outlook brighter. I reckon the Hun will crack smartly as he is well on the run in Russia, not in what one would call a healthy position in Italy and, once we get going in France, I think he will wonder where in the hell he can go next. There appears to be a bit of a revolt over in Hunland, which is of interest and will probably build up a bit.

Most of the shows we have done have been bomber escorts and it is certainly amazing the amount of stuff we are sending over these days. Although it must brighten the ears of the English troops, the Hun must have other ideas. We've been in far further than we ever dreamed of this time last year – not a sausage anywhere. We've been as far as Evreux, Argentan and Livarot, beyond Caen and Rouen.

I've got my flight now so I've got the boys to keep in order. They are a pretty good mob and I'm glad and proud to be in their command. I'm really lucky to have a flight in a squadron as there are such a lot of Flight Lieutenants around the country and a number of pre-war pilots. It is an interesting mixed mob of Aussies, Cannucks, NZ and British.

We went to a social do held by 485 Squadron, which I must admit was rather a blow-out and I got rather stinko. The other was a couple of nights ago when the sergeants had a dance – as a dance it was not so good but as a booze-up very high-powered.

I've got the place fairly well organised. As well as eggs we get plenty of lobster and have the odd duck now and again. Phil Tripe, our future boss, and I went to an egg merchant and did some pigeon shooting. We got about 20 and had a good feed a couple of evenings later.

Good to hear Digger was over to visit you and I'm also glad he has lost his beard, as it was not what I would call very handsome. I don't think he had a very good spin over here but that is the run of the game.

It won't be long now before we will be able to go down to good old Manly again – that will certainly be the day. My only worry is as it has been all along: what am I going to do to earn a living?

Well, I'm afraid I've no more news and I've got a job to do over here so I'll close.

Love to all of you,

Doug

On 4 August we moved on to Tangmere to convert to Spitfire XIVs and by the 10th the whole squadron was fully qualified. We then moved as 130 Squadron to Lympne.

We spent from 12 August to 30 September at Lympne. Our primary duty at Lympne was chasing 'doodlebugs', V1s, and the entire time we only got one, I was fortunate enough to get that. Operations told me when it was coming and would shortly cross the coast. I was down in position when it crossed the French coast near Gris Nez. I came down from 6000 feet and got a perfect interception at about 3000. It didn't explode, it just went down in the sea.

We only had 60 shells in each cannon so we only had about 10 seconds of firepower plus what was in the guns.

Our patrol area was from the French coast to the guns about three miles off our coast. The guns covered from there inland two miles and the Tempests patrolled from there to London where the balloons were. The Tempests and the guns got most of them, but for us it was really a waste of resources. There was a fellow, Jim McCaw, flying Tempests in 486 Squadron and he got about 20 V1s. His technique was to come alongside and knock tip them with his wing tip. The Gyroscope was used to maintain direction so when the gyro was toppled the V1 lost control and down they went.

The V1s were frighteningly noisy things. I recall there was one flying around in a circle above us. It eventually came down with a hell of a wallop and landed about 100 yards from our mess, which was Philip Sassoon's house. There was only superficial damage to the plaster on the ceiling.

Londoners were terrified of them. There was a theory that if you heard them you didn't get hit. Johnnie Checketts and I got wind of a Black Market dealer in the hills south of London. We went up there with the intent of blackmailing him into 'procuring' meat and other rationed goods. He ran a good set up. We were at the house negotiating and he was getting somewhat upset during the process, when all of a sudden there was a 'ping' sound. One of the V1s had hit the balloon defence wire. We heard nothing until the 'ping' and it made a hell of a mess. For better or worse he had all the windows open. There was no structural damage but everything on the tablecloth got sucked out the window. We left in a hurry and didn't negotiate any further.

Over the period at Lympne we did quite a lot of operations. Colin Gray was Wing Commander Flying and I led 130 Squadron. We did a lot of escorts for material moving to the continent and ramrods for Halifaxes and Bostons.

We did one dangerous trip where we flew at 2000 feet along the course that the gliders were going to fly for the drop on Arnhem, Nijmegen and Grave. Our job was to plot the flak path when we were fired at. I thought a lot of us would be shot down but despite the risk we only lost one aircraft. Several of us had holes in us but apart from that nothing serious.

We also did a bit of air to ground. We fired at trucks and other transport as well as attacking the V1 'doodlebugs'.

September 23 was the real show and all the Fighter Squadrons were escorting the airborne forces to Arnhem, Nijmegen and Grave. We did the escort for gliders to Nijmegen and Eindhoven but it was a disaster. The weather wasn't good but visually it was an incredible sight with the gliders being towed and the aircraft with parachutists. The drops were spectacular but unfortunately, when they landed at Arnhem, the Germans were all there waiting for them.

It was fairly common knowledge the push was coming in that area for some time so it would not have been difficult for the German spies to pick up what was about to happen from pub talk. The hierarchy must take some of the blame for letting it out of the bag. This will have contributed to the number of Allied casualties and extended the war unnecessarily. Loose tongues!

Lympne
Monday, 14 August 1944

Dear Mum, Dad and Girls,

The job we are doing now is purely defensive, seeking out VIs. This will give us experience with the faster Mk XIV aircraft so we can later put them to good offensive work.

Jack Henry is with us now and in my flight. He was with us two years ago in 485 Squadron. He lost a half ring to get back on ops and is as happy as a lark and I must admit that I'm fairly pleased about the whole thing myself as he is quite a lad and we get into a lot of trouble together. He had a good six months in Canada and has some great yarns to tell.

We have got a grand mess where we are now: a very large modern house, which used to belong to a chap, Sir Philip Sassoon. The gardens are extensive and as the weather is pretty good now it gets used regularly. We are in easy reach of Folkestone and when we get the time we will hunt the town out and see what action we can find.

The Army is doing well, thanks to the help of the RAF! The weather has been perfect for about ten days and looks as though it will hold so it appears that the 'Powers That Be' are on our side after a doubtful start. The boys over the 'other side' will be having the time of their lives bashing up the Hun transport. I'm trying to get Stan Browne into the squadron as he will be fed up with OTU by now.

Lympne – postcard of Sassoon residence, our mess at Lympne

Poker school

One of the big shots is expected this afternoon so I've got all the boys cleaning aircraft and the dispersal, and believe me they are rather 'brassed off'. It is damn silly with all the flying we do to have to keep one's aircraft in top line.

I received an airgraph from Gus Taylor a few days ago and he told me Jock McGruther had been killed, which shook me a lot. When you see Mr or Mrs

130 Punjab Squadron

McG, express my sympathy. Gus said his boys adored him and he was a very brave and gallant soldier.

Well I must close for now. Fit and well,

Doug

Lympne
Monday, 11 September 1944

Dear Mum, Dad and Girls,

I've not been able to go on leave yet as the other Flight Commander went base over apex at our squadron dance.

We have had some fun straffing and amongst the lot I got were two good truckloads of Huns, few of whom I should say survived as the driver elected not to stop – two beautiful flamers. With the new Mark we are flying there have been some long trips.

The 485 Squadron boys were here for a few days not so long ago and we had rather a bash up. They had not tasted beer for about two weeks so they needed

130 Squadron September 1944 prior to leaving for Grave, Holland. On plane: Standish, Pollock / Back: Bugs Keating, Dodds, D H White, Kenny Riordon, Eddie Edwards, Geoff Hudson, Fred Riley, Wally Brown, Ron Meadows, _ / Front: Marty Hume, Don Wilson, Mac McConnell, Stotty Stott, Doug, W/C Colin Gray, CO Phil Tripe, Scotty Scott, Keith Lowe, Capt Delara, George Earp, Adj Williams

refueling in no mean manner. I've got Marty Hume with me now attached to this unit and though he has lost his S/L rank, he is damn glad to be on ops again till he gets a better job. On Friday Marty, Colin Gray and I popped up to Farnborough. We were called upon to act as guinea pigs for decompression chamber tests on equipment and body. It was an interesting experience. As the air pressure reduced, our stomachs expanded, Marty's greatly so as he was rather portly before the exercise. The tests were carried out to the point we were almost induced to unconsciousness. As a reward we got to keep a new Mae West jacket, which was a great improvement on the bulky standard issue and a smaller oxygen mask more in the German style.

Jack Henry got a flight in another squadron. He went to Brussels with one of the Belgian boys the other day but I'm afraid he did not enjoy the trip much as he pranged when landing. He put a nice gash in his forehead and another at the back of his head, in all involving some ten stitches so he spent the night in sick quarters and came back yesterday by air ambulance. He looks very sorry for himself and will have to have an X-ray to see if his head is cracked and will be off for several weeks.

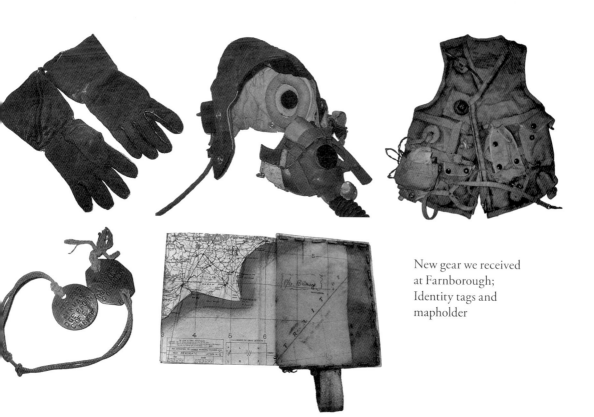

New gear we received
at Farnborough;
Identity tags and
mapholder

The weather still continues to keep up and now we are having coolish nights but beautiful days which all help bring the war nearer to ending. I've had your air letter dated 16 August, so this service seems pretty fair and means airgraphs have been knocked to leg as far as time goes.

Oxted
Saturday, 16 September 1944

Dear Mum, Dad and Girls,

Since I last wrote we have done some escort jobs, which have enabled us to get deep into Hunland due to the extra range from the Mark XIV. On Tuesday we got as far as Wanne-Eikel, near Essen. The only thing I don't like about the trips is that we get sore bottoms and no Hun aircraft.

I arrived here in the Ford 8 on Wednesday evening and had a few beers in the local and attended a small party afterwards. On Thursday I went to Big

Smoke. I went shopping and got a tin trunk and ordered and was measured for a new uniform, a couple of pairs of gray flannels and a sports coat. As the war is as well as finished I thought it would be a good idea to get a few clothes.

Yesterday was rather a quiet day and I spent the morning visiting the locals and in the afternoon I played around with the car and had a round of golf with Norman Roberts. I had a quiet night last night, attending a picture followed by a few beers and a lobster supper at Norman's. This afternoon I'm going to chase the dogs around the track with Norman and a few of the cronies.

The war goes well and I don't think it will be long now, so have a job organised for me, Dad!

Cheerio for now, give my love to all,

Doug

Oxted
Thursday, 21 September 1944

Dear Mum, Dad and Girls,

Last Saturday I got into trouble at the dance with a NZ Fleet Air Arm Wallah Jack Mason from Dominion Road after a very unprofitable day at the dogs. We had a few too many.

Garry Barnett was here the night before last. He will be going on rest within the next couple of days and is trying to get himself a good job, failing that he will try to get back home and out of the Air Force. He got a DFC the other day. Johnnie Checks is a bit annoyed as he has got the month's leave he deserves. He has worked damn hard during the past few months. Johnny Pattison has now got the 485 Squadron and should prove his worth. There is a chap Shaw whom I went to school with who has joined 485 and he also trained with that chap Abbott who you gave my address.

My leave has gone quickly. It might be the last I get for a while as we are expecting to be sent in the direction of Hunland.

Love, Doug

FROM	TO 1326 TO 1331	DISTANCE	A.S.I.	TRACK	CO.(M)	TIME E.TA LEG	TOTAL
BASE	N. FORELAND	28	180/220	%/550	052	7	1349
N. FORELAND	OSTEND	68	220	550	103	14	1357
OSTEND	ANTWERP (R/V)	61	"	"	101	13	1410
ANTWERP (R/V)	HECHTEL	42	'	"	101	9	1419
HECHTEL	LDG. STRIP	46	"	"	011	12	1431
LDG. STRIP	HECHTEL	46	'	'	215	12	1458
HECHTEL	ANTWERP	42	"	"	288	13	1511
ANTWERP	OSTEND	61	"	'	288	20	1531
OSTEND	N. FORELAND	68	"	'	289	22	1553
N. FORELAND	BASE	28	"	"	242	8	1601

N° 1018 H.Q.F.C. MAY 1943 000,005:1 Scale of Statute Miles S/c 1336

Ops schedule – for 23 September airborne escort to Eindhoven

Lympne
Wednesday, 27 September 1944

Dear Mum, Dad and Girls,

Marty Hume has got a flight in the squadron and is jolly glad. The CO is away at present so I'm the big cheese and knocking the boys into shape! I've only done a couple of trips so far since I came back. One was with Airborne Forces to Eindhoven and though we did not meet any opposition or see the parachute jumps it was a grand sight to see all the tugs and gliders on their way. I did some low flying coming back over the towns and villages of Belgium and there are certainly large quantities of flags flying from shop windows and houses. I had a good look at the place where I got clobbered by flak between Ostend and Bruges. It looks rather a pleasant place on the canal now with the odd bicycle wandering along the road.

The other trip we did was one of my longest – 2 hours 40 minutes – a Dakota escort to Grave for a supply drop. The planes landed and dropped their supplies on a prepared bit of land and then took off again as though

Spitfire Mk XIV at Lympne. IMPERIAL WAR MUSEUM IMAGE CL001354

nothing had happened.[74] My arm is a bit rickety today as I had the needle three times to keep me out of harm's way for a while. I'll probably be over the 'other side' before long and closer to the Hun.

The weather lately has been very iffy but now it looks as if we may have a good spell – let's hope so for if we get a dose of good weather the war could finish this year. Then all we have to do is finish off the Japs, and then it will be curtains.

Cheerio and keep smiling,

Best love,

Doug

---

74 I did not know it at the time but we were about to be posted to Grave. The reason for the haste unloading the Dakotas was Grave was still under enemy attack.

Occupation

*

GRAVE/DIEST

Operation Market Garden 17–25 September was the largest mobilisation of Allied Airborne Forces. The objective was to hold the bridges over key tributaries of the Lower Rhine in German-occupied Holland and then push through into Germany. Following initial success at Grave (R Maas), Nijmegen (R Waal) and Eindhoven (R Dummel), progress stalled.

On 30 September I led the squadron from Lympne[75] to Antwerp-Deurne. Antwerp was then being held partially by British and German forces. We were fired at as we landed and we were fired at as we took off for B82 Grave the next morning. The night in Antwerp we went for a jaunt around the town in a Jeep. It was an eerie set-up as part of the town was still occupied by Germans. We had strayed from the safety of the Allied-occupied area and the engine began to play up. Steam was coming from the radiator and the Jeep stopped. We were in an uncomfortable situation and had to get back to camp pronto. We decided to pee into the radiator. Whether it was the top-up or the cooling time, we got the engine started again and made it back.

75 Our CO, Phil Tripe, pranged when his wing collapsed on take off. He turned up in Grave a few days later with a new plane but didn't take part in operations. He was born in Canada in 1918 and drowned in Trout Lake, Ontario 1982 when his ice-yacht went through the surface.

Grave

Grave
Holland
Tuesday, 3 October 1944

Dear Mum, Dad and Girls,

Well I'm on the continent at last and what few days I've been over have been full of trouble and excitement. I've looked forward to getting over here since the invasion started and was more or less giving up hope. The notice we got was naturally little and all we had time to do was get one's kit and inoculations sorted and away we went. Marty and I took our cars up to Oxted and as Colin Gray and Jack Henry came up we had rather a hard night. Garry Barnett was there also. He will be in to see you so please do him well as he is a grand lad. We had a few of the paratroopers in the mess next day and they certainly had some tales to tell.

We landed for our first night at Antwerp, Belgium, and what a grand place it was. Food is scarce but booze plentiful and bags of bars. We started off in the best and worked downwards, getting to base at 2 a.m. full of beer, Champagne and Cognac. What amazed me was that even though the drink was fairly cheap, all the joints turned on a six- or seven-piece dance band to which we did justice. We shifted next day to Holland. We are now nearer the Hun and well into the country and as I see it the only civilisation we will see is when we next get leave – if we do. The Hun seems to be fighting fairly hard and as they are now more active in the air I'll be very surprised if we don't clobber a few.

Yesterday there was a dogfight over the drome and a Spit bought it and hurtled into the deck at a high speed. We've been shelled and bombed a little but I think Jerry has more to worry about than us. We've got quite a good set-up for the squadron: we've taken over half a house and have used the owner's orchard to put up the tents which the chaps who were not flying did today. It should prove to be the goods. The weather has not been what we want for it has rained ever since the tents went up.

RAF Authorisation Card to permit driving on the Continent

This letter will be a bit disjointed as I am writing it at odd intervals. If it does not 'spell sense', you will understand. I'm wondering when I'll see England again. I have a lot of gear with me that I'll never use so I'll put the hard word on the Winco to let me take the Spit over to Blighty for a night or so. The gen is to wear clothes till they fall off as the only washing we are likely to do is nil. When and if we get into Hunland we should be able to select accommodation at will enabling us to get some pretty good set ups for billets and mess.

I expect you will all be looking forward to a spell at Manly, petrol allowance permitting. I wish I could be with you all but I'm afraid it will not be this year so here's hoping for the next New Year at the beach.

Tons of love to all,

Doug

P.S. Don't worry about me. I'm fit and well and enjoying life.

Grave
Monday, 9 October 1944

Dear Mum, Dad and Girls,

We are in the thick of it with little distance separating ourselves from the Huns. We are reminded throughout the day that there is a war on by the continual noise of guns and ack-ack. I've seen no Hun aircraft up close but

have had a lot of good straffing and during the past few days have built up a
bit of a score in transport ruined. Damn good fun as long as you steer clear
of the flak areas. It has been cold at night but we have moved from our tents
and all the boys are now in four houses close together. It is consequently
more comfortable so if we are here over the winter period we won't have to
chop each other out of an iceberg to get weaving. The little Dutch kids come
to dispersal with baskets of fruit, which is plentiful and jugs of milk, which
they dish out to all and sundry. We give them English cigarettes in return and
they are as pleased as punch. Nightlife is non-existent as there are no towns
to speak of nearby and what there are has no beer anyway. We have a café as
an anteroom and drink Champagne which works out at 12/- a bottle and we
smoke German cigars. The Huns have been damn good to us on the whole as
some Army mob captured a terrific supply of Hun rations which the Army
and RAF over here have been living on – German food is good but their cigars
not so hot. Marty Hume and I run a 1939 Packard around: it was taken from
the Huns and we are looking forward to another push so that we can fix up a
few more of the boys with the same means of conveyance.

What I wouldn't give for a nice hot bath! We have a lack of washing facilities
here and our clothes pong to high heaven. There is no one to object so what
the hell! My current shirt I've had on for over three weeks and I reckon it is just
getting worn in. I got an air letter from you, Mum, dated 19th of last month. I
did not even know Harold Cavaghan had been killed.[76] I will drop them a note
as soon as I've finished this epistle to you. Boy it would be good to be at Manly
now and have a good dose of sun and sea to swim in. The beach house must
be a pretty posh outfit now with H and C water, pull the chain cistern – all the
mod cons. Don't forget an electric digger for the annual rubbish hole.

Love to all. Keep smiling.

Doug.

On 1 October I took the squadron up to B82 Grave-Keent. We joined 2nd TAF
83 Group. The aerodrome was only two miles west of the bridge that had been
taken on 24 September. We had 14 aircraft and no ground support staff with us.
All we could get in the Spit was a couple of blankets and a few 'dog' biscuits. We

---

76 Harold was 19 and in the Border regiment. Killed on 1 August 1944. Hottot-Les-Bagues Cemetery.

130 Squadron Spitfire XIV at B82 Grave with markings AP S flown at times by Doug.
IMPERIAL WAR MUSEUM IMAGE MH006848

spent the night in a café on the boundary of the drome. This was the best on offer as sleeping quarters but they had no food!

The next morning we went up on patrol. We saw about 70 Huns. I made the decision not to attack as we had not been refuelled and did not have enough petrol to chase them if we got into trouble. We used our brains and came back and landed at Grave. The ground crew and back-up arrived that afternoon of 2 October. After the tents were erected for the officers' mess, a German Me262 came over and dropped anti-personnel bombs and killed the adjutant and chef. A few of the others were injured. These bombs were quite anti-social and in my view not in accordance with 'fair play'. They exploded into many smaller bomblets above ground, spreading shrapnel everywhere.

There we remained without food and slept in the café for another couple of nights until the mess was resurrected. We started off with our own squadron and 125 Wing was augmented with 402 Canadian (Winnipeg Bear) Squadron also flying Spitfire XIVs and 80 and 274 Tempest Squadrons.

For the next few days I led 130 out on dawn patrols over Nijmegen and Arnhem. We were usually first up at dawn but we rotated the patrol duties of the wing's four squadrons throughout the day.

Subsequently we became more involved in armed recces over Germany, taking out transport. We were restricted by the weather as it was a particularly harsh autumn with incessant rain and poor visibility. There were days the runway was such a bog that we couldn't take off.

On 5 October, Geoffrey Page who was the Wing Commander Flying returned from one such recce and got into some trouble, did a forced wheels-up landing and caught fire. I rushed out and helped pull him out but that was the end of it for him. He was burnt in the Battle of Britain and naturally he had reached the end of his operations. The XIV were prone to becoming 'flamers' due to two 13-gallon wing tanks. After the war Geoff Page held a high-level post at Vickers, the manufacturers of the Supermarine Spitfire.

The next day we had a successful time destroying a number of barges and trains.

Then George Keefer, a Canadian, came in as Winco Flying. On the 11th we had another occasion when an Me262 came and dropped a bomb amongst the Canadian squadron. They were refuelling when the bomb hit the petrol tank and they lost most of their aircraft. The crew were fortunate and flew back to Britain where they had a week's leave before they returned with new aircraft.

Grave
Monday, 16 October 1944

Dear Mum, Dad and Girls,

Firstly I must apologise for not sending you the customary cable for your birthdays. I received your air letter dated 18 September in which you mentioned the fact, Dad, and it has worried me ever since. I guess you thought I had 'bought it'.

We are now running a two-squadron mess in part of a school – nothing flash, a couple of fairly large rooms, one for an anteroom and bar and one for a dining room as well as a back room for the kitchen. We are having large poker sessions at night and more by good luck than good management I'm about square on the series up to date. The Nuns are not bad souls and have given us bags of apples, tomatoes and beautiful grapes. The Hun cigars are lasting out (possibly because they are lousy) so we all sport them whilst dabbling with the cards.

As well as a lack of food and having to live mainly on 'bully beef' we have limited water. There is one tap for the entire wing plus all the support staff. For three weeks we have not had a wash. After Nijmegen was taken, Marty and I decided to send the boys up there in five-ton trucks to have baths. The baths proved to be showers and though we had to queue up for some two hours

I enjoyed myself as the water was good and hot and I reckon I lost a bit of weight in dirt that day.

We nearly lost P/O Edwards. We were doing a patrol at 30,000 feet when he was singing jibberish on the R/T. The lines are supposed to be kept clear except in an emergency. I realised he may be suffering from a lack of oxygen so talked the squadron down immediately. Fortunately Eddie Edwards came around and lived to see another day.

Yesterday afternoon was damn wet so I took four of the boys in the Packard and headed south, seeing what damage the war had done. We eventually came to a little café where we consumed a fair quantity of lager, which, though nice to drink, had no bang in it at all. It was a change to get out of the camp and have a look around. We followed one road and came to a sign: 'If you want to keep healthy don't go any further', with a dirty big swastika painted on it, so being brave airmen we turned the car around and retraced our steps smartly!

Best of love,

Doug

P.S. I have made a decision and don't wish to stay in the RAF after the war.

Grave
Monday, 23 October 1944

Dear Mum, Dad and Girls,

These air letters seem to be the form, all right. I received yours, Dad, dated 2 October, and considering the mail takes about five days from England it seems a fair thing. I notice also that you have been receiving my mail in good time so we can't really wish for more as you get a fair amount of gen in the few pages provided.

The war for me has been restricted by bad weather and we've not flown for some days. If we were near a town such as Antwerp, the boys could have quite a bit of fun. The few towns around here are very clapped out. Booze is almost non-existent as are the girls. The Hun must have taken one hell of a gaggle away as factory workers or for other purposes. I was told there was a bit of perfume at one town some ten miles away near the front line, so I took along the Packard and a pile of cigarettes to do some trading but found nothing. If I do run into any I intend to bring it back with me. When I got to the town, all I did was have a shave. I gave the cigarettes away as they are well appreciated in this part of the world. Another way we while away time is to go up to the front line after trophies, but it can be dangerous.

The other day three of us went to a town on the front line and were shelled and mortared for about an hour before we got out – damn unpleasant. One of the boys picked up the first Hun helmet he saw and unfortunately Jerry's head was still in it. A couple of the boys hit a mine in a Jeep and though only suffered minor injuries are rather shaken. We seem to have learned the hard way we are better to stay put in Grave.

The CO, Marty Hume, and I think we are onto a good wicket. The Groupy got a Collaborator's caravan some 70 feet long and we are hoping to talk him out of it. As there are three bedrooms, a sitting room and a kitchen, it would be as good a billet as you can hope for. Our mess goes well and we have now taken over a café as a bar and it is pretty good. Marty and I had a night in Groupy's caravan the other night and cleaned up a bottle and a half of Cognac for him. He also brought out some stuff a French farmer gave him, which is a type of home brew: the concoction being distilled cider. Personally I thought it was rotten and it nearly lifted off your head at each mouthful.

The boys are going on 48-hour leave now and it was damn funny to see four of them in a couple of Austins setting course for the nearest large town. Being the highly exalted Flight Commander I hope to take a Spit back to England as I want to get rid of some gear and see some civilisation!

After I've finished this I'm taking a few of the boys to a nearby town to get a hot shower apiece – the second I will have had since I've been over here. I did some washing a day or so ago and I'm afraid I'm not much class at the job. When cleaned and dried it looked just as dirty as when I started and believe me it was certainly dirty!

The boys are playing poker at a high rate of knots but I've been skinned of all my dough so I can sit and watch others go down the sink. Bridge is now becoming more popular in the mess at the moment – there are some six fours hard at it.

Tons of love,

Doug

Grave
Sunday, 29 October 1944

Dear Mum, Dad and Girls,

The rain has turned to fog and mist. It is rather unpleasant as the ground stays damp and also gives the troops little chance of getting their clothes dry.

The weather has curtailed flying and my guns are 'rusting up' a bit! I had a rather thrilling ten minutes or so the day before yesterday. I was leading the squadron, looking for Huns over Hunland, and just as I gave a turn I noticed large black puffs behind me and so ordered a climb. As I went about there was one hell of a bash and I knew the worst had happened so handed over the squadron to Marty and headed home. I was damn lucky really as when I got down I saw there were 20 holes in the kite but none in a vital spot. Almost every part of the aircraft let in a bit of air and I had a lump come in just behind my bottom. They can certainly shoot, these Jerries, as we were at a good 12,000 feet at the time. Another score to settle in the near future!

A majority of the boys have got Hun pistols but I've not bothered. One day an Army type was giving me the gen on a Walther P38 pistol and the inevitable happened: it went off and got another Army boy in the thigh some two or three feet from me. Rather stupid. The fellow was given a shot of morphine and did not worry much about life after that. We have been looking for cars for the squadron and have procured a damn good Fiat Ten, which will come in handy for 48s.

We have looked over a few Hun prisoners and for the most part they are a dumb-looking mob. One chap reminded me of a monkey at the zoo as he sat on the straw and had a scarf out, which he scrutinised in no mean manner, and every now and again would bring his thumbnails together on some prey. The guards reckon they are a dirty mob and stink to high heaven when first brought in so they apply Keating and such flea and bug powders liberally. One chap there had been a pilot in the Hun Air Force. He did not give much gen but I understood that he was shot down when training and his nerves must have packed in, so he ended up a private in the infantry – lucky fellow! Our troops have certainly been hardened in this war in Europe. They take no cheek from Jerry and shoot first with no worry at all.

We now have a regular run to a town some 12 miles away and at another place they have showers and a large swimming pool, which is piping hot and rather popular. Unfortunately, now that word has got out, they are generally packed so we have a roster going with the Army. The boys look forward to a good wash and a bit of fun in the baths.

Tons of love,

Doug

Our main occupation in Grave was bomber escort, air to ground and shooting up trucks. It was discovered that the Germans could flood the aerodrome as we were right on the River Maas, one of the tributaries of the Rhine. They were in fact preparing to do this so the wing split up.

The day before moving from Grave I flew down to Diest to organise billets and mess. The Army Major in charge of the town met me and I decided a couple of small hotels adjacent to one another would be suitable for pilot accommodation and a hall in a nunnery for messing. The English Major had great pleasure in telling me they were unavailable but I had done my homework. As the airfield was within three miles of the town the Air Force had jurisdiction and I had the right to take over the requested buildings. It wasn't often that we got one over the Army!

Next day I led our squadron to B64 Diest about 30 miles east of Brussels.

Diest

We reached Diest-Schaffen in early November. It was a small aerodrome, which the Germans had condemned. It only had mesh on it and if you went off the mesh the aircraft went on its nose. It was a one-squadron aerodrome.

We made ourselves at home in the prearranged hotels and nunnery which had been occupied by the SS. We all messed together with no distinction for officers. We all ate the same food and built up a good rapport, but the meals were awful. Corned beef for breakfast, cold corned beef for lunch and the same mixed with dehydrated vegetables for dinner.

We were primarily employed on air-to-ground and we had the job of following the V2 rockets. On the first morning we did a pre-dawn patrol to plot the trails of the rockets coming up from the eastern side of the Zuiderzee. I saw no more than four or five rockets but a 262 appeared. I turned into him and fired but he was out of range and promptly disappeared. The 262 was little trouble to us. They

Aerial view Diest-Schaffen today, note slope of runway uphill away from camera

were based around the Rhine but only had a range of 40 minutes. The Tempests used to wait for them on the return journey. They got a lot that way but often got caught themselves in the flak.

A couple of weeks later I saw the trail of 20 or so V2s. Very few of them got to England, either due to mechanical fault or them being hit and the gyro being upset. Their range was fairly limited, but they could be set up quickly. On one occasion they were directed towards Brussels and flew over us en route.

Diest
Belgium
Monday, 6 November 1944

Dear Mum, Dad and Girls,

You will notice the change of address. We are near the town of Diest. The change is like going from Aria to Auckland. We have a good set-up and have got all the boys in a couple of pubs, which is good and handy for mustering them together as the mess is only about 100 yards from the billet. The town is full of cafés, which do good trade, and fruit shops, which have plenty of grapes that are really good and run on an average at about 15 francs per pound. The Belgians are a grand mob and nothing is too much for them. Les Belgique's are most popular with the troops. As regards the female line here, I've not seen many. Two reasons that have been put forward are firstly that at present it is a Holy Week and they, being RCs, are very religious and stay put for the most part, and secondly that some 400-odd were treated in the usual manner as collaborators and don't come out to show their shaved heads to the populous.

We have naturally enough had some rather boozy evenings. There is plenty of variety as well as ample stocks so quite a few of the lads have to walk around for a major part of the next day with their eyes closed to stop them bleeding to death! Yesterday evening the CO, Marty, and yours truly set course for Brussels some 12 miles away and visited all the cafés and dives imaginable and finished up at a rather high-powered joint, the Café de Paris, at 3.30 a.m., winning the war left, right and centre. The CO and Marty failed to show any signs of life till lunch but I managed to struggle out not long after eight to eat a hearty breakfast of sausages and bacon, washed down with about a gallon of tea. We have acquired by fair and foul means, mostly, the latter, another three cars: an Airflow Chrysler and a couple of Fiats, one of which is in good nick but the other has got more towing hours to its credit than hours under its own steam.

The Army boys seem to be plodding along at a fair speed and meeting with little or no opposition. It should not be long now before Holland is cleaned up. I pray it will be very soon so we can get some food into the place. The issue has arisen as result of the Bastards flooding a fair part of the country, ruining the crops. It will take years to bring the land back into production. It's a great pity we cannot do the same to them.

At present I've got rather a painful rash or skin infection under my chin so it keeps me on the deck, for a day or so anyway. As soon as the weather clears we'll be flying again, much to the Doc's annoyance.

I received a letter from Bruce Wallace. He is with Mac and hopes to leave at the end of this month. Mac has apparently got himself engaged, so all goes well. Bruce had a bad time also in West Africa and got most of the tropical diseases they dish out down that way.

Best love to you all,

Doug

Diest
Sunday, 12 November 1944

Dear Mum, Dad and Girls,

The weather has been rotten and a couple of days ago we received a small dose
of snow. It did not get a chance to stay very long as it rained very hard prior to
the snow and afterwards came down in buckets. We only did a couple of shows
this last week. The first we got some Hun horse-drawn vehicles and on the
next we got damn all and received quite a bit of flak as a gesture. Today is a real
stinker, drizzling rain, which is good for nothing as far as we are concerned.

The boys have been nipping off to the towns in the vicinity as well as
Brussels. The CO, Marty and I are organised in a place called Tirlemont about
40 minutes away and we go in the Chrysler or the Doc's Mercury. The Doc
with us is also an NZ chap, Cross by name and his father had a practice in
Auckland. He came over here some time ago and, after finishing his medical,
joined the RAF. He is a damn fine fellow and he has seen a lot in this war going
through France and getting out at Dunkerque. He was a Squadron Leader
then and has been a Winco for some time. When the invasion started he
dropped his half ring in order to get over here as he has no intention of staying
in the RAF after the war and is going to go back to NZ.

I reckon if this war is not over by about March I'll try and get home. They
will probably kick me out after my three months leave as I've done too much
on ops to squeeze in another tour unless they keep me as an instructor. I think
I would rather get out as I reckon I want to get organised on a job as soon as
possible.

Well I've not given you much news this week, a lot of piffle really – I must
be getting homesick. I hope to go back to England for a week about the
middle of next month, which I'm looking forward to.

Love, Doug

While operating from Grave and Diest, we had a few successes. The Germans
were skilled at hiding their transport in the bush and trees. We seemed to do
quite well after it was raining. One day, 19 November, I saw a motorbike going
along the road, so I led the flight of four down. We'd crossed the Rhine and were
in Germany and I was determined to get this guy on the bike. I fired at him but

couldn't get the nose down far enough so missed the target. He spun out on the side of the road, probably due to fright. As we pulled out we noticed a number of trucks on the road between two sections of wood that would otherwise have been unsighted from the air. I brought the squadron down and we got staff cars and about 20 trucks, mainly 'flamers' and presumably full of petroleum.

In that second tour, on the air to ground attacks, I was hit seven times but none causing serious damage. We had to be careful as the Huns were setting traps. There might be a train with engine steaming but with flak at the ready on all sides. There was no chance of getting through the flak. If you attacked you were a goner. Ironically, as the Allies were gaining the ascendancy, the situation became more difficult. We used to go into towns like Hertogenbosch and get pistols and sell them to the Americans. It seemed that we as Squadron Leaders had less money than US privates.

The German prisoners were held in a huge field in Hertogenbosch. I was talking to a British officer and enquiring about any SS. He said they got a lot of SS but only kept one and shot the rest. It had become tough and ruthless on both sides especially since the Germans realised they were losing the war. There was a successful bombing raid by Tempests and Typhoons which cleaned out SS headquarters in Holland. From then on they took no prisoners. The war was at the stage whereby any aircrew who force-landed or parachuted into German-occupied Holland or Germany and fell into SS hands were immediately shot.

Diest
Sunday, 19 November 1944

Dear Mum, Dad and Girls,

Today has been a perfect day, but the drome rather soft, which has meant only one show from which I've just returned and it was a field day. I got rid of all my ammo and we got results so that the dreaded Hun is minus quite a bit more transport, boats and a high-powered loco. The other time I've been out this week I saw damn all apart from flak.

My social activities have quietened down somewhat, though I pay the odd social call to my popsy about 20 miles away at Tirlemont. I am now – *un bel homme* – so they think, which is good for morale. We have been playing a bit of bridge and I'm getting pretty hot, though at times my partner, whoever the unlucky man may be, reckons I'm a bit clueless. We are expecting Jack Henry and his mob of roughs any day now – trouble ahead! Vic Hall was here to see us a day or so ago and was in his usual form, but I'm glad to say did not stay the night so we were let off lightly. Al Deere is expected any day to pay Marty and me a call, so it looks like trouble for one night. He has got a staff job now, I think, and is rather brassed off. The Army is still advancing towards the Ruhr and within shelling range. The sooner they get there the sooner this show will finish.

I had an airgraph from Noel a few days ago. You must have done them well at the dinner party as both Bob Gyllies and Noel Taylor have written and said what a damn good night they had. I was surprised to hear that they had called Bob up for the Army. Surely there must be some mistake as he has had a dose of TB, which I should think would exempt a person from the Army for good.

Best of love,

Doug

Diest
Sunday, 26 November 1944

Dear Mum, Dad and Girls,

I procured three bottles of perfume yesterday, which I posted in the afternoon. Funnily enough, good perfume is not easy to obtain. I was really looking for Chanel No 5, but that is only procurable on the black market. The perfume I got was bought for me by an agent for Chanel, and she reckoned that the stuff I've sent you is far better. All three bottles in one so I hope it reaches you. We are allowed to send one parcel duty-free to the value of £2 so you will understand why it is valued at 36/-.

We are putting on a ginormous Xmas party for the local children between the ages of five and eight on the 9th of next month, which will go well, and we are expecting over 400 to be there. The pilots in the squadron are putting on a pantomime and the G/C has dragged me in as Santa Claus, so I'll have my work cut out for the afternoon. In Belgium Xmas Day is 6 December – Saint Nicholas Day!

Last Thursday, seven of us had one big bash-up in Brussels. We got there at about three and it was just like going up to Big Smoke when released. We did the local cafés around the Gare du Nord and at 6 p.m. set course for one of the many officers' clubs. These clubs are damn well run and NAAFI have certainly got their fingers out for once. The one we went to on Thursday night had a tremendous horseshoe bar, which sold all kinds of grog – including whiskey, which is usually scarce in these parts – at very cheap prices. Whiskey and Cognac at five francs a tot. We had a grand meal there in a massive hall, which had about six large chandeliers and a string orchestra playing in a box some 20 feet above the floor. Very best Burgundy and other wines 35–40 francs a bottle and in an adjoining room a dance floor. I'm afraid the rest of the night was rather a shambles as we all lost each other and did not rendezvous till about midday next day.

The Frogs did a damn good push the other day and I hope we can get established over the Rhine, which will signal the end, bar the shouting. The sooner the better – I'm sure dying for the day when I go through the gates of 7 Bourne St. It should not be long now.

Tons of love and a very Happy Xmas to you all,

Doug

Diest
Saturday, 2 December 1944

Dear Mum, Dad and Girls,

Old Father Weather has come to the fore again, keeping us on the deck. We used to moan about English weather and I'm beginning to think that after all it is not the worst in the world. There never seems to be a happy medium in flying: in summer you get too much and in winter you don't get anywhere near enough. When we are on the ground over here the Intelligence Organisation pulls its fingers out and organises damn good lectures and films.

This week I took a crafty 48 hours off and spent a lazy time at the home of my girlfriend Anna at Tirlemont. Anna's auntie always seemed to be present whenever we met. At night the aunt insisted that she give me a drink which consisted of heated red wine with sugar and cinnamon. She reckoned it was good for the old bronchial tubes. It was a shrewd move on her part as both nights all I remember is putting out the light. It was good to sleep between sheets on a really soft bed. What a grand brew, both to drink and for medicinal purposes, as both mornings my coughing hours were reduced considerably.

The days were spent wandering about and eating. I take them down the odd bit of food and though I object considerably, they insist on giving me something in return. They gave me a cigarette box and a miniature of the Manneken-Pis (the statue in Brussels), which I wear on my battledress. It is the envy of all and sundry as they are impossible to acquire in the shops. I've also got a bracelet and a ring, which are going to be engraved. They are damn good people. As a matter of fact, Anna is a great girl – attractive, sincere and a good cook. Don't worry, I'm not about to get hitched! Anna speaks Flemish which I don't understand, and she doesn't understand English.

As I look out of the window of this distant land, watching the rain pelt down, I think of good old Manly. God bless the place – what memories – the family together, sun and bags of tennis and abundant fishing.

Tons of love to all,

Doug

Diest
Saturday, 9 December 1944

Dear Mum, Dad and Girls

We have had snow all morning and I've got a slight dose of flu. The ground is wet underfoot and it is damnably cold. We have had a bit of activity this week with a few patrols and yesterday had a bang-up day. In the morning we did an armed recce and, though we found little, managed to get a bit of Hun material. In the afternoon, also on a recce, Hun kites poked their noses in and got a bit of a shock having three shot down and three probables to worry about. We lost one. I was not on the afternoon show, as the morning do fixed my ears for me and the dreaded lurgy came on rapidly during the day. I hope to get a flip or two in before I go on leave. When I go I'll get the gen on going back to NZ as I intend to get on my way when this tour is over. To tell you the truth, the old nerves are getting a bit fidgety lately, but should hold out for a

while. I think I've done my dash and will be too clapped out for another tour – I've passed the 500 hours ops now, which is not bad going.

Social life has been quiet this week and, apart from a dance and a visit to Anna, I've been in bed early. I got a small pair of clogs made in Holland when we were there and I had them painted by the Chief Inspector of Police in this town. He made a damn good job of them, painting them sky blue with RAF wings on them and the colours of France, Belgium and Holland. I'll send them over when I go on leave.

Give my love to all,

Doug

On my last operational trip I destroyed a white VW car. Jerry used any means to camouflage their transport, including Red Cross vehicles. Our instructions were to destroy anything that moved.

Unfortunately my health was deteriorating rapidly. I had bad facial eczema which would not improve and with hindsight I'm sure I was suffering a nervous breakdown. George Keefer suggested it was time I moved on as I had done about 150 hours and in theory my second tour was as good as over. I indicated I'd like to stay until the end, which he agreed to, but suggested I go to London for a few days rest.

Finale

*

I returned to London and discussed the situation with Noble Lowndes and Fergie and decided that since there was nothing set up for me when I returned to New Zealand that, at the age of 25, I should consider getting back. Noble suggested I return before the rush as there was no doubt that when the war ended there would be an influx of people looking for work.

Oxted
Saturday, 16 December 1944

Dear Mum, Dad and Girls,

I've finished my second tour and will do just the odd trip. I've completed over 500 ops hours and as the last couple of trips I've been a bit windy it is the best thing to do. I've been to NZ Headquarters to arrange a trip home and I should be on my way some time in February.

I had a hell of a trip to England as the weather was duff in the morning and we did not get away till about 2.30 in the afternoon. We finally plonked down at Odiham with Jamie Jameson also on leave to the UK. It was a pea-souper. Even the local trains were delayed about four hours. I finally got to Fergie's, very cold and hungry, at about two in the morning. However, I managed to

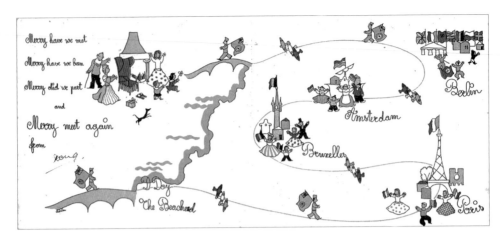

Xmas card, 1944

ring him up *en route* and he had one of his potent stews on brew, which did good service. I will go to Katie's tomorrow for a couple of days and set sail back to the Continent for Xmas with the boys.

I had a night with Mac Sutherland who will be repatriated minus a leg. He is very fit and happy considering all and when he gets fitted up with a new tin leg will go home. He gets around on his crutches pretty well and I think the only thing that worries him is self-consciousness of his disability. He hates anyone giving up a seat for him or trying to help him in any way.

My stinker of a cold persists and has made me rather miserable at times. I think I've still got one lung left, which seems to do the job OK! A bit of NZ sun will fix it.

Cheerio for now,

Doug

Mac was lucky to have survived his ordeal when shot down in August 1943. His aircraft was immobilized and he was hit in the right leg by cannon-fire. He told me he temporarily lost consciousness but came to just in time to bale out. His next recollection was on the ground from where he was taken prisoner and admitted to a hospital near Rouen, surrounded by an 8-foot barbed-wire fence.

His leg was amputated without anaesthetic. He was given Cognac with egg to keep his blood pressure down and also received transfusions from the doctor's blood.

While the doctors and nurses were kind Mac and an Englishman Guy Pease became bored and decided to plan an escape. This was quite a mission given that Mac had one leg and it was now mid-winter. Over time they made a key and found some clothes.

They made their escape on 21 December but both injured themselves on the barbed-wire fence. There were many German soldiers around and progress was slow. The rain and cold were unbearable and their cuts from the barbed-wire became infected so they had no option but to give themselves up. They spent Xmas Day 1943 in solitary confinement! Mac spent four months at Sagan camp and was repatriated via Sweden in September.

Diest
Monday, 25 December 1944

Dear Mum, Dad and Girls,

Xmas Day in Diest. We had a programme laid on, which would have been pretty good, but a big shot has flown in to speak to the boys and has more or less cancelled a bit of the activity. When he arrived I sneaked off to drop you a line or two. The cold has developed well and last night I could not speak a word – today a faint cackle issues forth. I feel such a damn fool for last night all the erks were asking me questions I couldn't answer.

I've handed my flight over and will probably go back to England around about New Year. If all goes well I should be on my way home sometime in February so I'll be seeing you all soon. I should get three months leave and then probably get rooted out. I'd like to do a quick tour against the Japs but we'll see what happens.

On the way back from leave another chap and I had a rather large-scale night in Brussels, which cost us a lot of money but we had a lot of fun. We were with a couple of popsies and at about two we decided to head for home. A taxi appeared and the driver said he would take us home for 400 francs paid on the spot. Sammy paid but I shrewdly took a note of the speedo and saw he was taking us for a ride. When we had delivered the girls I put the pistol against his head and said, 'OK, next stop the police station!'

We had a small argument and the Civvy Police didn't want to know and said go to the Service Police which I was all for. Once outside the driver got the wind up and we got all the 400 francs back and had quite a good trip for nothing. There is a hell of a lot of that sort of racket going on but I don't think that bloke will be trying to rip anyone off for a while.

Accommodation that night cost us nothing either. We entered a small hotel and at that time of night there is no receptionist. Knowing the system, we took a key off the hook for room six, walked upstairs and had a good sleep. In the morning we replaced the key on the wall and simply walked out.

I had a bit of trouble returning to Diest. The Battle of the Bulge was in full swing and had cut off the main road. I had to detour north and was very pleased to eventually find base. I didn't want to take any risks, having survived everything the Air Force has thrown at me over the last four years.

Well I must away and get weaving on the Christmas celebrations. I expect tonight I will again be mute and use the deaf and dumb language.

Best of love,

Doug

Before I left the Continent I did one last recce to England to supplement the coffers. While the NZ boys were employed by the RAF tax-free, unfortunately the UK pilots were taxed on their meagre salary. There was a shortage of coffee in Belgium so I did a return visit to England and came back with as much coffee as I could stow. We flogged it off on the black market to give the UK pilots in 130 Squadron a small bonus.

Oxted
Saturday, 6 January 1945

Dear Mum, Dad and Girls,

Xmas dinner went well at Diest, although my voice petered out completely. The troops had their meal at midday and we dished out the goods to them. We had our meal in the evening with plenty of Champers and what-have-you to go with it. I was an honoured guest – why, I don't know – and at the G/C's table. I did no more flying but had quite a few parties with the boys and eventually left on the morning of the 29th. I had to make a trip to Eindhoven where I spent the night, and next morning set course for the coast via Brussels.

What a trip – in the back of a three-ton truck from 9.30 a.m. till 6.30 in the evening, apart from a stop of about half an hour in Brussels for lunch.

New Year's Eve went well. I spent it on the Belgian coast and had a fair quota of booze and finally hit the hay a little after three. I got up at about eight in the morning and after about five cups of tea got the wheels rolling for the trip over. Saw the Doc, got my gear together and generally mucked about. We hopped on another three-tonner and after about an hour arrived at the port of embarkation and sat or rather stood around the wharf waiting for the good ship to come in. It was damn cold and needless to say I was a bit browned off over the whole thing. We eventually left port at about three and did not disembark on this side till after midnight. We went through all the usual procedure and eventually hit the hay a little after two.

I did not hurry myself next morning as the train journey would involve numerous changes to Oxted, plus I had gear to cart around. I was up early next morning and set course for NZ Headquarters where I got the gen. I ran into Chalky White and Bill Compton there so that meant staying the night. Next day we had a fling at the Kimul. We had intended a quick drink but we were delayed by the likes of Jack Henry and Sailor Malan. We got properly lost on the way to Oxted and did not get there till after six. We had a high-powered meal and then took Fergie and Norm Roberts up to Biggin where we had another small session. I got all my gear from the tailors, which cost me close on 40 quid for really very little – however, the deed is done now.

At the present moment I'm at an NZ repatriation centre and awaiting the return of the Adjutant to find out what the form is and see what paperwork I have to fill in. I'll probably have to stay here the night, but I've got my car here so I'm not unduly concerned. I should get a few weeks leave and then set course for Bonnie New Zealand – how, I don't know, but I should think in all probability via USA. The only trouble with that trip is the lack of money, for I feel sure we will not be allowed to take much out of this country.

Hope you had a good New Year,

Doug

Oxted
Tuesday, 9 January 1945

Dear Mum, Dad and Girls,

I last wrote from the Repat Base prior to going through all the balony which is required before returning home. I set course for two weeks' leave, with a possible extension depending on the boat position. I don't quite know the exact form yet but I should not be kept waiting long. These days I feel ashamed to take my pay for, as I see it, for the next six or seven months I'll be doing next to nothing for the Air Force. I guess as it is from the Government I care a little less about it.

It has snowed during the night and continued for some time this morning so that there is an inch or two on the deck, but this time tomorrow it will have vanished and it will be rather wet underfoot. I'm trying to buy something respectable for the Fergies before I go, but it is so hard to get things these days. I'll have another scout around London tomorrow.

On Friday and last night I took the Fergies to the flicks. On Saturday night I went to the local dance, which developed into quite a party where I met an NZ Navy type who trained with Lewis Eady and sees a fair bit of him. Lewis is apparently in good fettle and sees a bit of the 'other side' where I've just been.

Tons of love,

Doug

Oxted
Thursday, 18 January 1945

Dear Mum, Dad and Girls,

There must be a fair number of chaps wanting to go home as I've had my leave extended and I know a boat departed not so long ago. This last week I've spent with Chalky White and Pat Patterson with Fergie's as headquarters and we have had a rather varied programme, visiting such places as Biggin and seeing all the roughs in that part of the globe. Monday night we had a dinner party at the White Harte Brasted. The party consisted of Mr and Mrs Fergie, Norm Roberts and his wife, a Mr and Mrs Manson, Pat, yours truly and Bill Robjohn – Marty Hume's cousin who has been on subs for a major part of the war and as an NZer is a visitor to Fergie when in this part of the world. The do was a great success and enjoyed by all. We had the odd drink before dinner and the meal they put on consisted of artichoke soup, goose, roast spuds, sprouts, cherry pie and cheese. We then resumed with the odd liqueur and, when the bar closed, returned to Fergie's.

I heard rather a good story the other day, Dad: Eisenhower and Montgomerie were on their landing craft on the way to the beachhead when a sly Hun submarine torpedoed them. When in the water, Ike asked Monty if he could help him as he could not swim. 'That's OK, old boy' said Monty and proceeded to drag Ike to the beach. When they had more or less recovered from the ordeal, Ike confided in Monty and said, 'Say, I hope you don't mind, Monty old fellow, but I would rather you did not say anything about this episode as I would hate my boys to think I couldn't swim.' Monty thought for a moment and replied, 'Yes, Ike, I think it would be a good thing to keep the matter quiet as I would hate my boys to think I couldn't walk on water.'

When I get home I should get three months leave and it will give me time to get organised for future life. What I'll have to choose between is farming on one hand and a good steady job or a business of my own on the other. If you see anything crop up, Dad, think it over.

Well I'm off to Rotary lunch with Fergie so I'll close.

Tons of love to you all,

Doug

Oxted
Surrey
Tuesday, 23 January 1945

Dear Mum, Dad and Girls,

I've just returned from Chichester. Pat and I took Fergie and Norm down for a couple of days and they thoroughly enjoyed it. Hawk Wells, Johnnie Checks, Vic Hall and a mass of others are all down that way. We arrived there on Sunday afternoon at about five and after a spot of tea I popped out to hunt out Checks and Co. We all came back to Arthur King's where Fergie and Norm were staying and were joined by Vic as well as Hawk and his wife, who is incidentally going to produce a little Hawk! I was up fairly early on Monday and after breakfast at the mess went down and got Fergie and Norm and motored to Midhurst. W/C Thomas, whom I was with at Milfield, is in the hospital with TB. He is in a pretty bad way, having the dreaded bug fairly well implanted but he was cheerful enough and glad to see us.[77]

When we left him I went on an egg mission and, after a quick beer in the Spread Eagle at Midhurst, returned to Arthur's for lunch. On to the flicks and then I popped out to the mess and had a bath and a general clean up, picked up Checks and off to another meal at Arthur's. After supper we took Fergie and Norm out to the mess where we had a good party and got to bed a bit after one. When I got to breakfast this morning there were three or four inches on the ground. I had breaker with Hawk, Checks and Co. I went down to the pub and had another breakfast with Fergie and Norm. Fergie and I set course just after 12 and it was rather a rotten journey. I could not get any speed up as the roads were very treacherous and the snow froze to the windscreen, so I had to get out and rub it clear at regular intervals on the way back. Mrs Fergie received a parcel of tea, sugar and cheese today, for which she wants me to thank you very much – they certainly appreciate things like that over here.

I was sorry to hear Ewie had been clobbered in the leg and lost a foot.[78] It will be very hard on him, as he will miss his main hobby in life – running – damn rotten luck. I'm sure the experts will be able to put on a slice of wood in place of his foot and enable him to do most things. I'll probably be back at the same time as him.

77 Tommy Thomas died in 1946 as a result of TB.
78 Ewie had competed in Egypt with Englishman Austin Littler, a competitor in the 1938 Olympics. Littler broke the Egyptian 800m record with a run of 1 min, 57½ secs.

I've been moderately quiet though we had a big night last Saturday. Pat and I took a couple of WAAF Officers to a party, which was to start at Shepherds. We got there and discovered the party consisted mainly of the fairer sex. The pub was overflowing so after paying respects and having a yarn to Bill Compton we popped off to the Dirty Duck where we holed up till it closed and then to the Coconut Grove, a local nightclub, which is now the best joint in London. We left about four and owing to the state of the roads we did not get back to Fergie's till just before seven in the morning – quite a night.

The weather has kept the golf course in a continual coat of white but the other day I forced myself out. I've never been so cold in all my life. It was the wind and it was so cold that in the latter part of the afternoon the tops of the hills were frozen – however, I had a good game and got in a bit of exercise.

I still don't know yet when I will be dispatched but the latest rumour is the middle of next month. I hope to get back by Easter to help you spend your 10 days leave, Dad – so I'll try and push the boat to help it on its way.

Goodbye now and tons of love to all,

Doug

Oxted
Wednesday, 31 January 1945

Dear Mum, Dad and Girls,

As you have no doubt read in the papers, the winter over here has been very cold and we have had plenty of snow and ice around the country, which has made life very uncomfortable for many, though I should say their discomfort is little to what the Huns are undergoing right now – living in camp, bags of snow and ice and the odd bomb to keep them on their toes – they deserve it all and more which will no doubt be dealt out to them before it is all over. The Russians are nearly through. I did not expect them to go any further than the Oder but it looks as if the aim is Berlin or bust. It will be a grand bit of work when Berlin is taken, though there will be a fair amount of Hunland still left. When we get a bit of decent weather on our front things should start to buzz. I would not be at all surprised to see the whole show close up with a bit of a bang.

Life here definitely breeds laziness and a general day for me is to report – just to say I'm around – between nine and nine thirty each morning when we are told if we have anything to do that day. After a small chin wag with the big chief we then go to a café, after which we might play snooker. If lunch is edible we have a little, if not we go off to a café, and following that we go to a local and over a beer decide what picture we will see. The flicks over, we come back, have supper and then do the rounds – what a life. I'm very fed up with it and will buzz off for a day or so if things do not brighten up.

I had a farewell night in Oxted last Saturday and the beer flowed fast and furiously. They are a grand mob and I will endeavour to see them all again before I leave, even if it is only for a few hours. They looked after me well and I think I almost became a local citizen.

Cheerio for now and keep your fingers crossed for Manly at Easter.
Best of love,

Doug

11 February 1945 – left England

Photo taken after Doug had left England: Tony Robson, Mrs Ferguson, Frank Transom, Marion and David Ferguson, Chalky White, Garry Barnett

AIR DEPARTMENT,
WELLINGTON C.1.

IN REPLY REFER TO
REF. No.

5/2/4262 DPR

20th June, 1945.

Mr E. B. Brown,
7 Bourne Street,
Mt. Eden,
AUCKLAND.

Dear Mr Brown,

      I have pleasure in informing you that a message received from Air Ministry states that your son, Flight Lieutenant Douglas Gordon Elliot Brown, has been Mentioned in Despatches for meritorious services.

      On behalf of the Air Board, I desire to express my sincere congratulations on your son's fine achievement.

      Yours faithfully,

L. a Barrow

AIR SECRETARY.

T.W.

Epilogue

*

THE LATER YEARS

When we volunteered, we did not know what we were in for. It was an adventure. There was a lot of drinking beer and socialising and some flying thrown in for good measure! For those of us who survived, the friendships we made lasted for the rest of our lives.

Many colleagues were killed training, in flying accidents or shot down. We all lost close friends. It did no good to dwell on it – if you did you were likely to be the next to go. Some of the boys used to play up to the girls and would say jokingly, 'Might be shot down tomorrow.' Although the odds were high and there was an element of luck, experience, skill and attitude came into the equation.

I did around 280 operational trips. On my first tour I may have only seen the Hun at close range 80 times. The second tour was mainly air to ground. Although we didn't see much of the enemy we still lost quite a few as the situation was exacerbated by running into our own flak and tiredness. I was hit by flak seven times, mostly from our own side.

My aircraft, at least until I pranged it was called 'Wine, Women and Song'. That was our life, we lived it to the full. The men we flew with became closer than brothers. When we flew we depended on each other and socially we played hard.

Towards the end of our tours many of us, myself included, suffered health issues as a result of the continuous pressure, poor conditions, lack of sleep and

ABOVE LEFT Noel Taylor, Bob Gyllies, Doug, Eve

ABOVE RIGHT Johnny Johnson visits NZ in 1960s: Ken Lee, Jim Porteous, Hal Thomas, Jamie Jameson, Johnny Johnson, Harvey Sweetman. NZ HERALD

enemy action. At the time we didn't know what it was and just pressed on as well as we could. It took a couple of years to get over my illness. I was a bit nervy for a while, especially if something like a car exhaust backfired.

I had started law at university before the war. I knew there was no way I was going to complete it – my dad was in law – I wanted to get into business of some sort.

I started work right away at Charles Palmer's machinery business. I learnt a lot from Charlie Palmer, initially in the warehouse and then 'on the road'. I spent some time in sales and it involved literally walking to our customers each day. One day it would be Ponsonby, then Otahuhu, Onehunga and so on. I bought into a business in December 1945 while I was still with Charles Palmer. The business was a one-man outfit and short of capital but they had premises which in those days were sought after. I continued to work for another year with Charles Palmer and then went for it in the business I had bought into, the RR Martin Equipment Company Ltd.

We bought out Bert Martin and over the years have acquired other businesses and added product lines. The business, currently named Hindin Marquip Ltd, is still in family hands and going strong as one of the leading NZ machinery and hand-tool wholesalers in New Zealand.

I married Eve Young on 17 December 1949 and, as predicted by the fortune teller in England, produced three children: Hamish, Rosalind and Fergus, who in turn produced me six grandchildren.

As the business became established I joined the St Cuthbert's College and King's School boards; some not-for-profit organisations and a number of private and public company boards, including Email Industries, Mirotone, Montana Wines, National Mutual Life, NZ Industrial Gases, NZOG and Smith Biolab;

and have been president of Auckland Rotary and the Auckland Golf Club. There is no doubt my wartime experiences prepared me for what life had to offer. From that point of view I have been lucky and made many friends through these associations.

*

Soon after the war Garry Barnett organised the first 485 Squadron reunion and these initially took place every second year. Max Collett's involvement saw the reunions become an annual event. Smaller groups of us would also get together for the likes of golf or family functions. Des Roberts organised a fishing trip for four of us to Mayor Island. Jack 'Freck' Frecklington and Herb Patterson arrived from Rotorua and I met them all at Tauranga. Freck emerged from the car ashen-faced and shaking as Herb believed full speed was the only way to travel. Freck took all weekend to recover and did not contribute greatly to the fishing. We divided up the catch but Freck refused to join Herb for the return journey and instead went by bus via Whakatane. The inevitable happened and his bag disappeared en route, only to turn up 3 weeks later complete with fish in an advanced state of decay.

RNZAF Whenuapai has adopted the number 485 and badge as 485 Wing. Those of us remaining from 485 Squadron are extremely proud to have this liaison

Mick Shand, Vic Hall, Eve Brown

485 Squadron reunion, 27 February 2010 David Fail (486 Sqdn), Russell Clarke, David Iggo, Maurice Mayston, Ken Lee, Owen Hardy, Max Collett, Doug, Vic Hall, Sean Perrett (pilot), Sir Tim Wallis, patron (in front)

with Whenuapai. At their HQ a pictorial museum has been set up showing pilots present and past. It is a splendid memorial and a personal thrill for 485 Squadron members who trained at Whenuapai to see the original arched hangar at the base when the reunions are held there.

The 485 Wing has recently honoured previous 485 Squadron Leaders Reg Grant, Johnny Pattison and Bill Wells by naming meeting rooms at 485 Wing Headquarters after them.

The 70th anniversary of the formation of 485 Squadron is in 2011. While the few remaining are able, the wing at Whenuapai is willing, and the families of those who flew continue to be interested, may the reunions continue with the exchange of stories old and new.

*

Now that I have more time to reflect and less time for golf my interest has been rekindled in the education system as my grandchildren pass through it. I reunite as often as I can with old flying colleagues and Manly beach is still a regular destination over summer months and holiday weekends as it was in the days of distant youth. Unfortunately the fish are smaller and less plentiful than they were in those days.

APPENDIX

NZ-born Wing Commanders while I was at 485 and 130 Squadron

Bill Wells

Bill 'Hawkeye' Wells

Bill 'Hawkeye' Wells was my first CO when I joined 485 Squadron at Kenley and subsequently W/C when Reg Grant took over the squadron in May 1942. Hawk was a good leader and popular, an aggressive pilot but did not take risks. Bill stayed in the RAF after the war and married Mary. They had a rural property bordering Salisbury and eventually retired to Spain. They visited NZ a few times and stayed with us. Further reading: *An Illustrated History of the NZ Spitfire Squadron* by Kevin Wells.

Pat 'Jamie' Jameson

In June 1940 Jamie had led a flight of Hurricanes to Norway to destroy German planes. When Norway entered the war, orders were to destroy the aircraft. Jamie decided they could land them on a carrier which is what they did – with sandbags under the tail instead of a hook. Unfortunately the carrier HMS *Glorious* came across the *Scharnhorst* and *Gneisenau* and was sunk. Jamie was a strong swimmer and along with 29 others made it to a Carley float, but only five survived. Over 1500 perished with the *Glorious*.

Jamie became a proficient Battle of Britain pilot and was our Winco at Wittering while our squadron was at the satellite base of Kings Cliffe from July 1942.

Jamie and Hilda were great friends of ours. After the war Jamie inherited Jameson's Whiskey which was established in Dublin in 1780. It was one of the few remaining brands in the Republic of Ireland. Whiskey as a business had suffered for a number of years due to prohibition and tariffs so the remaining manufacturers merged in 1966.

Al Deere (image p. 228/229)

I first met Al at Kenley when he was Flight Commander of 611 Squadron. When I received my commission we were returning from a session at the pub and Al demanded the officers' mess bar be opened. The Corporal in charge refused to open up so Al took him out with a single blow to the nose and promptly demanded to know where the keys to the bar were. Al mysteriously disappeared the next day. However, he had a moral victory by being rapidly reinstated to another squadron.

When 485 relocated to Biggin Hill in July 1943, Al was the Winco. On one occasion Jack Henry had come to visit after a tour to the ME. We had a big night and ended up at the WAAFs' mess. Unfortunately, Jack Henry was discovered next morning in bed with one of the WAAFs and the 'Queen Bee' demanded an enquiry. Al went through the motions of reprimanding us sufficiently in front of the 'Queen Bee'. Much to Al's embarrassment I couldn't keep a straight face so that was the end of that sham!

The only time I flew with Al was at Biggin. One cannot say enough about Al's war record and skill as a leader. He was shot down a number of times during the Battle of Britain, hence the resulting book, *Nine Lives*. He was a cracker, a really great guy. Eve and I spent many a happy time with Al and Joan in the UK and NZ after the war.

Al's name lives on through the efforts of his nephew Brendon Deere who has restored a Spitfire IX with initials AL as identification. This Spitfire is housed at Ohakea and actively flies. It is greatly appreciated by surviving Spitfire pilots and aircraft fans.

Bill Crawford-Compton
Before war broke out, Bill had been impatient to join the RAF. He had signed up as crew on a yacht, *Land's End*, visiting Auckland. There were four on board but the yacht was wrecked off New Guinea. They drifted to a small island and he eventually obtained a passage to England, arriving in September 1939, signing up immediately.

Bill Crawford-Compton, Bill Wells

After serving in 485, Bill became a Flight Commander in 611 Squadron. Bill was a 'go-getter' and was Winco Hornchurch while we were at Biggin Hill. At our station was a Reverend King with whom Bill enjoyed some 'light' banter. Whenever Bill visited us he would set off an explosive device under the Rev's bed.

He had a most successful war record and stayed in the RAF after the war, rising to the rank of Air Vice Marshall. He visited NZ in April 1945, shortly after I returned. We spent the week partying and playing golf at Middlemore. He married Clöe and they visited NZ again in the 1970s.

Johnnie Checketts, Wing Commander at Horne, May 1944
Checks and I were very close friends, even though he was six years my senior. Johnnie joined 485 Squadron when I was at Kenley but he didn't get on with Reg Grant. It was just one of those things and he was posted elsewhere. Checks was an excellent shot and had the ability to position himself well. When going down on the Hun you

Johnnie Checketts.
RNZAF MUSEUM

have to be able to judge relative speeds well and be perfectly positioned to shoot at the right time. Checks shot down a number of aircraft with this skill. I was a poor shot and couldn't hit a cow in the arse with a handful of wheat.

Checks' luck ran out on 6 September 1943 when he was shot down on a trip we did to Rouen. He eventually escaped by French fishing boat from Le Havre seven weeks later. The skipper assumed a huge risk in concealing the escapees, included among them was Terry Kearins. Terry was coincidently Johnnie's No 2 when he was shot down on 15 July almost two months prior to Johnnie.

A year and a day after Checks had been shot down, he and Al Deere returned to the village near Lille where Checks had been hidden. Unfortunately the Gestapo had taken away the man and woman who had nursed him.

Checks came back to NZ before me and went up to Fiji. He married Natalie, whom he was acquainted with before leaving NZ for the war. Johnnie joined the RNZAF and became Station Commander Taieri in Otago. We remained good friends after the war and I stayed with them whenever I went to Dunedin on business.

Unfortunately he had an altercation with the hierarchy at the RNZAF. As a civilian he continued flying Tiger Moths as top-dressing planes. It was very dangerous and he was lucky to survive this endeavour.

I was visiting Checks a few days before the book release, *The Road to Biggin Hill*. Vincent Orange the author was also there. Three whiskeys each had been poured – quite unusual for Checks as it was rare to get one out of him. Sensing that something was up, and with no desire to have my glass refilled again, I asked bluntly what the 'occasion' was. It transpired that extensive reference had been made in his book to material contained in my letters home and the publisher had deemed it necessary to seek my permission as the book was going on sale the next day. I had no prior knowledge of this. On questioning them how they came by these letters, Checks nonchalantly replied, 'We asked your father to copy them.'

Colin Gray

Colin Gray was briefly attached to 485 Squadron when we were at Kings Cliffe in September 1942 awaiting a posting as CO to another squadron. I considered Colin to be the best NZ fighter pilot I flew with. He was a good shot and a good leader and was also ex-Battle of Britain.

Al Deere told me one day: 'I was lining up on a Hun when all of a sudden it disappeared and I hadn't fired. Colin came down out of the blue at right angles and had hit it.' Some didn't get on with Colin but I found him a great chap.

When I was CO of 130 Squadron at Lympne during the V1 incursion he was Wing Commander. He ended the war as NZ's most successful ace with 27 kills. He retired from the RAF in 1961 as a Group Captain and had a successful career with Unilever.

Post-war we thoroughly enjoyed Colin and Betty's company and we occasionally managed a 'reunion' golf match against Mick Shand and John Palmer.

Prisoners of War at Stalag Luft III

A number of 485 Squadron spent a significant part of the war restrained in Stalag Luft III. The camp was situated in Poland about 20 miles east of the border with Germany.

John Palmer and I were at Wanganui Collegiate together. John was head boy. He took life seriously and was a steadfast citizen and friend. He was shot down on my first operation, baled out into the English Channel and lucky to be picked up. The next time he was shot down was on 10 April 1942. He was captured and became the first we lost to Stalag Luft III, to spend the next three years in POW camp.

From outside Stalag Luft III, January 1942.
GETTYIMAGES.COM REF 3241959

The second to go from Kenley was Ross Falls, shot down on 1 May 1942. He Married Ngaire Nilsson after the war and was a sharebroker in Napier/ Hastings. Good golfer!

Mick Shand was a Battle of Britain veteran. Mick was shot down on his second operation and was hospitalised for a year before joining 485 in October 1941. This was typical of the period during the Battle of Britain when new pilots were put into front-line squadrons with inadequate training and often as little as 20 hours flying time in a Spitfire. The following is condensed from a letter Mick wrote from the hospital:

'I soon found we were right in the thick of all the activity which was then at its height. A mere two or three scraps a day against many times our own numbers was all in the day's play and I must admit it was exciting. On the first day up when I heard over the radio telephone that our squadron of 12 was approaching 80 enemy, I got a funny feeling in my stomach and began to think I must have misheard the numbers, but I got quickly used to it and it was an advantage as there were so many targets to aim at. I got my packet about 7 o'clock after being in the squadron a little less than a week. From our home base we go to operate from forward bases right on the coast. We were a good target as we were silhouetted against the clouds below. A couple of cannon shells ripped past me

ABOVE LEFT Stalag Luft III rugby team Mick Shand on right
ABOVE RIGHT Stalag Luft III barracks. Mick Shand on left

and exploded on the instrument panel. I didn't know I had been hit in the arm and couldn't understand why it was practically paralysed. The engine had conked and all this while the plane was doing most peculiar antics at several hundred miles an hour, four miles up. I put myself in the hands of the Gods and tried to get the plane under control. I got it out of its final spin about 500 feet up and made a landing safely in a field right on the coast. A Jerry followed me down all the way and hovered over me for a few minutes before going away. I have never sat so still in all my life.'

Mick was B Flight Commander while we were at Kings Cliffe until he was shot down during a rhubarb in November and became a POW in Stalag Luft III. He was the last one out of the tunnel in the Great Escape 24 March 1944. A guard was preparing to shoot when he was distracted and the shot missed. Of the 76 who got out of the tunnel, three got away, 52 were shot and the rest including Mick were recaptured.

Mick and his fellow escapees were taken to an SS prison. They were led out six at a time and Mick assuming they were returning to Stalag Luft III tried to swap positions with one of the selected men to get back to camp early. He offered him some cigarettes and chocolate but the offer was turned down. It wasn't until later that Mick discovered those taken out were shot as a reprisal for the escape attempt.

Mick married before returning to NZ and grew berries in Greytown before purchasing a sheep farm in Pirinoa. We enjoyed many happy times together socially (some I am pleased to forget) with Mick and Phil and their family. We had holidays together and used to go fishing together at Manly.

In 1990 Mick travelled to England for 50th anniversary celebrations of the Battle of Britain and in 1994 for a reunion of Great Escapees.

In 1943, when we were back in 11 Group at Westhampnett, we lost five killed and two to POW camp, Bruce Gordon and Tony 'Slim' Robson.

I formed a close bond with Tony Robson during and after the war. We had some exciting times together fighting the Hun and had a number of near misses doing rhubarbs. He was shot down on 18 February 1943 and was a POW for the duration. I was his best man when he married Lyn and he was a groomsman when Eve and I married. He farmed in the Hawkes Bay where we often visited as a family as our children were of a similar age. He often sent a sheep up on a truck to go in the freezer. Duck shooting was a regular event at Slim's.

On one occasion in the early 1990s he came to visit on very short notice. He made no mention of the fact he wasn't well and he died soon after. It was one of the few occasions he had discussed life in the POW camp. He related how Mick Shand had found a pumpkin seed and planted it. Mick nurtured the plant that grew and kept watch over the single pumpkin produced. Day and night he would keep guard over his prized possession. He was so nervous someone would steal it he picked it green and made it into soup.

At the beginning of 1945 the Russian offensive penetrated Poland. The Germans ordered the evacuation of the POW camps. Stalag Luft III had over 10000 prisoners who were marched around 100km to Spremberg from Sagan. It was mid winter with heavy snow and the POWs were not in peak fitness. Some died during this forced march in difficult conditions. During the march Mick had a child's pram loaded up with his camp belongings. After a while one of the wheels fell off and so Mick continued hobbling along with this unbalanced pushchair. Food was in short supply during the march, so to supplement their diet Slim would climb over the fence to rustle sheep, which he deposited in Mick's pushchair.

Jack Rae was already at 485 when I joined and he was another of our pilots who was a great shot and got about 14 in his two stints at 485 and Malta.

He went off to Malta at the end of 1942. I was tempted to join him but was made Deputy Flight Commander and commissioned, so I decided to stay put.

Jack returned to the squadron in April 1943 but was shot down in August and became another guest of Stalag Luft III.

Although he was short in stature, Jack had an aggressive nature and before long had devised an escape plan. There was an aerodrome with FW190 aircraft about 10 miles away. Jack had obtained information giving him cockpit layout and he was confident he could fly one back to the UK. Jack and a Canadian pilot Reg Probert planned to crawl along the ground, camouflaged with sheets part painted and rubbed with soil. One night they made their way along an indentation in the parade ground towards the fence. Unfortunately, the usually regular passes of the German guard were interrupted due to the cold and his need to run the patrol rather than walk it. When cutting the wires, the guard sighted them and they spent 30 days in solitary. This probably saved their lives as it was during this time that the Great Escape took place.

When the camp was evacuated under forced march, Jack had heard a rumour the prisoners would be shot. As the march left Stalag Luft III, Jack and a friend made a successful escape by peeling off unnoticed. They headed for the drome where he had intended previously to fly off in a German plane but found after all it was a no go. They came across a naval POW camp and effectively knocked at the door to be let in. There he remained until the US Army arrived.

During the war, Jack was a wild character, but afterwards he changed completely to a mild and gentle soul. He married Vera, sister of Reg and Ian Grant. Jack Rae's account of the war appears in the book, *Kiwi Spitfire Ace*.

Coincidentally, Mick Shand and Jack Rae died on the same day, 20 December 2007.

Camps and Bases Attended and Flying Hours

Date	Location	Group	Hours	Primary Transport
22/12/1940	Levin			
9/2/1941	Whenuapai	No 4 EFTS	45	Tiger Moth DH82
30/5/1941	Moose Jaw	No32 SFTS	87	Harvard II
9/10/1941	Grangemouth	No58 OTU	6	Miles Master
			35	Spitfire I
5/12/1941	Kenley	485 Sqdn	137	Spitfire VB
10/7/1942	Kings Cliffe	485 Sqdn	142	Spitfire VB
5/1/1943	Westhampnett	485 Sqdn	113	Spitfire VB
1/7/1943	Biggin Hill	485 Sqdn	78	Spitfire IXB
8/10/1943	Aston Down	Fighter Leader School	118	Spitfire VB
29/1/1944	Milfield	Pre Invasion School	68	Spitfire VB
31/5/1944	Horne	130 Sqdn	46	Spitfire VB
20/6/1944	Westhampnett	130 Sqdn	9	Spitfire VB
27/6/1944	Merston	130 Sqdn	22	Spitfire VB
4/8/1944	Tangmere	130 Sqdn	7	Spitfire XIV
12/8/1944	Lympne	130 Sqdn	40	Spitfire XIV
1/10/1944	B82 Grave, Holland	130 Sqdn	23	Spitfire XIV
1/11/1944	B64 Diest, Belgium	130 Sqdn	9	Spitfire XIV

B82 refers to TAF code for airfield
Total flying hours   985

Colleagues at Arms

Name and nickname	Birthplace	Occupation Post-war or date killed
Baker, Reg 'Baldy'	Dunedin	12/2/44: Shot down in Mosquito, 487 Squadron
Barnett, Garry	Wellington	Accountant
Black, Lindsay	Wellington	5/3/45: Accident Fighter Leader School
Browne, Stan	Wellington	
Burke, Jim	Timaru	25/2/42: Accident in Magister, 485 Squadron
Checketts, Johnnie 'Checks'	Invercargill	RNZAF / Top-dresser
Clouston, Dave	Auckland	Doctor of Psychiatry
Collett, Max	Napier	Accountant
Crawford-Compton, Bill	Invercargill	Air Vice Marshall, RAF
Dasent, John	Hawkes Bay	22/12/43: Flying accident in Spitfire, 485 Squadron
Falls, John R 'Ross'	Hastings	Stockbroker
Frecklington, L Jack 'Freck'	Rata, Feilding	Farmer
Gaskin, Peter 'Gasman'	Auckland	
Gibbs, Bruce 'Gibby'	Utiku	Farmer
Grant, Reg 'Dumbo'	Woodville	28/2/44: Engine failure at take off in Mustang
Grant, Ian	Woodville	13/2/43: Shot down, 485 Squadron
Griffith, Lyn 'Griff'	Levin	Commercial Pilot
Hardy, Owen	Auckland	RAF
Henry, David JV 'Jack'	Invercargill	Painter Decorator
Houlton, John	Christchurch	Top Dressing Industry
Hume, Marty	Martinborough	Farmer
Jameson, Pat 'Jamie'	Wellington	RAF / Jameson's Whisky
Kearins, Terry	Dannevirke	Farmer
Lee, Ken	Auckland	University Lecturer
Mackie, Evan 'Rosie'	Waihi	Bay of Plenty Power
Maskill IPJ 'Mick'	Alexandra	Maltster Castlemaine Brewery
McNeil, Arnold 'Mick'	Opunake	25/2/42: Accident in Magister, 485 Squadron
McNeil, Ian 'Tusker'	Gisborne	Farmer
Metcalfe, Murray 'Killer'	Wellington	16/9/1943: On high cover operation
Moorehead, George	Christchurch	30/5/1943: Accident 485 Squadron
Palmer, John	Havelock North	Farmer
Pattison, John	Waipawa	Farmer
Porteous, Jim 'Pranger'	Auckland	Property Valuer
Rae, John 'Jack'	Auckland	Ladies' Clothing Manufacturer
Roberts, Des 'Red'	Stratford	Insurance Company Manager
Robson, Tony 'Slim'	Poukawa	Farmer
Shand, Michael 'Mick'	Wellington	Farmer
Stenborg, Gray 'Dutch'	Auckland	24/9/1943: On operation 91 Squadron
Strang, Robert 'Jack'	Invercargill	25/1/42: Oxygen failure in Spitfire, 485 Squadron
Sutherland, MG 'Mac'	Port Chalmers	Hastings Gas Company Manager
Sweetman, Harvey	Auckland	Builder / Property Management
Thomas, Hal	Cambridge	Marac Finance
Tucker, Hugh 'Tommy'	Palmerston Nth	Farmer
Wells, EP 'Hawk'	Cambridge	RAF
White, LSMcQ 'Chalky'	Gore	Farmer
Wipiti, Bert	New Plymouth	3/10/1943: On operation 485 Squadron

ABBREVIATIONS

A/C	Aircraft
AA	Above average
AFC	Air Force Cross
ATA	Air Transport Auxiliary
ATC	Air Training Corps
ATS	Armament Training School
AWOL	Absent without leave
BSM	Barracks Sergeant Major
CFI	Chief Flying Instructor
CGO	Chief Ground Instructor
CNR	Canadian National Railway
CO	Commanding Officer
CPR	Canadian Pacific Railway
DFC	Distinguished Flying Cross
DFM	Distinguished Flying Medal
DSO	Distinguished Service Order
E/A	Enemy aircraft
EFTS	Elementary Flight Training School
F/Lt	Flight Lieutenant
F/O	Flying Officer
FANY	First Aid Nursing Yeomanry
FLS	Fighter Leader School
G/C	Group Captain
ME	Middle East
MO	Medical Officer
NAAFI	Navy Army and Air Force Institutes
OTU	Officer Training Unit
P/O	Pilot Officer
POW	Prisoner of War
R/T	Radio telephone
RAFVR	Royal Air Force Volunteer Reserve
RFC	Royal Flying Corps
RNZAF	Royal NZ Air Force
SFTS	Service Flying Training School
TAF	Tactical Air Force
u/s	Unserviceable
V/R VR	Volunteer Reserve
W/C Winco	Wing Commander
WAAF	Women's Auxiliary Air Force

BIBLIOGRAPHY

Sortehaug and Listemann *No 485 (NZ) Squadron 1941-1945 Spitfire*
Errol W Martyn *For Your Tomorrow*

INDEX

Numbers in bold refer to illustrations